Case Studies in
Generalist Practice

www.wadsworth.com

www.wadsworth.com is the World Wide Web site for Wadsworth and is your direct source to dozens of online resources.

At *www.wadsworth.com* you can find out about supplements, demonstration software, and student resources. You can also send e-mail to many of our authors and preview new publications and exciting new technologies.

www.wadsworth.com
Changing the way the world learns®

#4 disappointing.
Its solely 1to1 practice, when worker + client
have same subculture + where agency job
does this work - no advocacy needed!

ok #6 1to1 engagement despite agency + supv barriers
see 3, 4 + 9 on pp. 40-41

#8 1to1 AODA teen + famly. eh

#10 ok bot no

#11 eh.

16 boring

18 6w notes - not engaging / pre-beginning

#22 compelling. Q: where usable?

Case Studies in Generalist Practice

Third Edition

Robert F. Rivas
Siena College

Grafton H. Hull, Jr.
University of Utah

THOMSON
™
WADSWORTH

Australia • Canada • Mexico • Singapore
Spain • United Kingdom • United States

Belmont CA: Brooks/Cole 2004

Executive Editor: Lisa Gebo
Assistant Editor: Alma Dea Michelena
Editorial Assistant: Sheila Walsh
Marketing Manager: Caroline Concilla
Marketing Assistant: Mary Ho
Project Manager, Editorial Production: Katy German
Print/Media Buyer: Jessica Reed

Permissions Editor: Kiely Sexton
Production Service: UG / GGS Information Services, Inc.
Copy Editor: UG / GGS Information Services, Inc.
Cover Designer: Ross Carron
Cover Image: Getty Images; Digital Vision
Printer: Victor Graphics, Inc.

For more information about our products, contact us at:
Thomson Learning Academic Resource Center
1-800-423-0563

For permission to use material from this text, contact us by:
Phone: 1-800-730-2214
Fax: 1-800-730-2215
Web: http://www.thomsonrights.com

BROOKS/COLE—THOMSON LEARNING
10 Davis Drive
Belmont, CA 94002
USA

Asia
Thomson Learning
5 Shenton Way #01-01
UIC Building
Singapore 068808

Australia/New Zealand
Thomson Learning
102 Dodds Street
Southbank, Victoria 3006
Australia

Canada
Nelson
1120 Birchmount Road
Toronto, Ontario M1K 5G4
Canada

Europe/Middle East/Africa
Thomson Learning
High Holborn House
50/51 Bedford Row
London WC1R 4LR
United Kingdom

Latin America
Thomson Learning
Seneca, 53
Colonia Polanco
11560 Mexico D.F.
Mexico

Spain/Portugal
Paraninfo
Calle/Magallanes, 25
28015 Madrid, Spain

Printed in the United States of America

1 2 3 4 5 6 7 07 06 05 04 03

Library of Congress Control Number: 2003102274

ISBN 0-534-52140-1

To Donna and Heather, my other and only
—R. F. R.

To Jannah, Mike, and Pat, who continue to teach me
about life and love
—G. H. H.

Contents

Foreword
Karen K. Kirst-Ashman
University of Wisconsin-Whitewater
xi

Part I
Micro Practice: Individuals
1

1
The Case of Trent
Iris Carlton-La Ney,
University of North Carolina, Chapel Hill
3

2
The Case of Trent Revisited:
A Single Subject Research Design
Cathy King Pike, Indiana University,
and Amy Webster Meschi, Bishop Jonathan G. Sherman
Episcopal Nursing Home
8

3
The Young Bears
Barbara Jacobsen and Mike Jacobsen,
Southwest Missouri State University
14

4
Nalani Ethel: Social Work with a
Hawaiian Woman and Her Family
Noreen Mokuau, University of Hawaii,
and Barbara Pua Iuli, Kapiolani Medical Center
22

5
Saundra Santiago
Diane Strock-Lynskey, Siena College, and Theresa Gil,
Hudson Valley Community College
29

6
The Case of Mrs. Miller: A Long Engagement
Earlie M. Washington, Western Michigan University
36

7
Late Night with Bea Rosen
Kay Hoffman, University of Kentucky, and
Mary Alice St. Clair, Cranbrook Hospice
42

8
Substance Abuse as Problem or
Symptom: The Smith Family
Robert E. Weiler, Indiana University Northwest
51

9
Una Rosa
Richard Furman, University of Nebraska
57

**Part II
Mezzo Practice:
Families and Groups**
63

10
Personal Growth and Self-Esteem
through Cultural Spiritualism:
A Native American Experience
*James Wahlberg (Deceased),
East Tennessee State University*
65

11
In the Best Interest of the Child
*Lettie L. Lockhart, University of Georgia, and
Alicia R. Issac, Clayton College and State University*
74

12
Between Two Worlds
Rupa R. Gupta, School Link Services
80

13
Sally's Saga
Charles M. Young, University of Wisconsin, LaCrosse
89

14
Brad: Consequences of a Dysfunctional Family
H. Wayne Johnson, University of Iowa
95

15
A Visit to Dwight's Hollow
Jody Gottlieb and Linda Gottlieb, Marshall University
102

16
No Mad Dog Looks: Group Work
and Mediating Differences
*Cynthia Duncan, North Central Education
Service District*
109

17
Deanna's Dilemma
*Jannah J. Hurn Mather, University of Utah,
and Robert F. Rivas, Siena College*
118

18
Ari and Simone: Notes from the Group
*James X. Bembry and Betsy S. Vourlekis,
University of Maryland*
125

**Part III
Macro Practice:
Communities and Organizations**
133

19
Project Homeless
*Gloria Alexander, Southwestern Vermont
Council on Aging*
135

20
Transitional Homes for Young Street Mothers
JoAnn Ray, Eastern Washington University
144

21
The Appointment Letters
Grafton H. Hull, Jr., University of Utah
151

22
The Evergreen Boys Ranch: A Story
about Jack and Diane
Robert F. Rivas, Siena College
155

23
The Willow River Developmental
Disabilities Center
Dennis D. Eikenberry, Aurora Community Services
162

24

Self-Disclosure and Client Discrimination
*Alicia R. Issac, Clayton College and State University,
and Lettie L. Lockhart, University of Georgia*
168

25

Managing Margaret's Care
*Kimberly Strom-Gottfried, University
of North Carolina at Chapel Hill*
174

26

From Case to Cause: My Name Is Jess Overton
Donna McIntosh, Siena College
180

27

Community Work with Refugees
Terry L. Singer, University of Louisville
189

28

When Life Changes in an Instant
Carla Sofka, Siena College
196

Foreword

How can you best depict to students the drama, depth, and diversity characterizing social work practice? This book provides a rich and realistic view into the heart of the field. Descriptive case examples offer one effective means of making course content come alive for students so that they might better comprehend what social workers do and how they do it.

Four themes characterize the organization of this book. First, vibrant cases offer students opportunities to understand and evaluate practice from a *generalist perspective*. It is crucial for students to recognize the complexities of any particular case—the fact that multiple systems are involved and intervention can potentially target any one or more of these systems. Content is structured to delve into a wide range of cases at the micro (individual), mezzo (family and group), and macro (organizational, community, and other large system) levels.

A second theme involves the focus on *diversity, populations-at-risk, and social and economic justice*. Cases include a wide range of client systems in many different contexts. In compliance with new Council on Social Work Education (CSWE) Educational Policy and Accreditation Standards (EPAS), new to this edition are cases involving national origin and international issues. Another new case addresses individual and community trauma, clearly relating to the new era of post-9/11 global and community crises.

The third theme emphasizes social work's *many practice contexts*, ranging from child welfare, to corrections, to health and mental health, to national and international public welfare, in addition to numerous others. Students can view slices of practice from multiple settings so they might understand the infinite variety and flexibility involved in social work practice.

A fourth theme focuses on the importance of *professional values and ethics*. Students must understand that all practice occurs within the context of ethical principles and the resolution of ethical dilemmas.

This book can be used as a primary or supplementary text in a range of social work courses. Cases are written clearly and concisely, reflecting interesting and relevant practice wisdom. Discussion questions following each case can be used to stimulate discussion of many facets of social work practice, policy, and research. Additional references to related readings are also identified so students might further pursue the issues involved.

The editors are among the most highly respected social work educators in the field. Both have extensive experience as social work program directors, authors, and members of both the CSWE Board of Directors and Commission on Accreditation.

This is a great book that both you and your students should find relevant and enjoyable.

Karen K. Kirst-Ashman, Professor
University of Wisconsin-Whitewater

Preface

Case studies have long been an important part of social work education. It's easy to imagine the first "Friendly Visitors" of the Charity Organization Societies and workers of the Settlement Houses learning about social work from the contributed, collective wisdom of their colleagues. Often, such wisdom was written in personal journals and case records or passed on through oral history and discussed in early "case staffings" and training sessions preceding formal social work education.

When considering the early writings of social workers and social reformers, we are struck by the vivid descriptions of cases they encountered. Although sometimes fraught with value judgments indicative of the period, such case narratives were effective in conveying the human conditions encountered in social work's early development (see, for example, Addams, 1910; Little, 1994). It is not surprising to see a renewal of interest in the case study as an educational tool for social work education. In addition to social work, case method learning has a rich history in law, medicine, business, education, and a number of other academic and professional curricula (see, for example, Christensen, 1987). Case studies help link the theoretical with the practical and provide learners with "an opportunity to vicariously participate in the process of doing social work practice" (LeCroy, 1999, p. xiii). New texts and new editions of established texts have supported the expanding research base of social work practice by including practical examples ranging from short case scenarios to full case analyses. It is also encouraging to see a new journal, *Reflections: Narratives of Professional Helping*, emerge as a medium for sharing case experiences among professionals and "to publish narratives with good literary quality that contribute knowledge on ways of helping others and creating social change" (Abels, 1995, p. 1).

At one point, the Council on Social Work Education provided published case studies as resources for schools of social work. With some popularity as teaching tools, these cases helped educate a whole generation of social workers by supplementing classroom experiences with discussions of *The Case of Mr X.* or the case records of *Mary Warson* or *Margaret Clayborn* (CSWE, 1964). Another generation of social workers encountered the classroom challenges of that classic, *The House on Sixth Street* (Pincus & Minihan, 1973), which ushered in a new vision of generalist practice for social workers. It seems time for a "next generation" of cases to be encountered that are relevant to the current educational needs of generalist practitioners. We hope some of those cases will be *Late Night with Bea Rosen, The Evergreen Boys Ranch: A Story about Jack and Diane, Deanna's Dilemma*, and *The Case of Trent*.

To the Learner

Preparing yourself for the wide range of generalist social work practice situations you will encounter is a complex and difficult endeavor. As a learner, you will be exposed to an increasingly diverse range of experiences in both the classroom and the field practicum experience. The case studies you will encounter in this text can be used to supplement and augment your learning about social work practice.

Cases help define and give texture to abstract or theoretical concepts. Social work roles (for example, case manager, advocate, broker, or mediator) lack full meaning without concrete examples of what actions are taken by workers who carry out these roles. Similarly, descriptions of social work values may not have sufficient meaning to you unless you struggle with decisions that require using those values.

If you are new to social work and have relatively little experience in social work organizations, or have limited helping encounters, we hope you can benefit from these case illustrations of practice from experienced social workers. In writing this text, we asked our contributors to use case examples or elements of practice from their own experience. We were pleased to see that our contributors, many of whom are social work educators, were able to "practice what they preach" and provide us with such rich, diverse, and useful case examples. As you struggle with some of the difficult issues in these case studies, remember that the authors have also struggled with the same issues. We hope you can learn from their work.

We also hope that these case studies will provide practical examples for you and that you will be able to use them to broaden your learning experience in the field of social work. Many social service agencies utilized as settings for field instruction are unable to provide sufficient breadth of coverage of diverse practice situations. Field instruction settings must sometimes rely on a narrow range of case situations from which to choose learning experiences for you, often assigning cases that are available rather than those with optimal learning value. Some field agencies may find it difficult to provide you with exposure to clients from diverse racial, ethnic, or cultural backgrounds. Others may have limitations in adequately providing you with the range of micro, mezzo, and macro practice experiences needed for you to fully understand generalist practice. In addition, many field instructors are specialized by education and practice focus and do not themselves bring a generalist perspective to the cases they assign their learners. Thus, case studies can be a valuable and broadening addition to your learning.

We hope this text will help you understand the varied dimensions of social work practice, identify practice principles in a deductive way, and increase your involvement in your own learning process. We also hope that the text will better prepare you for practicum and supplement your practicum by providing experiences that might not universally be afforded all learners.

We have attempted to provide examples of key aspects of generalist practice. Cases can demonstrate important elements of the general problem-solving method, describe practice skills, highlight social work values and ethics, explore diversity, work with systems of varying size, and work in different fields of practice. The cases included here contain examples of these elements for your discovery and discussion.

The General Problem-Solving Method

Each case is written to demonstrate the rational, orderly steps in the problem-solving process, generally following a framework that includes engagement, data collection, assessment, goal planning, contracting, intervention, evaluation, and termination. Although problem solving is hardly ever a completely linear process (and indeed some of the best problem solving takes place by nonlinear reasoning), we have attempted to capture the beginning, middle, and ending phases of each case in an ideal, orderly process. The cases also show that social workers often simultaneously carry out several steps in the problem-solving process and that not all social work is done in a step-by-step fashion.

Practice Skills

The case studies give examples of the practice skills used by workers in various stages of problem solving.

Some cases tend to stress skills inherently important to engagement—for example, the skills of being a good listener or questioner. Other cases contain a good deal of information you can use to practice your skills of assessment. Although not all cases provide substantial illustration of every skill needed, overall the cases document a wide range of skills that await your discovery and analysis.

Social Work Values and Ethics

One of the most important aspects of becoming a social worker is learning the values of the profession and the principles contained in the *NASW Code of Ethics*, which guide us as professional social workers. Special efforts have been made to ensure that you will encounter important value issues in each case, such as client self-determination, confidentiality, social justice, and many more. As in actual social work practice, each case will present you with ethical choices or dilemmas, some solved and some unresolved, that characterize the struggles of the individual worker. You will find that often there are no simple, adequate, or satisfying answers to questions of ethical consequence.

Diversity

Learning about social work practice with diverse racial, ethnic, or cultural groups and with populations at risk for prejudice, discrimination, oppression, or other forms of social and economic injustice is an important element of social work education. Although the cases chosen for this text do not represent all possible groups in these categories, we are proud of the range of diversity represented here to excite, stimulate, and challenge you. Efforts have been made to portray the strengths of various populations, particularly since case studies tend to be rather problem focused and often do not include positive information about the background of the people involved in them. We hope you will be excited by the diversity you encounter here. If you are from a geographic region that lacks population diversity or if your experience includes limited exposure to clients from differing cultural backgrounds or special populations, you might have your first encounter with the "other" in some of these case studies. We hope this will be an exciting part of your learning. We have also added to the diversity in this edition by including cases that will illustrate a global perspective on social work and its mission to seek social change.

We caution that although attempts have been made to include many diverse groups in these cases, the complexity of culture, gender, sexual orientation, disabilities, and other population characteristics cannot be fully understood in a limited number of case studies. No individual case adequately represents a particular population, and you should take care to avoid overgeneralizing about a population based on only one case study.

Range of Client Systems

As social workers, you will confront practice situations that require you to work with systems of differing sizes. Understanding practice with individuals, families, groups, organizations, institutions, and communities is facilitated in three ways. First, the text is organized into three categories of cases: micro (individuals), mezzo (families and groups), and macro (organizations, institutions, communities, and large system change). Second, many cases have implications for multiple system interventions. For example, you will encounter a case in which the social worker helps a child experiencing difficulty in a school system, involves the family of that child in the intervention plan, works with the larger organizational system to carry out an intervention plan, and confronts the issue of institutionalized racism at the community level. As in actual practice, you must be prepared to work with a variety of systems, sometimes working from case to cause. Third, several cases incorporate material appropriate to multiple curricular areas: human behavior and social environment, social work practice, social welfare policy, social work research, ethics and values, diversity, populations-at-risk, and social and economic justice.

Fields of Practice

Finally, the cases presented here represent a wide range of practice settings, fields of practice, and social problems that characterize the richness of social work practice. There are cases involving the fields of child welfare, school social work, corrections, health, mental health, housing and homelessness, gerontology, managed care, developmental disabilities, substance abuse, domestic violence, public welfare, rural social work, and international social work. While not totally representative of the diverse fields in which social workers practice, we believe there is sufficient variety in settings and problems to challenge you and provide a good beginning overview of the fields in which social workers work.

To the Teacher

Case method learning can help you create class conditions conducive to active learning (Kowalski, Weaver, & Henson, 1990) and can initiate an empowering and active experience for learners. It has been suggested that this model of learning encourages "student-generated analysis rather than teacher-manufactured solutions" (Silverman, Welty, & Lyon, 1992, p. xv), which can be important to the development of critical thinking skills in learners.

Case method learning can increase the potential for student involvement and participation in their own learning. The beginning learner can start to understand the purposes of social work and get a "sense" for social work simply by reading and reviewing the actions taken by the social worker in the case. The more advanced learner can get "inside" a case by analyzing the dialogue presented between the worker and the client system and identifying the major practice issues and principles inherent in the case.

Although all too evident, we are amazed at how often we remind ourselves and our students that learning takes place within the learner. As you know from experience, lectures or didactic presentations are important parts of teaching, but class discussions are often significant features of courses that have maximum learning value. In case study learning, class discussion is one of the methods that reinforces active learning. It is important for learners themselves, individually and as a group, to discover and develop data that will help them understand a case. Learners need to struggle with understanding the meaning of a case and the principles it illustrates. You can assist them with these tasks by leading class discussions that help them assess and analyze a case situation, evaluate the interventions used, and suggest differential courses of action. Finally, your class discussions can aid in the more abstract, conceptual work of summarizing and applying critical thinking skills that will reinforce learners' abilities to transfer new information learned to other practice situations encountered in field practicum and, eventually, in professional social work practice.

Using Diverse Learning Techniques

Case analysis and class discussion employ several different styles of learning. Some may learn best by abstract conceptual thinking, and they can use case analysis to deduce practice principles and identify and analyze conceptual issues.

Some learners prefer to participate vicariously by listening to class discussions or by "listening" to the external and internal dialogue presented by workers and clients in the case. Other learners immerse themselves in a case situation and, by presenting and discussing various aspects of a case in class discussions, learn by doing. Thus, the case method allows the teaching-learning encounter to encompass multiple learning styles. If used to its full potential, case study can meet a variety of student learning needs.

As part of the class or field seminar experience, case studies can be an exciting addition to the learning encounter. We offer several suggestions for making case studies work based on recent work with several of the studies included in this text.

Making Case Studies Work in the Classroom

Learners should be assigned to carefully read each study and come prepared to discuss the case in class. It is helpful to have learners prepare written comments or summaries and answer the learning questions at the end of each case. In addition, learners can be encouraged to explore the suggested readings at the end of the case. We have found that requiring learners to search the literature and abstract two or three readings that detail practice principles relevant to the social problem or to the population in the case to be a worthwhile experience.

Discussion of the case is one of the most important aspects of the teaching-learning encounter. Since the case study method is based on involving students in their own learning, it is often helpful to assign particular students or teams of students to present the case to the rest of the class. If students prepare for presenting by working in groups, an additional layer of discussion will occur that will add to the depth of analysis possible, and it can raise the quality of case presentations.

Teachers should act as discussion leaders, posing important learning questions and challenging observations and statements made by learners. The best discussion group will often be characterized by spirited student discussion rather than frequent teacher intervention. All students in class should be encouraged to raise relevant issues and should be responsible for adding to the discussion. Teaching under these circumstances involves skillful leadership of group discussion rather than responsibility for providing answers or didactic lectures. Learners should be encouraged to learn on their own.

To further prepare for case discussions, several other questions can be addressed. We have provided examples of some of the general questions applicable to many of the cases. Learners can be encouraged to complete these questions prior to class discussion, and the questions can serve as a general discussion guide. These general questions are included at the end of this section. We hope these will be helpful.

What's New

A third edition of *Case Studies in Generalist Practice* would not be possible were it not for the tremendous support of colleagues and students who used the first edition in their teaching and learning. Their suggestions and ideas for improving the book are always most welcome. In this edition we have added three new cases dealing with topics that include working with refugees, international work, and a multisystem approach to individual and community trauma.

In the previous edition we added topics such as managed care, substance abuse, domestic violence, and rural social work. We have also revised the grid in the front of the book to assist instructors to identify which cases cover which CSWE Curriculum Policy Statement content areas. In this way, the cases may be used in curricular areas other than practice to demonstrate aspects of human behavior and social environment, policy, research, diversity, values and ethics, populations-at-risk, and social and economic justice. We hope this will be a valuable assist to our colleagues.

Acknowledgments

We wish to acknowledge all undergraduate social work educators, whose support for and dedication to generalist practice made this book a joy to prepare and revise. In addition, we thank our many contributors for sharing a small part of their lives and their practice with us. We wish to acknowledge the staff at Brooks/Cole for the encouragement, support, expertise, and patience that made this project possible, particularly Lisa Gebo, sponsoring editor; Alma Dea Michelena, assistant editor; Katy German, print production manager; Heidi Allgair, production editor; Kiely Sexton, permissions editor; and Vernon Boes and Ross Carron, designers. We thank the following manuscript reviewers for their hard work and suggestions: Linnea F. GlenMaye, Wichita State University; Virginia David, Nazareth College of Rochester; Robyn Snider, Jacksonville State University; Kaaren Strauch Brown, Eastern Michigan University; Cheryl Waites, North Carolina State University; and Cheryl Whitley, Marist College. Their insights have been folded into the overall manuscript. Becky Lübbers and Mary Moran of the University of Utah provided significant support to the third edition of this project.

Shameless Cat, computer expert extraordinaire, continued to provide me word processing assistance. Tempest Jerry Garcia, golden retriever of the North, taught me to balance work with long walks in the woods. Their assistance is acknowledged (R. F. R.). Stonehearth's Majestic Prince, golden retriever par excellence, gave up many of our walks so that I could work on the book. His forbearance is acknowledged (G. H. H.).

Robert F. Rivas
Grafton H. Hull, Jr.

Readings

Abels, S. (1995). Salutory, *Reflections: Narratives of professional helping, (I)*, 1-3.

Addams, J. (1910). *Twenty years at Hull House*. New York: Macmillan.

Christensen, C. R. (1987). *Teaching and the case method. Text, cases, and readings*. Boston, MA: Harvard Business School.

CSWE (1964). *The case of Mr. X., Mary Warson, Margaret Clayborn*. New York: Council on Social Work Education.

Kowalski, T., Weaver, R., & Henson, K. (1990). *Case studies on teaching*. New York: Longman.

LeCroy, C. W. (1999). *Case studies in social work practice (2nd ed.)*. Pacific Grove, CA: Brooks/Cole.

Little, K. B. (1994). *Maria Love, the life and legacy of a social work pioneer*. Buffalo, NY: Heritage Press, Western New York Heritage Institute, Canishius College.

Pincus, A., & Minihan, A. (1973). *Social work practice: Model and method*. Itasca, IL: Peacock.

Silverman, R., Welty, W., & Lyon, S. (1992). *Case studies for teacher problem solving*. New York: McGraw-Hill.

Contributors

ROBERT F. RIVAS, A.C.S.W., is Professor and former Director of Social Work at Siena College in Loudonville, New York. He has also been the Baccalaureate Program Director at the School of Social Welfare, SUNY-Albany. Professor Rivas has published in several fields, including social group work. The fourth edition of his text *Introduction to Group Work Practice* (2001), published with Ron Toseland, is used by undergraduate and graduate programs across the country and in several other countries. He has served on both the Board of Directors as well as on the Commission on Accreditation for CSWE.

GRAFTON H. HULL, JR., Ed.D., C.I.S.W., is Professor and Director of the Baccalaureate Social Work Program at the University of Utah. Dr. Hull is the co-author, with Karen Kirst-Ashman, of *Understanding Generalist Practice, Generalist Practice with Organizations and Communities, The Macro Skills Workbook,* and *The Generalist Model of Human Services Practice*. He is the author or co-author of articles, book chapters, and monographs in several areas of social work education and practice. Dr. Hull is a past member of the CSWE Commission on Accreditation and the Board of Directors. He is also past President of the Association of Baccalaureate Social Work Program Directors (BPD), the Iowa Confederation for Social Work Education, the Wisconsin Council on Social Work Education, and the Missouri Consortium of Social Work Education Programs.

GLORIA ALEXANDER, A.C.S.W., L.C.S.W., is Coordinator of the Mom to Mom Program at the Burdett Commons Community Center in Vermont.

JAMES X. BEMBRY, M.S.W., Ph.D., is Associate Professor of Social Work at the University of Maryland, Baltimore County.

CYNTHIA DUNCAN, M.S.W., is Director of Student Support Services in the North Central Education Service District, Wenatchee, WA.

IRIS CARLTON-LA NEY, Ph.D., is Professor at the School of Social Work at the University of North Carolina at Chapel Hill.

DENNIS D. EIKENBERRY, M.S.W., A.C.S.W., B.C.D., is a therapist with Aurora Community Services in Rice Lake and Eau Claire, Wisconsin.

RICHARD FURMAN, Ph.D., is Assistant Professor of Social Work at the University of Nebraska.

THERESA GIL, M.S.W., is Assistant Professor at Hudson Valley Community College.

JODY GOTTLIEB, M.S.W., is Chair and Professor in the Social Work Department at Marshall University, Huntington, WV.

LINDA GOTTLIEB, C.P.A., is an accountant with Huntington Plating, Inc. in Huntington, WV.

RUPA R. GUPTA, Ph.D., is a Prevention Analyst for School Link Services in Santa Clara County, CA.

KAY HOFFMAN, M.S.W., Ph.D., is Professor and Dean of the College of Social Work at the University of Kentucky in Lexington.

ALICIA R. ISSAC, M.S.W., D.P.A., is Adjunct Professor in the Social Sciences at Clayton College and State University in Atlanta, GA.

BARBARA PUA IULI, A.C.S.W., is Director of the Social Services Department at the Kapiolani Medical Center at Pali Momi in Aiea, Hawaii.

BARBARA E. JACOBSEN, M.S.W., M.B.A., is retired.

MIKE JACOBSEN, L.C.S.W., Ph.D., is Professor and Director of the School of Social Work at Southwest Missouri State University.

H. WAYNE JOHNSON, M.S.W., is Professor Emeritus and former Director of the undergraduate program at the University of Iowa School of Social Work.

LETTIE L. LOCKHART, M.S.W., Ph.D., is Professor in the School of Social Work at the University of Georgia.

JANNAH J. HURN MATHER, M.S.W., Ph.D., is Professor and Dean of the College of Social Work at the University of Utah.

DONNA MCINTOSH, M.S.W., is Associate Professor and Program Director at the Siena College Department of Social Work in Loudonville, New York.

NOREEN MOKUAU, D.S.W., is Professor and Chair of the Ph.D. Program at the School of Social Work, University of Hawaii.

CATHY KING PIKE, M.S.W., Ph.D., is Associate Professor of Social Work at Indiana University-Purdue University of Indiana School of Social Work.

JACKIE PRAY, M.S.W., Ph.D., is owner of Social Work Unlimited, LLC in Duluth, GA.

JOANN RAY is Professor Emeritus at Eastern Washington University School of Social Work and Human Services.

TERRY L. SINGER, Ph.D., is Dean of the School of Social Work at the University of Louisville.

CARLA SOFKA, Ph.D., is Assistant Professor and Field Coordinator for the Siena College Department of Social Work.

MARY ST. CLAIR, M.S.W., A.C.S.W., is a social worker at Cranbrook Hospice and in private practice in Bloomfield Hills, MI.

DIANE STROCK-LYNSKEY is Professor of Social Work at Siena College.

KIMBERLY STROM-GOTTFRIED, Ph.D., L.C.S.W., is Associate Professor at the University of North Carolina at Chapel Hill School of Social Work.

BETSY S. VOURLEKIS, M.S.W., Ph.D., is Professor in the Department of Social Work at the University of Maryland, Baltimore County.

JAMES A. WAHLBERG, M.S.W., D.S.W. (Deceased) was Professor in the Department of Social Work, East Tennessee State University, Johnson City, Tennessee.

EARLIE M. WASHINGTON, M.S.W., Ph.D., is Professor and Director of the School of Social Work at Western Michigan University.

AMY WEBSTER MESCHI, M.S.W., is a social worker at Bishop Jonathan G. Sherman Episcopal Nursing Home.

ROBERT E. WEILER, M.S.W., is a lecturer in the Division of Social Work, Indiana University Northwest, and a doctoral candidate at the University of Illinois- Urbana-Champaign.

CHARLES M. YOUNG, M.S.S.W., is Emeritus Professor in the Department of Social Work at the University of Wisconsin-Lacrosse.

About the Authors

Robert F. Rivas is Professor of Social Work at Siena College in Loudonville, New York. He served as the Siena Baccalaureate Program Director for over ten years and has taught extensively in field instruction, practice, policy, and research. He served two terms on the Council on Social Work Education (CSWE) Commission on Accreditation and has been an active member of the CSWE, the Association of Baccalaureate Program Directors in Social Work, and the New York State Social Work Education Association.

Professor Rivas held a previous appointment to the School of Social Welfare of the University at Albany, where he served as Field Coordinator and Program Director. On his recent sabbatical he taught as a Visiting Professor at Minot State University Social Work Program and at the Turtle Mountain Chippewa Tribal College in North Dakota. He is co-author of *Introduction to Group Work Practice* with Ron Toseland of the University at Albany. He lives in upstate New York with his wife Donna Allingham Rivas, and they have one daughter, Heather Allingham Rivas.

Grafton H. Hull, Jr. holds a Master's of Social Work (MSW) degree from Florida State University and a doctorate in education from the University of South Dakota. He has 29 years of experience in BSW and MSW programs and has served as a member of the Council on Social Work Education Commission on Accreditation and the Board of Directors. Dr. Hull is past president of the Association of Baccalaureate Program Directors and three state social work education associations. He is the author or co-author of six books and numerous journal articles and monographs. Dr. Hull's biography appears in *Who's Who in America* and *Who's Who in the World*. He is married to Dr. Jannah Hurn Mather and has two sons and two stepsons. He is currently a Professor and Director of the Undergraduate Social Work Program at the University of Utah.

General Questions to Assist in Case Analysis

1. What are the relevant facts in the case? How would you write an abstract of the most important facts?
2. What important facts were developed about the client system?
3. What were the thoughts of the social worker involved in the case? What feelings did the case circumstances evoke in the social worker? How did the worker deal with those feelings? What feelings would you have had? How would you have dealt with those feelings?
4. What important value and ethical issues were raised in the case? What other value and ethical issues might be raised? What value dilemmas were raised? How did the social worker deal with these? What alternative ways of dealing with the value and ethical issues would you suggest?
5. What did you learn about any or all of the steps in the generalist problem-solving method?
6. Which social work roles were demonstrated? Which roles seemed most important? Could other social work roles have been used by the worker?
7. What skills did the worker use to engage, collect data, assess, plan goals, contract, intervene, evaluate, and terminate in this case? How well did the worker do? What mistakes did the worker make? How would you have handled any of the situations differently?
8. What population did the case study involve? What effect did race, ethnicity, culture, gender, sexual orientation, disability, or other special characteristics have in the case situation? What did you learn about special populations from the case? Did the worker deal with the case demonstrating sensitivity to the population involved? What appropriate interventions were differently applied based on the nature of the population

represented in the case? What effect did prejudice or discrimination or oppression have in the case? What examples of overt or institutional discrimination or oppression were there in the case? What issues of social justice were raised in the case?
9. What systems were discussed in the case (individual, family, group, organization, institution, community, larger system)? What interventions were carried out at differing system levels? How did the worker involve multiple systems in the intervention?
10. What social problems were demonstrated in the case? What relevant information about the problems did you obtain from the case or from the readings? In what field of practice did the case situation take place? What did you learn about social work in that field of practice?
11. What relevant information was collected on which to make an assessment? What other information should the worker seek to do a full assessment?
12. What theoretical base informed the worker's assessment and intervention in this case? What other approaches might have been considered?
13. How were research skills utilized to inform the worker? How would you design a research project to evaluate the program involved in the case or to evaluate the worker's practice or the client system's outcomes?
14. What policy implications were raised for you in the case? How did the facts in the case link practice and policy? How did the worker influence policy at various levels (organizational, community, societal)?
15. What practice principles can be derived from the case study? How can these principles be transferred to other case situations?

I

Micro Practice: Individuals

The cases in this section demonstrate work done primarily with individual clients. Although several cases involve other significant systems, such as families, organizations, and natural helping networks, all cases tend to have the individual client system as the focus for worker intervention. In this section, we include a diverse group of cases, some stressing a completed service plan and others left incomplete by design.

Completed cases give an overview of the helping process and demonstrate the steps in the problem-solving process. Incomplete cases allow the reader to struggle with the problems remaining and answer the question, "What should happen next?" The section begins with two cases related to each other that were written by different authors. In *The Case of Trent*, Iris Carlton-La Ney offers the story of a social work student who helps a young African American student change his behavior in a climate of institutional discrimination, stressing the steps in the problem-solving process, especially problem identification and assessment in a cultural context. After reading this case, we felt it would provide an excellent opportunity for students to learn more about micro skills and research design, so we "commissioned" Cathy Pike and Amy Webster Meschi to write a follow-up case, *The Case of Trent Revisited: A Single Subject Research Design*. Their work follows the student worker back to a field seminar where she obtains assistance in designing a research project to measure Trent's progress. Pike and Webster's collaboration demonstrates operationalizing problem behaviors, collecting and organizing single subject data, and documenting outcomes. Both cases do a marvelous job of demonstrating aspects of behavior modification with young children and, taken together, provide an excellent exemplar of the generalist "practitioner-researcher" in action.

Barbara and Mike Jacobsen write the account of a young man in a school system and the worker who advocates for his self-determination in *The Young Bears*. This case gives the reader an inside view of case staffing in a school system and stresses assessment within a Native American cultural context. The reader is left with a major question about what to do in this case—this should provide some interesting class discussions. Noreen Mokuau and Barbara Pua Iuli contribute the case of *Nalani Ethel: Social Work with a Hawaiian Woman and Her Family*. It provides a fascinating view of Hawaiian culture and stresses the importance of culturally sensitive practice. The authors demonstrate how a native Hawaiian worker uses her knowledge of Pacific Islander culture to empower a young mother to realize her potential.

In the case of *Saundra Santiago*, Diane Strock-Lynskey and Theresa Gil follow a social worker in a domestic violence shelter who tries to help a young Latino woman in an abusive relationship. This case stresses the dynamics of spouse abuse as well as data collection and assessment. The ending of the case leaves the reader with several unanswered questions and provides an opportunity to practice assessment skills.

In *The Case of Mrs. Miller: A Long Engagement*, Earlie M. Washington tells the story of two adult children of a chronic mental health patient who ask for help with their depressed, isolated mother. The case demonstrates the persistence needed to engage and provide outreach services to a hard-to-reach client and how linking her to community resources can be an effective part of generalist practice.

Kay Hoffman and Mary Alice St. Clair contribute a case documenting extensive work with an aging widow, stressing grief counseling, termination, and the strength of the individual helping relationship between client and worker. *Late Night with Bea Rosen* begins with a mysterious letter written by one student to another, handing over the continuing responsibility for the case of Bea Rosen. As the reader will discover, there is much to be learned about termination with a client as well as termination and graduation from a Bachelor of Social Work program. Graduating students will appreciate the parallels in this case.

Robert E. Weiler provides a case involving substance abuse and a 16-year-old boy. The case illustrates each step in the problem-solving process. Because intervention included work with both the boy and his family, it is a good lead-in to the next section on social work practice with mezzo systems. Rich Furman adds a global perspective in an account of his student's work with a young woman from Guatemala and her struggles to survive trauma. Using an empowerment perspective, the social worker performs a multisystem intervention in the case *Una Rosa*.

The cases in this section provide a view of social work at the micro level, with its emphasis on individual relationships, social work roles and practice skills, and the problem-solving sequence. There is a strong emphasis on diversity in this section. Readers will be able to explore many differing cultural issues and can expand their understanding of populations at risk. In addition, this section provides a broad view of the role of social work in an assortment of settings and with a variety of social problems.

1

The Case of Trent

Iris Carlton-La Ney

Two weeks ago, Jo began her field placement at Carver Elementary School. She was excited about this opportunity inasmuch as she planned a career in school social work after completing her degree. She was also enthused about her new field instructor, wanting to learn his approach to working with children in a school setting. Jo was told she would be working closely with the school psychologist and a number of other professionals. The prospect of inter-disciplinary collaboration greatly appealed to her.

Because Jo had some beginning ideas about her role as a school social worker, part of her daily routine included a morning walk through the school to acquaint herself with the teachers and support staff, to learn children's names and have them recognize her, and to make herself available for referrals. As she was walking through the freshly painted and brightly decorated school halls one morning, she noticed a small boy yelling and screaming loudly, begging for his mother. A somewhat frustrated looking teacher aide hovered over the boy, responding to him with similar yells and screams and trying to force his small rigid frame into a chair placed in an isolated section of the corridor used for time-out.

Initial Engagement

Jo approached the teacher aide quizzically, hoping to find out the nature of the problem. Trent, a small, attractive, bright-eyed 5-year-old African American child, looked relieved that someone was coming to his rescue. The teacher aide told Jo that throughout the day Trent had been totally disruptive, rowdy, and aggressive toward other children in the classroom. She explained that the usual method of time-out, sitting quietly in another teacher's room, did not work for Trent. Therefore, placing him in the hallway was her only option. Jo spoke briefly to Trent, informing him about the time-out process and asking him to cooperate with the teacher aide. She explained that his time-out would begin only after he stopped crying and could sit quietly. Jo said, "By the time I count to five, you should be perfectly still and quiet. Then your time-out will begin." Trent responded appropriately, and Jo stayed with him for his two-minute time-out session.

The next morning, Jo spoke with Trent's teacher, who confirmed the aide's version of Trent's behavior. Both the teacher and the aide were certain the only option for Trent was to have him tested for behavioral and emotional handicapped (BEH) certification and evaluated for intensive services such as placement in a self-contained classroom.

Because school had been in session for only two weeks, Jo was both surprised and concerned that Trent's teacher had so quickly reached such a drastic conclusion about Trent's needs. She was also curious as to why such a young child was causing such an uproar. Jo also found it difficult to understand how Trent could be described as "rowdy" and "aggressive," when his behavior seemed to her to be rather deliberate and slow. Jo wondered whether Trent's teacher had tried any systematic interventions other than time-outs. Jo understood that African American children, especially boys, are often labeled very early in school and that these labels follow them throughout their education. She remembered that labels influenced how teachers and other staff react to kids and could compromise the quality of education that children obtain.

Data Collection and Assessment

Jo's enthusiasm showed when her field instructor told her to pursue Trent's situation and see what she could do to help. She began by consulting the school psychologist. Together they decided that Jo should gather as much information as possible. This would help her test her idea that Trent was labeled in error. It was suggested that Jo try every possible alternative to get needed information before making a referral.

Further discussions with Trent's teacher revealed that she had not really tried other intervention strategies with Trent, nor had she talked with others at the school about ways to handle him. Jo was concerned that Trent's teacher, a white female, was operating with some preconceived ideas and stereotypes about African American male children. Because Trent was slow moving, deliberate in his speech, and inattentive, Jo feared that his teacher had labeled him a slow learner with behavior problems and was seeking confirmation for her assessment. Jo, who was also white, tried to be sensitive to her own role in working with an African American child. She expected that Trent's family would be more guarded in their interaction with her, and the issue of race might need to be discussed with the family. She knew that it was important for her to develop an early positive relationship with them to understand the family dynamics and to help Trent. Jo was aware that for African American families there are often key decision makers and networks of support within the extended family. She concluded that it would be important to get to know the significant family members and include them in working with Trent.

Jo set her plans into action over the next two weeks. Her first steps included contacting a BEH specialist to observe Trent and determine whether he should be tested for exceptionality; gathering information from the school on family background as a preliminary step to conducting an in-depth social history; and scheduling one-on-one sessions with Trent to complete a developmental evaluation.

The BEH specialist saw Trent within the week, and she and Jo discussed Trent's behavior since the beginning of the school year. The BEH specialist observed that Trent appeared to be a very intelligent child who was very slow in his movements and mannerisms. She felt that the crowded and visually stimulating classroom was too much for Trent to process quickly and easily. The specialist and Jo agreed that a plan should be implemented to help Trent succeed in kindergarten.

Jo began investigating Trent's family situation by reading the school record and speaking by telephone with Trent's father. It was apparent that, until recently, Trent had been living with his mother. A few weeks ago, Trent's mother enrolled in graduate school and decided Trent should live with his father and stepmother while she completed graduate work. Trent's stepmother had two older daughters who lived in the home, so Trent was introduced to a new family living situation. Trent's father tried to make the transition easy for him, often spending Saturday alone with Trent. To avoid imposing Trent on his new wife, Trent's father took full responsibility for his care. Unfortunately, Trent's father treated him like a toddler instead of a 5-year-old, requiring little responsibility from Trent. The stepmother did little for Trent and did not participate in disciplining him.

Jo tried to complete a genogram to better understand the family dynamics. The genogram would allow her to collect and visualize data about several generations of family members, their significant life events, and other family patterns. As Jo suspected, the father and stepmother were responsive, yet guarded, during their first meeting at the school. The interview provided Jo with very little information and left her feeling frustrated and ineffective. Jo knew that African Americans sometimes feel alienated from formal systems, and she tried to convince her field instructor that this might explain some of the resistance to disclosing family information. The field instructor assured Jo that the school was the best place to schedule the second interview and cautioned her that a young white woman might not be safe doing an in-home interview in that neighborhood. Jo argued that because of the problems with the first interview, a home visit was the best strategy. Against her field instructor's judgment, Jo scheduled the second interview a week later in the father's home.

Jo arrived at the home a little late. The family greeted her warmly and appeared to be much more relaxed. Jo told the couple that she had gotten lost trying to locate their home, and she apologized for her tardiness. She also told them the route she had taken and admitted being a little scared. They empathized and said that they would have also been uncomfortable in that area and told Jo of a safer route to and from their home. Admitting that she was uncomfortable relieved Jo of much of her anxiety and simultaneously helped Trent's family see Jo as a sincere person genuinely concerned about Trent.

During the second interview, Jo explained the purpose of their meeting and discussed the genogram with them. The father and stepmother provided information. Jo knew a more complete picture was needed and later contacted Trent's mother for additional information. Upon completing her interviews, Jo was able to complete a genogram that revealed a stable and functioning extended family. It also showed a grandmother who played a significant role in Trent's life, providing childcare while his mother worked. Jo remembered that grandmothers often play an intricate role in African American families and add major strengths to the family unit. Jo also found that prior to moving in with his father, other members of the extended family were routinely involved with Trent.

To complete Trent's developmental evaluation, Jo scheduled half-hour sessions with him twice each week. The sessions allowed Jo to further develop a helping relationship with him. During these meetings, Jo asked Trent to complete several activities that required him to use classification skills, to show evidence of understanding concepts of conversation, and to identify common symbols (for example, letters of the alphabet, stop signs, and so forth). Trent completed each task without difficulty. He was able to form patterns with various colored and shaped blocks, read simple words, and identify the letters of the alphabet in various contexts. Trent showed no developmental delays in physical ability and was able to run, hop, skip, and gallop when asked. He was skilled at catching, throwing, and kicking a large rubber ball, and his fine motor skills appeared appropriate for his age. Essentially, Jo found no evidence of cognitive or physical developmental delays.

Intervention

After several meetings with the school psychologist, the teacher, the teacher aide, and Trent and his parents, an intervention plan was devised. Jo helped identify goals for Trent, including being able to maintain appropriate behavior at school and being able to act responsibly at home. Jo decided to follow Trent's progress at school by using a chart illustrating four behaviors: (1) obeys the teacher and classroom rules, (2) keeps hands and feet to himself, (3) uses good manners, and (4) walks in line/sits in seat correctly. Trent participated in making the chart, including decorating it and deciding the types of stickers he would like to use to reward appropriate behavior. With his interest in animals, Jo was not surprised that Trent selected brightly colored zoo animals for his stickers. Participating in the construction of the charts and selecting stickers helped invest Trent in the behavior change process.

In addition to the behavior chart and task list, Jo suggested that Trent's care plan include a small social skills group. Five other boys from Trent's class were in need of some special attention in the area of social skills, and Trent was included in this group. The members of the group also functioned as a potential source of friends for Trent, since he had not made many friends after moving in with his father. The group also provided an opportunity for Trent to learn and practice socially appropriate behavior through group interaction in a safe setting.

Jo paired Trent with a seventh grader who would act as his "lunch pal." This student, an African American youngster, would have lunch with Trent three times during the week, serving as an older role model and reinforcing appropriate social skills. Although Jo felt Trent's father was an excellent caregiver and role model, she was concerned that there was a lack of understanding and appreciation of African American culture within the school setting. Jo felt that choosing an African American youngster as a lunch pal might minimize the negative effect of the school culture on Trent and enhance his school survival skills. Jo also assigned Trent a science tutor. The science tutor could nurture Trent's lively interest in science and nature by spending time with him in the science center of the school. This allowed Trent to explore his interest in animal life and learn new responsibilities.

Evaluation

Jo maintained regular contact with Trent's mother and father, teachers, and the other support personnel. The parents cooperated by maintaining behavior charts at home, while Trent's teacher followed Trent's progress by charting his behavior in the classroom. The teacher and Trent's parents reported positive changes in Trent's behavior and maturity level. By Christmas break, Trent was interacting with his classmates with much more ease and confidence. The teacher and the aide were relieved that Trent spent time outside the classroom in regular sessions with Jo and with the science tutor. They identified fewer disruptive outbursts and were better able to manage the ones that did occur. Jo felt confident that she had been effective in her work with Trent. Her plan helped him to modify his behavior and to adjust to kindergarten.

Jo remained skeptical and concerned that Trent was at risk in the public school system because of the discrimination African American males have historically faced within that system. She decided, as a long-range career goal, to address this problem by researching the extent to which African American males are treated differently within the schools. She suspected that differential treatment would be found and that a wider change effort would be necessary to remedy this condition. She wondered how she could help the school milieu become more sensitive to African American males.

Readings

Chand, A. (2000). The over-representation of Black children in the child protection system: Possible causes, consequences and solution. *Child and Family Social Work, 5*(1), 67–77.

Hamer, J., & Marchioro, K. (2002). Becoming custodial dads: Exploring parenting among low-income and working-class African American fathers. *Journal of Marriage & Family, 64*(1), 116–130.

Tucker, C. M., Herman, K. C., Pedersen, T., Vogel, D., & Reinke, W. M. (2000). Student-generated solutions to enhance the academic success of African American youth. *Child Study Journal, 30*(3), 205–222.

Discussion Questions

1. *How might Jo go about determining whether African American males are treated differently in the schools?*

2. *What theory was Jo using by employing behavior charts and stickers to reward Trent?*

3. *What was the rationale for involving Trent in development of behavior and task charts?*

4. *Why was it important to avoid giving Trent a label this early in his academic career? What theory was Jo aware of that supported her efforts not to stigmatize Trent by diagnosing him as behaviorally disordered?*

5. *Why might Jo anticipate that Trent's family would be guarded in their interactions with her? Was this a reasonable assumption on her part?*

6. *What effect did Jo's self-disclosure about being scared have on Trent's father and his wife? What are some of the potential purposes for using self-disclosure when working with clients?*

7. *Jo was engaged in an assessment of Trent, whereas the teacher was focused on a diagnosis. Why was an assessment a more appropriate and useful approach to helping in this case?*

8. *What is the purpose of a genogram? How might it help in this case?*

9. *What role might Trent's mother's decision to leave him in the care of his father have played in Trent's later behavior in school?*

2

The Case of Trent Revisited: A Single Subject Research Design

Cathy King Pike
Amy Webster Meschi

Staffing Trent's Case in the Field Seminar

Jo's field placement included a weekly seminar with other students and the field coordinator, Janet Campbell. During these seminars, students discussed cases in their field placements and received feedback from their peers and Janet on their efforts in placement. Jo looked forward to these "case staffings" because the cases were always interesting and the students and Janet usually offered great ideas for improving their work with clients. Today Jo would present the case of Trent to the class. She was pleased to have the chance to consult her colleagues before actually implementing her plan of intervention. Jo was very excited about the lunch pal, social skills group, and science tutor interventions, but she had some questions about how to proceed with the behavioral aspect of her intervention with Trent.

As Jo had expected, her colleagues and Janet were as enthusiastic as she was about the various interventions with Trent. Jo had planned to have the lunch pal document the extent to which Trent used good manners during lunch, but Janet suggested this could be detrimental to the intended results. Janet said that the beauty of this intervention was the chance it gave Trent to interact with a "big guy" and to benefit from the older child's modeling of appropriate behaviors. Janet suggested that direct measurement of this intervention could result in Trent's feeling that it was a punitive treatment rather than an interesting and exciting opportunity to "hang out with a big guy." Jo hadn't thought about this and was glad to have the feedback. Janet suggested that the lunch pal could have a marvelous effect on Trent's manners simply by modeling good manners himself and then complimenting Trent when he used good manners in the lunchroom.

Another aspect of this case that Jo hadn't considered was posed by one of the class members, Sam. Sam suggested that Trent seemed to be experiencing parallel difficulties. He noted that Trent's recent move to his father's home, his separation from his mother and grandmother, and the beginning of kindergarten were all major adjustments, each of which could have caused considerable upset in Trent's usual coping mechanisms. Sam proposed that many of Trent's problems might actually stem from the combination of all these changes rather than from a significant lack of social skills.

One concern Sam posed was that Trent might not know exactly when he would see his mother and grandmother and might even feel they had abandoned him at a time when he was expected to adjust to new rules both at home and at school. Sam suggested that Jo further explore with the family when Trent would see his mother and grandmother. Specifically, Sam thought visits should be scheduled at regular intervals and should include time for Trent to be alone with his mother as well as with his grandmother. Sam suggested that Trent should be informed of the schedule and helped to understand the intervals between visits by charting on a calendar the days left before he would visit his mother or grandmother. In this way, Trent would know that he wasn't abandoned by his mother and grandmother and might even begin to enjoy having his father take a more integral role in his life. Janet agreed that it was very important that Trent not connect his father's expanded role in his life to feeling abandoned by his mother and grandmother.

Jo wondered about using visits with his mother and grandmother as incentives for improvements in Trent's classroom behaviors. Janet advised against this because these "connections" for Trent were too important to be used as reinforcements, the point being that they could be withheld when the targeted behaviors weren't achieved. Janet pointed out that because the provision of love should never be contingent on performance, visits with Trent's mother and grandmother should not be used as reinforcers. However, Janet suggested that visits with cousins might serve as good reinforcers for Trent. Jo questioned why visits with cousins could be used as reinforcers but visits with Trent's mother and grandmother could not. Janet answered that Trent's mother and grandmother were primary love objects, whereas Trent's cousins probably fell into the category of "friends." Thus, good behavior in school reasonably could be rewarded with spend-the-night get-togethers, a trip to the zoo, or other social activities with his cousins.

During the seminar, Jo discussed with the other students and Janet how to organize and implement Trent's behavioral program. Janet suggested that Jo needed to attend to several considerations in designing and implementing a behavior-modification program. For instance, Jo would need to specify the target behaviors to be measured and operationalize these behaviors, develop appropriate rewards for immediate use and as reinforcers for extended periods of success, determine the timing of reinforcements, and consider how to measure and implement these rewards with Trent's teachers. This sounded like an overwhelming challenge to Jo, and she wondered aloud if she had the ability to carry out this part of the intervention. However, she said she would be interested in hearing suggestions from Janet and the class members about how to do all of this. Janet reminded Jo that she really was a long way toward having the program established because her assessment was comprehensive and involved multiple sources of information. According to Janet, Jo just needed to more highly specify some aspects of the behavioral program before implementing it.

Janet suggested that Jo first identify the target behaviors Trent's teachers and she believed were needed in the classroom. Jo had already developed targeted behavioral goals and had listed four behaviors in the initial assessment. Those four were: (1) obeys the teacher and classroom rules, (2) keeps hands and feet to himself, (3) uses good manners, and (4) walks in line/sits in seat correctly.

Janet said these behaviors were a good place to start, but she had a few suggestions that would help with measuring the behaviors. One tip Janet mentioned was that any behavior will increase in frequency of occurrence by virtue of the measurement of that behavior. Jo said, "Wait a minute. You mean that any behavior you measure will increase if a client knows it is being measured?" Janet said, "Exactly. That means you should never measure negative behaviors. Instead, you should measure only those positive behaviors you want to see substituted for the negative behaviors already occurring."

The second suggestion Janet had was that Jo carefully specify what she meant by each of the four behaviors she had identified. For instance, she suggested Jo list the behaviors that demonstrate that someone is obeying the teacher and classroom rules. On the second targeted behavior, Janet said that Jo should specify exactly what Trent would be doing with his hands and feet when he was keeping them to himself. In a similar fashion, good manners would be operationally defined as those behaviors that demonstrate the presence of good manners. The fourth behavioral category, "walks in line/sits in seat correctly," also needed to be defined in specific behavioral terms.

Janet suggested that Jo could measure the specific behaviors that led to obeying classroom rules, good manners, and walking in line and sitting in the seat correctly. Then, those behaviors in each category could be combined into a larger constellation of behaviors to be graphed. In this way, Janet would have not only a measure of the total category of behaviors indicative of a given type of behavior but also measures of each specific behavior.

Janet suggested that Jo develop two types of rewards Trent would be motivated to earn: immediate rewards for specific behaviors and intermediate rewards for sustained behaviors. Immediate rewards would be given as soon as target behaviors were observed, and intermediate rewards would be provided after a specified number of days in which Trent was able to sustain the targeted behaviors in the classroom. Janet reminded Jo that those immediate rewards would have to "fit" within the regular classroom environment. That meant that the rewards couldn't be obtrusive or provoke envy among Trent's classmates.

Until these new behaviors were established, rewards should be provided each time Trent was observed engaging in the targeted behaviors. Janet said that Jo's contacts with Trent, observations of him with his classmates, and discussions with Trent's family, his teacher, and the teacher aide could help her determine what rewards would be likely to motivate Trent.

Planning and Implementing the Single-Subject Design

Jo left the field placement seminar thinking she was glad she had staffed Trent's case. Her colleagues and Janet had suggested several great ideas for Trent's case, and she was excited about the prospect of trying them.

The first thing Jo decided to do was to break those four behavioral goals into specific, discrete behaviors. It seemed to Jo that all of Trent's problematic behaviors could be subsumed into three categories: classroom conduct, physical use of self, and general courtesy. Jo thought about the behaviors that would be included in each of these categories. For instance, behaviors that evidenced good classroom conduct included raising his hand and receiving permission from the teacher to speak; keeping quiet when the class was working on a task; following the teacher's instructions; and listening to the teacher by looking at her face as she spoke, while remaining still with his hands folded in the lap. Appropriate use of self would include walking at a moderate speed directly behind the person he was following and keeping his hands at his side; sitting in his seat with both feet on the floor and facing forward; keeping his hands in his lap or on top of the desk when not using them to write or work; and speaking quietly during group exercises in class. Behaviors that related to general courtesy were saying "please" and "thank you"; waiting for others to finish speaking before he speaks; speaking with a moderate tone of voice; and sharing the classroom toys and activities during group time.

Each of the three categories included four specific behaviors Jo believed Trent could accomplish. Before her next meeting with Trent, Jo planned to observe his behavior at different times during the day for a week. By comparing these initial observations to those made after program implementation, Jo would know how well the program worked for Trent. Jo also wanted to make sure she had not missed an important behavior that needed to be included in Trent's behavioral program.

Next, Jo met with Trent's teacher and the teacher aide to determine the extent to which they thought these behaviors sufficiently addressed Trent's needs and to decide which immediate rewards could be given to Trent during the course of the day. Jo had prepared a chart in which the specific target behaviors were listed by category and gave a copy of the chart to Trent's teacher and teacher aide (see Table 1).

Trent's teacher and the aide agreed that the behaviors Jo had included were a comprehensive list of behaviors they wanted Trent to develop, but they wondered how to implement immediate rewards that would not be intrusive or cause the other children to envy Trent. Jo suggested that the use of both immediate and intermediate rewards could help prevent problems. She suggested that Trent's teacher use a checklist of each of these behaviors. When one of them "caught" Trent engaging in one of the targeted appropriate behaviors, she could place a mark next to it. At the end of each day, the behaviors in each category could be counted to obtain an overall rating for the day. In addition, verbal praise and a pat on the arm could serve as immediate rewards. The teacher and teacher aide thought of additional ways to incorporate reinforcements already used with all students. For instance, they planned to focus strongly on reinforcing Trent for these behaviors when they had a session—called "Good for You Time!"—in which they discussed the things students had done well that day.

Jo met with Trent's family and discussed the behavioral program with them. Both Trent's father and stepmother approved of the plan and began thinking of ways to provide intermediate rewards Trent could "earn" with a certain number of points for the day and week. These intermediate daily rewards included having a special story read at bedtime, looking at the family photo album, or helping his father work on a project. Larger weekly rewards would further reinforce the changes in Trent's behavior.

At her next meeting with Trent, Jo carefully reviewed those behaviors expected of him. Trent said he knew how to do all the behaviors and was very excited about the rewards. To make sure Trent knew exactly what was expected of him, Jo and Trent practiced each behavior listed in the chart. Trent demonstrated each behavior, receiving only limited prompts from Jo on speaking quietly and in a moderate tone. Trent demonstrated a remarkable understanding of the concept and behaviors included in sharing, and Jo made quite a fuss over these skills. Next, Jo and Trent developed the checklist that would be taped to Trent's desk. Jo and Trent found pictures demonstrating each behavior listed in the chart, and Trent colored some of the pictures that were cut from a coloring book. Jo made a note to ask Trent's teacher to let him finish coloring the pictures between classroom activities.

Monitoring Trent's Progress

Jo followed Trent's progress for the next eight weeks (see Figure 1). The teacher aide kept track of daily behavioral charting and gave the behavioral chart to Jo each week. Jo continued meeting with Trent at scheduled times and followed up with telephone calls to his parents. After the baseline period, Trent continued to make steady progress toward his goals. Occasionally, he had a "bad" day, as might be expected of anyone, but Trent recovered quickly and returned to previous behavioral levels. His teacher and teacher aide faithfully carried out their responsibilities in providing immediate rewards to Trent. At the end of the intervention, both said they had enjoyed working with Jo and had appreciated all of her work to develop a plan that would work for Trent.

Table 1
Target Behaviors for Trent

Classroom Conduct
1. Raises hand and receives permission before speaking
2. Is quiet during work
3. Begins work on each activity the teacher instructs the class to do
4. Looks at the teacher's face when she is speaking to the class or him

Physical Use of Self
1. Walks directly behind the person in front and holds hands at sides
2. Sits in desk with both feet on the floor and facing forward
3. Keeps hands in lap or on top of the desk when not using them to work
4. Speaks quietly during group exercises

General Courtesy
1. Says "please" when asking for something and "thank you" after receiving it
2. Allows others to finish talking before speaking
3. Uses a moderate tone of voice when speaking in the classroom and at lunch
4. Shares classroom toys and activities during group time

Readings

Gardner, F. (2000). Design evaluation: Illuminating social work practice for better outcomes. *Social Work, 45*(2), 176–182.

Miller-Cribbs, J. E., Cronen, S., Davis, L., & Johnson, S. D. (2002) An exploratory analysis of factors that foster school engagement and completion among African American students. *Children and Schools, 24*(3), 159–174.

Nugent, W. R. (2000). Single case design visual analysis procedures for use in practice evaluation. *Journal of Social Service Research, 27*(12), 39–75.

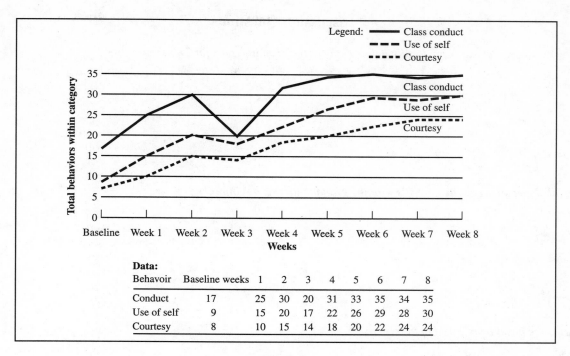

Data:

Behavoir	Baseline weeks	1	2	3	4	5	6	7	8
Conduct	17	25	30	20	31	33	35	34	35
Use of self	9	15	20	17	22	26	29	28	30
Courtesy	8	10	15	14	18	20	22	24	24

Figure 1
Trent's Progress by Behavioral Categories

Discussion Questions

1. Why was it necessary to behaviorally define many of the primary goals for Trent?

2. Why did Janet stress not using visits with the grandmother as a reinforcer?

3. What is the baseline referred to in this case?

4. What was the value of case consultation received from Jo's peers and her supervisor?

5. One of the important purposes of research on practice is that it helps us learn what interventions produce a given set of outcomes. From a research perspective, what is the problem in identifying what caused the changes in Trent's behavior?

6. *In your own life, identify people who are your primary love objects. How would you react to their time with you being contingent on your performance in school?*

7. *What is a reinforcer? How does it differ from punishment?*

8. *Why were both immediate and intermediate rewards important for Trent?*

9. *What potential problem was involved in having Jo observe Trent for purposes of establishing a baseline prior to the intervention and then having the teacher and teacher aide monitor behavior after the intervention?*

3

The Young Bears

Barbara Jacobsen
Mike Jacobsen

Presenting Problem

Josh Klinkhammer had attended other special education staffings, but this would be his first at Wilson Junior High, located in the town of Macaby. As an MSW social worker employed at the Central City Family Service Agency, he worked with troubled youngsters and their families, often acting as counselor, advocate, problem-solver, and general resource person for people who needed his help.

As Josh drove to Wilson Junior High, he was struck by the beauty of the scenery in Macaby, a small college community of about 2000 residents. There was a New England feel to the community, with large, well-maintained older homes, well-kept lawns, and a small but busy downtown district. The Macaby community was well known for antique shops and highly competitive athletic teams. Josh did not know any of the professional staff at Wilson Junior High, but he had been told of the school district's reputation for high academic standards.

Josh recalled the reason for his trip. He had been contacted by Janet and John Young Bear and had been asked to attend the special education staffing for their 16-year-old son, Dan Young Bear. Josh had conducted four counseling sessions with Dan and his parents about Dan's academic and behavioral problems. In addition, Dan's older brother and younger sister had attended the second session, revealing that Dan and their mother used to fight a lot. Dan's siblings were quite verbal about his "problems."

Data Collection

Dan's mother reported that since the fourth grade Dan had worked with a learning disabilities teacher for three to four hours each week. Although Dan had experienced difficulty in school since the first grade, according to his parents, his problems increased significantly during junior high. As a result of Dan's difficulties, the school set up an "end of the year" case conference for Dan.

Dan and his family moved to Macaby approximately four years ago. Janet Young Bear, Dan's mother, "discovered" the community when she was assigned as the school social worker in a neighboring community. She had developed personal and professional friendships in this community that were rewarding for her. John Young Bear, Dan's father, reported that people in Macaby were polite and friendly, but he did not really feel a part of the community, which he attributed to his Native American background. This did not appear to particularly bother him. Although college educated with a criminal justice degree, he preferred outside construction work and was often away from home.

In their sessions with Josh, Dan's parents had expressed their individual frustrations, both with their son and with the school district. Dan's mother appeared particularly discouraged by her son's behavior and said she felt like giving up. At one point, she realized she was working harder on the problem than her son was. She decided to request a transfer out of her son's school district to get "out of the middle." She found it difficult to be simultaneously a parent and a professional when dealing with school officials and wished to be "just a parent." Since Dan entered junior high, Janet and John had been "invited" to school frequently to discuss their son's plans, lack of progress, or behavioral difficulties. Janet had attended most of those meetings alone due to John's work schedule and Dan's refusal to attend.

Dan was identified as learning disabled when he entered the school district in the fourth grade. About one year later, he was diagnosed as having an attention deficit disorder (without hyperactivity). Since entering junior high two years ago, Dan's problems had worsened, with Dan exhibiting many somatic complaints and other behavioral problems. Matters were complicated by the fact that Dan's two siblings, an older brother and younger sister, were doing well both academically and socially. Dan's mother reported that other parents in the district had often complained to her that their children experienced more difficulty in seventh and eighth grades. She had hoped that by knowing the staff at the junior high she could help Dan avoid these problems, but she was not feeling very successful.

Josh was feeling at a loss as to how to best advocate for Dan and his family. Although Dan's mother had been quite verbal in their family sessions, Dan's father, though articulate, was generally contemplative and seemed much less upset about the situation. Dan, too, could be quite eloquent, particularly when argumentative, but he was often only superficially involved in the counseling discussions and problem solving. When he did speak of his teachers, he spoke very disdainfully of some, making fun of their individual quirks. Unfortunately, Dan was funny and engaging in these conversations, as opposed to his usual sullen demeanor, and he received subtle reinforcement this behavior from his parents and siblings. Apparently, Dan had also gained some notoriety with his classmates for his storytelling capabilities.

As Josh prepared to enter the conference room, his thoughts turned to Dan. Josh noted that Dan was a tall, slightly overweight, good-looking young man with long dark hair. His general physical appearance, which favored his father, seemed at odds with his immature behaviors. In addition, there was a special quality about Dan that Josh could not quite identify. Josh wondered how he could explain that quality in words, but words did not immediately present themselves.

Dan's Case Conference

Janet Young Bear had warned Josh that the conference was likely to be difficult. As he glanced around the room, looking at the folded arms, listening to the stilted conversation, Josh could sense the tension in the room. Dan and his father were seated at one end of the table. Josh was seated close by. Although Josh did not know anyone, he noticed that no one made an attempt at introductions. To relieve the tension, Josh turned and introduced himself to the teacher sitting next to him. The principal informed Josh that they would make introductions as soon as everyone arrived. When Dan's mother arrived, she took a seat several chairs away from Dan, since the other seats were taken. She greeted Josh and several of the teachers by name.

As soon as the physical education teacher arrived, the school principal made formal introductions. Josh was asked to introduce himself. He told the school staff that he was a family counselor with the Central City Family Service Agency and had been meeting with Dan and his parents for the past four weeks. He indicated that he had also met with Dan's siblings. At this point, Mrs. Schenk, Dan's science teacher, interrupted Josh. She immediately indicated she had never had any difficulty with Dan's older brother who was, in her opinion, an excellent student. Mrs. Schenk went on to report that of particular concern to her was that Dan, though equally capable, was so irresponsible about his studies. Although he was maintaining a C and B average on her exams without studying, he was doing none of the other work. He was, therefore, failing. Josh was forced to suppress a smile. Dan's impression of Mrs. Schenk's commanding presence had been pretty accurate! His mother, however, had indicated that Mrs. Schenk was an excellent, well-respected teacher who had won awards for her teaching. Mrs. Schenk indicated that Dan was seriously disruptive and careless in her labs, which made it difficult and even dangerous for the other students to work with him. As Mrs. Schenk became more flushed and agitated, the principal intervened, indicating that they would go around the table, hearing from the

school psychologist and learning disabilities teacher first, and then the remaining teachers.

Mrs. Miller, the psychologist, described Dan as an interesting young man whom she had first evaluated when he arrived in the district four years ago. Her testing indicated that Dan's full-scale IQ was approximately 130, and if his distractibility and skill deficits could be eliminated, he would probably test even higher. Technically, Dan was a gifted student. He scored particularly low on the digit span and coding subsets of the Wechsler Intelligence Scale. These results suggested problems with span of attention, visual rote learning, and immediate visual and auditory recall. His greatest strength, revealed by the Wechsler, was in picture completion. This suggested strengths in visual alertness, awareness of detail, and power of observation. Finally, she indicated that she did have some question about the degree of severity of the attention deficit problem, as Dan had been quite consistently attentive during the testing. She described Dan's various trials on specific medications, with apparently mixed results. Dan did not like medication and refused to take it. Dan's medication was discontinued.

The learning disabilities teaching specialist, Ms. Madigan, described Dan as very enjoyable at times and yet the most frustrating student she had worked with in a long time. She outlined Dan's tremendous progress in developing his writing and reading skills over the past two years. She revealed that it took great determination on her part to get Dan to work but that once he "settled in," and if he was in a good mood, he was able to concentrate and work fairly well for about 30 minutes. She reported he worked best alone, especially without other students present. Although Dan continued to have some significant deficits, they were not sufficient to explain his failing grades. She received daily complaints from Dan's teachers about his difficulties in their classrooms, and she, in turn, would talk with Dan about them. The complaints were primarily about his failure to work in class, his immature behaviors, and his disrespect for teachers. Looking at Janet Young Bear, Ms. Madigan indicated that she was "sorry that things have worked out like this." To Dan and his father she revealed how rewarding it had been to learn about Native Americans, the reservation, and "your customs." Gazing at the principal, she closed with, "I believe we have provided all the support and guidance that can possibly be expected. Dan has made considerable progress but has just not applied himself sufficiently."

The English teacher, Mrs. Hurley, was introduced and, prompted by the principal, described her "considerable" difficulties with Dan. She indicated that she did not find Dan enjoyable in any sense of the word and suspected Dan felt the same way about her. Dan's glare confirmed her statement. After two years together in the seventh and eighth grades, she would not, under any circumstances, consider taking Dan back into her classroom. In fact, for the past few months, at his mother's urging, Dan had been sent out of the classroom to the resource room for English. Although she understood that Dan had disabilities, in her opinion, his biggest problem was "just plain laziness, and a foul mouth to boot." He had completed no assignments in the last term. His general fidgety nature was very disruptive to a class. She revealed that she had enjoyed her experience with Dan's older brother who, in her opinion, was apparently an exceptional young man, given the situation. She stated, her voice shaking, "In my nearly 40 years of teaching, I've learned that there are just some students who do not respect and will not follow the rules. Languages are predicated upon rules. Dan doesn't like rules. He's often tardy to class, he chews gum when he's not supposed to, he violates our dress codes with impunity, and with that long hair." Her last comments were directed at Dan's father.

Josh counted . . . three teachers to go. He could feel his own anxiety rise. What could he possibly say to help defuse this situation? Dan's mother appeared unfazed, but his father had pulled up to the table. Dan was sitting with his arms folded, rocking back precariously on his chair and exhibiting a slight smile. Before Josh could say anything, the principal indicated that they would continue around the table and hear from everyone else.

The mathematics teacher, a much younger male teacher named Mr. Forbes, immediately responded, "Math has a lot of rules too, and while Dan may forget some of the rules, he understands mathematical concepts very well. His test scores are generally in the B range with an occasional A. He doesn't complete all of his assignments, but he does work in class. Technically, he cannot pass—not enough earned points. This is unfortunate, because I feel he understands the work. Dan really has not been disruptive in my class, although we individualize most of our assignments. Actually, Dan and I have had a fairly good relationship. Right, Dan?" Dan shrugged, but responded grudgingly with "I guess so." Mr. Forbes continued, "I've offered individual tutoring after school and during free periods. Dan has considerable potential in math and may even be gifted, but he hasn't taken me up on my tutoring offer. The offer still stands. Are you going to summer school, Dan?" The principal, while scrutinizing the mathematics teacher, indicated that summer school and tutoring might not be realistic given the situation.

The history teacher, Mr. Robertson, went on to talk about incomplete and missing assignments but indicated that he was sometimes quite surprised by how Dan participated in classroom discussions. "He particularly likes more complex or controversial topics, or to challenge me when he thinks I'm wrong, and sometimes I am. He seems quite aware of the history of his people. Most of the time though, he just sits and does nothing. But he is quiet and not disruptive. Actually, I think he enjoys history and has the potential to be a good student."

The physical education teacher, formerly introduced as "Coach," was asked for his report. "He rarely attends, and I will not go looking for him again. When he does show up, he refuses to dress and participate. The kid won't even take his coat off during classes. That just doesn't work; he's got to get with the program. And I won't tolerate any more of his back talk. There's been two years of this now, and enough is enough." The coach closed with, "You know, it's a shame. I think he has some athletic ability. He's certainly big enough, but it seems that a lot of kids don't care much for Dan. Some students make fun of him during PE. I think he's basically a good kid. Maybe if he got involved and went out for a sport, like his brother, this whole situation might change. As it stands now, his attitude problem keeps him stuck. He could probably make the football team or even might make a pretty good wrestler. I'm done talking though. This kid just won't listen. It's a damn shame!"

Again, Josh was struck by Dan's caricature of the Coach. When he looked at Dan, Dan grinned, apparently reading Josh's mind. Dan continued to rock on two legs of his chair, but the rocking had slowed a bit. His father sat with his arms folded, legs crossed, chair slightly pulled away from the table, and his facial expression fixed but attentive. His foot was keeping time to the movements of his son's chair.

The learning disabilities specialist again spoke up, talking about using star charts, daily communications to home, and frequent phone calls. She detailed the many efforts of the school system. She stressed that Dan's parents had been cooperative, but that Dan frequently "forgot" or "lost" books, paper, and notes to and from his parents. He rarely had a pen or pencil. She indicated that he was terribly disorganized. He carried the entire contents of his locker in his backpack in order to have what he needed with him. It was frequently necessary to help him organize the material in the backpack in order to find anything, and Dan resented and resisted this. She reported that in her efforts to help organize Dan's possessions, she had frequently found completed schoolwork that was too late to be accepted.

The school counselor, Mr. Hoover, reported that Dan seemed reluctant or embarrassed to see him. He wondered if Dan wasn't actively avoiding his assistance. The few times they had talked, Dan indicated that he just wanted everyone to get off his back but couldn't determine how he might change his behavior to make that happen. The counselor went on to report that he was concerned about Dan's appearance: hair uncut, jeans with holes, and bad friends. Given the friendships Dan was cultivating, he could be headed for trouble. The counselor closed with, "I'm pleased to see that your family is in therapy. Dan just won't talk to me about those things."

Dan's mother related that efforts to support Dan at home were difficult. His Dad often traveled, and at times she worked at night or attended school functions for their other children. Generally, Dan reported having no work to do, or if he did, he had brought home the wrong book or couldn't find the assignment sheets. When he did have the book or assignment, the quality of his work was so poor that they would end up fighting about it. Dan appeared to resent the help. She indicated that it felt like she was "pushing a boulder uphill." She attributed Dan's present situation, in part, to the fact that she had backed off, realizing she didn't want to spend the rest of her life organizing her son. As a result, their relationship improved. She also reported that when someone at school would call her about Dan's behavioral problems, she would ground him. Dan, silent until now, retorted, "Yeah, I spend my life grounded." His mother agreed, saying, "Now I'm worried that Dan just sits, with nothing to do, while the rest of the household stays very busy. As long as I have no expectations of Dan, schoolwork or housework, he is pleasant and we get along all right."

The principal then summarized the meeting to that point, stating that Dan had failed all of his eighth grade classes and appeared to have significant attitude problems. He did not feel that Dan was ready for ninth grade and could not in good conscience reward him by sending him forward with this kind of record. Also, in his opinion, it rarely helped to retain a child in eighth grade under these circumstances. Some of his teachers had expressed reluctance or concern about having Dan return to their classrooms, in some cases for the third time. He invited the special education coordinator to describe options available to Dan.

At this point Dan's father quietly addressed the group. "I understand that Dan failed, and it makes sense that he works until he gets it right. Why don't the teachers want him to return?"

The science teacher quickly responded: "Dan disrupts my class. When he is there other students don't work, and he shows me little or no respect."

In an equally quiet but firmer voice, Dan's dad replied, "It seems like Dan has enough problems of his own without holding him accountable for how other students behave or your difficulties with discipline in your classroom. You are going to have to have a better reason than that to send Dan out of Macaby and away from his friends and family."

Flushed, the science teacher responded, "I have to think of my other students. I feel it would do no good to send your son to school here next year. I would refuse to take your son back in my classroom. He is dangerous and disruptive and a very bad influence on my serious students. As you have heard, others feel the same way." Coach agreed, saying that Dan often "pushes people's buttons." The mathematics teacher said, "It sounds like Mr. Robertson and I are the exceptions."

Gazing at the mathematics teacher, the principal responded with "Let's move on" and quickly introduced the special education coordinator who then described the special education options typically used by the Macaby School District in such situations—the Resource Classroom, in the Aureala District, approximately 25 miles away, or a self-contained learning program room in the Manchester District, approximately an hour away by special bus. She indicated that perhaps other private arrangements could be made in the Central City District as she knew that Dan's mother worked in Central City. Transportation and tuition would be provided by the Macaby District through funds pooled by several districts for special education students. There were some limitations to the money available for private schooling arrangements.

At this point, Dan became visibly uncomfortable for the first time and blurted that there was no way he would go to those "dummy classes." Nervous and shaking, he flatly stated that he would not go to school next year if he was forced to attend those kinds of classes.

Dan's father reiterated his original position regarding an out of Macaby placement. However, he thoughtfully offered a new option. "Dan should not be required to spend time with people who obviously have no respect for him. Schooling can come at any time in life. I myself didn't finish high school until I was ready and needed the diploma. Earlier in my life, I had some of these problems too. Maybe this is just not Dan's time for school. He could work with me for a while during the day while we sort all of this out," offered the father in a calm monotone. "Or perhaps he can live with his grandmother or my sisters on the reservation and attend school there next year. It's apparent that Dan doesn't get along with most of these people, and they really don't want him around. Why force the issue? He has a right to respectful treatment in life. So do his teachers."

Dan's mother turned and said to her son, "I don't know what else to do, Dan. You've indicated both by what you've said and what you've done that you will not work for these teachers. In this district, they are the only people teaching these subjects. We can't afford to move, and I don't want to see you fail again. I guess I would agree to an outside school placement to give you a fresh start. I can't agree to your dropping out of school. I think that it would be a big mistake to return to the reservation. They have no special classes or teachers there for you."

An uncomfortable silence prevailed. The principal summarized the situation by coolly stating, "Dan has failed every one of his classes. Teachers complain about him. He is apparently making some poor choices for friendships here at school. Dan is developing a serious attitude and behavior problem. He once spit on me, and I cannot allow him to treat staff like that. He has been disciplined in a variety of ways for his behaviors. Under these circumstances, we will not forward Dan into high school in this district. We will not allow him to return to our eighth grade. Other educational arrangements outside of this district will have to be made for Dan next year. Are there any questions? Mr. Klinkhammer, do you have anything to add?"

Assessment

Josh contemplated Dan's situation, recognizing that he had only a minute to make an "on-the-spot" assessment. He reviewed the behaviors presented by Dan and contrasted these with some of Dan's strengths and potentials. He briefly thought of the statements of rejection expressed to Dan by many of his teachers and looked for sources of potential support for Dan among the school personnel. Josh thought of Dan's family situation, recognizing its strengths and frustrations. In addition, Josh, if no one else, knew that there were cultural issues that affected this situation based on Dan and his father coming from a Native American background.

Josh knew that the principal was exceeding his authority in determining that Dan could not return to school, and under state education department law, the whole staffing might, in fact, be illegal. Josh asked the group if a final decision on this matter had to be made during this meeting. The principal indicated that plans had to be made by the opening of school next fall. The special education coordinator stressed the need for further assessments and discussion. The final decision would be made by the Area Education Agency, taking into consideration the district's recommendations. Josh suggested that perhaps he could meet with the family to assist them in sorting out their options and work together with them and the special education coordinator to reach a resolution.

The principal closed the meeting with, "Dan, it seems that you're going to have to make some hard decisions about next year. Let us know if we can be of some further assistance. I wish you and your family well in the future."

Intervention

Present in Josh's office were Dan and his mother and father for their previously scheduled counseling session. Josh asked the family where they wanted to start. "I guess I would like to work with Dad this summer and move to grandma's house this fall," Dan immediately offered. When Josh asked if that included attending school, Dan responded with, "I guess so, if I have to." "I'm not sure that would be the best," replied Dan's mother. "We're finally making some real progress in building this family, and I hate to see us lose you just when things are looking better. We love you and want you to live with us. This school situation is just one part of our life, and I think we can work things out here in Macaby. You do have some other educational options."

"Please, Janet," Dan's father interjected quietly, "My mother is a part of this family too, as are my sisters, my uncles, and their families, who would be very close if Dan moved there. It would be moving home. He would have friends again who would understand him. People like us. This Macaby business is just not working out for Dan."

"But what about the special supports and services that he needs? When the kids left the reservation they were behind in school. Dan is potentially a gifted student, but he needs special services. He won't get them on the reservation," replied the mother. "And besides, Macaby is basically a good community. We have a lovely house, it's close to my work, we're finally paying all of our bills, Sam and Elizabeth are doing well, there's a college in town, why can't we just stay here and make a go of it together as a family?"

"I hate this town," Dan responded, "and they hate us. Anyway Dad, Sam, and me. Maybe they don't hate Sam but he's such a *wasichu*, such a suckup and good white boy. He cuts his hair. Just because he likes basketball and studying doesn't make him such a big deal. Things were better before you guys got married, had Elizabeth, and we moved here."

When Josh asked why Dan felt that the town hated his father, brother, and him, Dan heatedly revealed that "Dad and I have no friends. They make fun of both of us behind our backs or won't have anything to do with us. They pick on me just because of my hair and other stuff, Indian stuff. I hate PE. They tolerate Sam because he makes their damn basketball teams win and he gets A's. If he didn't do that, he would be just another 'redskin' like Dad and me. They really don't like Elizabeth either, but they do like Mom, she's white. This is a white town." "Dan, we had to move off the reservation," his mother asserted, "there just weren't jobs for both your father and me. Financially, we just couldn't make it, particularly because we helped support John's family and clan members. Besides, I didn't earn my MSW to never practice social work. Things were tough for me as a practicum student there. We were also concerned that your sister Elizabeth, because she is a part-blood, might have similar problems. Some of the people just don't accept partbloods, you know that. She really has no clan, and because of her lineage she could never be a full tribal member. And she's your sister."

"White people in this white town won't accept her either," Dan retorted angrily. "Like it or not, to them, she's a breed. She's little now, but it will get worse. She'll have to take a science or English class, worse yet PE, in junior high from these wasichu. Then there's that damn principal; he'll get her too. They'll never accept her." "Dan, don't you think that part of your difficulties in Macaby emerge from your learning problems? You will take those with you wherever you go, and at least here there are some real resources available for you," replied his mother in an encouraging manner. "You have so much potential, can be so much fun. I've seen you be much happier, and we could have that here as a family. We can make it here financially. This can all work out." Dan's only response was a glare.

Josh asked Dan's father for his perspective on this situation. "Dan, I agree to some extent with your mother. Please get used to the fact that many people are just racist, can't handle differences, and that's their problem. It doesn't have to be yours. Just stay away from them. Ignore them. I still don't know about all of this disability stuff, apparently your mother does, and I respect that. To me, it just seems like your way, just as I have my way, your mother has hers, Sam has his, all human beings have their own way. So if your way makes school difficult, find something else that you can do, that you like, and do it. If you are gifted, that will come out. I don't believe you should have to spend time with people who disrespect you just because of their rules. I guess it's your decision."

"So do you and your father agree on this matter, Dan?" Josh inquired. "About some things, I guess," was the response. "And you, John?" Josh asked the father. "I'm sorry but I can't answer that question. I can't speak for Dan. Some things he does and apparently thinks I understand and would do too. Others, I don't understand and think are mistakes. His feelings are his feelings, not mine. I am concerned, he is becoming pretty inactive and reactive. I think he needs to discover and get on his own path," John responded thoughtfully. After pausing for a moment, he continued, "It seems to me that we are getting off balance here. We came here because of family troubles. Janet thought you might be able to help. Dan does have some problems with school, but they are not our only problems and, in my opinion, they are Dan's problems. He helped make them, and he can choose to fix them or not. At home he would be treated more like a man, he is almost a man, just look at him. Human beings must make their own choices. We will help all we can."

"From your perspective, John, what are those family problems?" asked Josh, sensing an opportunity. "I am becoming very worried about all the shoulds and musts," was the measured response. "We don't have to live any particular place, have a specific kind of house or car, Dan or Sam or Elizabeth don't have to end up any certain way because of potentials or opportunities or anything else. It is up to us to decide. Other people's ways are not necessarily our ways. More and more it seems like we are trying to live up to the shoulds and musts that come from other people. Janet seems to understand and like those ways, Dan doesn't, but both seem increasingly unhappy. I think Sam could live anywhere, and who knows about Elizabeth. Maybe we should have stayed on the reservation and found a way to live. Even Janet seemed happier then."

Janet replied, "John, you know that we just couldn't make it on the reservation. There were no decent jobs and really no resources for Dan. You're right, I'm not happy right now. But I think we are much closer to being happy as a family. I loved some parts of living on the reservation but not others. Our life has changed a lot since Elizabeth arrived and Dan began to have these problems. We have to provide for their future."

"Janet, it seems that both Dan and John believe that returning to grandma's house is a viable option for Dan. How do you feel about that?" asked Josh. "I think Dan's diagnoses of ADHD, LD, and gifted are probably quite accurate. John, I've been telling you for years that I feel like I am parenting Dan and the other children all by myself, and it has been one of the most difficult challenges of my life. Dan, I've really come to love you, but you are trying. John, I think that if Dan returned to the reservation he would probably have to relive a lot of your life, and you know your life has been really hard. I respect and love you for what you've accomplished, but why should Dan have to go through the same things? If he would just accept them, there are plenty of resources here to help him adjust and succeed. And, as much as he irritates me, I want to continue living with and raising Dan; I love him. Besides, I have a right to a life too. There are just no professional opportunities for me on the reservation. No, I can't agree with Dan returning to his grandmother's or dropping out of school." Janet paused and then finished, tears welling up in her eyes, "and I feel exhausted, I've tried so hard."

Dan reached over and touched his mother in a comforting way and said, "So, Mr. Klinkhammer, what do you think we should do?"

Readings

Barkley, R. A. (1990). *Attention deficit disorder: A handbook for diagnosis and treatment.* New York: Guilford Press.

Coleman, M. J., & Minnett, A. M. (1992). Learning disabilities and social competence: A social ecological perspective. *Exceptional Children, 59*, 234–246.

DuBray, W. H. (1992). *Human services and American Indians* (pp. 33–60, 127–174). St. Paul, MN: West Publishing Company.

Good Tracks, J. G. (1973). Native American noninterference. *Social Work, 18*, 30–35.

Hull, G. H. (1982). Child welfare services to Native Americans. *Social Casework, 63*, 340–347.

Richardson, E. (1981). Cultural and historical perspectives in counseling American Indians. In D. W. Sue (Ed.), *Counseling the culturally different* (pp. 216–255). New York: Wiley.

Toseland, R., Ivanoff, A., & Rose, S. (1987). Treatment conferences: Task groups in action. *Social Work with Groups, 10*(2), 79–94.

Discussion Questions

1. *How should Josh Klinkhammer, MSW, respond to Dan's question in the last line of the case study?*

2. *What are the strengths of the Young Bear family?*

3. *Identify three strengths that Dan exhibits.*

4. *How do the cultural backgrounds of the family members, and of both the reservation community and the community of Macaby, affect family member functioning?*

5. *To what extent is Dan the only problem in this family? Are there other potential clients?*

6. Given basic social work principles, who should be the primary client or consumer of services at this point in the Young Bear family's life? Who is the primary client at this point in the case?

7. How could Josh learn more about Native Americans to more appropriately assist the Young Bear family?

8. Identify all the potential systems (micro through macro) that could be targets for change in this case.

9. What did Dan's father mean when he said "Maybe this is just not Dan's time for school?"

10. Why did John and Janet support John's family and clan members financially when they lived on the reservation?

4

Nalani Ethel: Social Work with a Hawaiian Woman and Her Family

Noreen Mokuau
Barbara Pua Iuli

Introduction: The Professional Social Work Context

Malia, a social worker for the Horizons project, provided services to families with children under 3 years old. The majority of the families with whom she worked were considered "environmentally at risk" residing in various low-income housing projects. Many of Malia's clients were of Pacific Islander descent, particularly of Hawaiian and Samoan ancestries. Malia's organization received referrals from pediatricians, family physicians, public health nurses, and other health care professionals.

While the "target child" was often the foremost reason for the referrals, the entire family was involved in intervention and were frequently assisted through provision of resources, networking, advocacy, counseling, and other services. The main objective of the Horizons project is to provide care coordination services to families with very young children who are at risk. As a care coordinator, Malia's primary responsibilities were to initiate contact with the families, help them identify their needs, and link them with appropriate resources for support. In addition, she monitored and evaluated the effects of these services on her clients.

In the early stages of intervention, Malia often worked with the mothers of the children referred to her. Since mothers were frequently the primary caretakers, once their situations were stabilized they were in a better position to care for their children. Work with the children was carried out after assisting the caretaker and the family.

Engagement: Development of the Relationship

A public health nurse at the state's Department of Health referred Nalani Ethel to Malia at the Horizons project. Nalani fit the criteria for referral due to her high-risk status as a parent with very young children. As a condition of the referral, Nalani insisted that she work only with a Hawaiian social worker. Thus, Malia, a Hawaiian social worker who specialized in practice with Pacific Islander families, seemed a compatible choice.

Malia noted in the referral that Nalani (24 years old) was married to Pohaku (24 years old), and they had a daughter, Kahea (4 years), and twin sons, William and David (16 months). At the time of the referral, Nalani was six months pregnant. Her high-risk status was reflected in several ways, including:

- previous experiences of homelessness;
- permanent removal of her oldest child based on findings of neglect by the court and the state's Department of Human Services;
- low socioeconomic status, with a gross family income of $10,000; and
- low educational attainment.

Nalani and her family resided in a high-rise, low-income apartment complex. Having worked with several Samoan and Hawaiian families from this neighborhood, Malia was very familiar with the surroundings and the people who resided there. However, her earliest home visits to Nalani were awkward. The first home visit was conducted in an open corridor of the building because Nalani said that her apartment was too untidy for visitors. The second home visit was conducted in a neighbor's apartment because Nalani again expressed embarrassment over the cleanliness of her own home. Nalani's hesitance to invite Malia into her home appeared to indicate both embarrassment about the condition of her home and perhaps a lack of trust in her new social worker.

Malia wondered about the best ways to establish trust with Nalani. She thought that there must be a way to help Nalani feel more comfortable with her, but she also recognized the need to make an actual home visit to Nalani's home, meet her husband and children, and assess her home situation.

The two earliest "home visits" illustrated the importance of trust in the evolving relationship between Malia and Nalani. The discussions focused on two issues: Nalani's challenge of the legitimacy of the "Hawaiian-ness" of Malia and Nalani's interest in her Hawaiian heritage. In the first home visit, Nalani expressed surprise at meeting a Hawaiian social worker with blond hair, fair skin, and blue eyes. Her expectation was that Malia would have dark hair, tanned skin, and brown eyes. Nalani's challenges to Malia's Hawaiian-ness appeared in a series of questions pertaining to Hawaiian culture:

Nalani: Where is your family from?

Malia: I was born and raised in Wai'anae (O'ahu), moved to the mainland for several years, returned to the islands, and now live in Wahiawa (O'ahu) with my husband and two children.

Nalani: How old are your children?

Malia: Kimo is 7 years old and Haunani is 5.

Nalani: So you have some young ones too! I guess you know about children.

Malia: I have been learning as I go along. Even my social work training hasn't prepared me much for some of the things I have to deal with as a parent.

Malia's ability to respond to such questions and to disclose in a culturally appropriate way assisted her in gaining Nalani's beginning trust. Malia recalled other events that assisted her in the engagement process, including the fact that she knew several people in Nalani's building and greeted them in culturally acceptable ways by physically embracing them and sharing information about each other's families. In the earliest meetings with Nalani, Malia used Hawaiian words interspersed throughout the interview, and her ability to speak the Hawaiian language was a definite asset. Finally, Malia shared other personal information about herself, including information about her family and background. This self-disclosure was then used to focus on identifying places, persons, and experiences she and Nalani might have in common. Establishing connections or "binders" with people is vital to building trust among Hawaiians and reflects their cultural norms of openness and sharing.

Data Collection and Assessment: Using Cultural Information

As Malia was able to establish a beginning relationship with Nalani, she collected additional information about her situation. The assessment phase focused on three areas, with the greatest attention being paid, in the beginning, to Nalani's self-development and identification as a Hawaiian. Nalani identified this initial focus as her most difficult problem, although Malia realized that Nalani's parenting skills and her relationship with her husband were also problematic. Typically, social workers from the Horizons project conducted assessments of the entire family. However, Malia recognized that Nalani's personal needs seemed to overwhelm her, so the nature of assessment tended to focus on her.

Self-Development

Nalani was very proud to be Hawaiian but was not quite sure what it meant to be Hawaiian. She was aware that genealogy played an important part in any Hawaiian family's self-concept because it is critical to identification and a sense of roots. However, there were gaps in Nalani's knowledge about her own family tree, and she could not fully remember the names of several ancestors. As Malia helped to explore Nalani's genealogy, it became evident that they shared some genealogical connections and were related. This connection served as another "binder" for the two women and further enhanced their relationship.

The exploration of genealogy became important for another reason. Proof of genealogy was a means to secure federally sanctioned homestead land. To qualify for Hawaiian homestead lands, it was necessary to provide evidence of "Hawaiian blood quantum." This meant that an individual's genealogy must include at least one native-born Hawaiian parent. The idea of applying for homestead land represented a beacon of light for Nalani, who recalled the anguish of being homeless and who currently resided in a less than ideal living situation.

Another critical issue for Nalani was not being able to understand and speak Hawaiian, the native language of her heritage. Malia recognized that in translating Hawaiian to English much of the meaning can be changed and sometimes distorted. Thus, for many Hawaiians who are seeking to establish their Hawaiian identities, learning the language becomes extremely important. Although many young Hawaiians are not fluent in their native tongue, recently more were making the effort to learn the language. Nalani appeared "hungry" for lessons on language, as Malia would often use Hawaiian words interspersed in their discussions and Nalani seemed interested in learning these words.

Nalani's strong desire to understand her Hawaiian heritage provided Malia with opportunities to work on other issues. Malia noted, for example, that Nalani mistakenly believed that child abuse was common among Hawaiians, stemming from cultural origins. It became apparent that focusing on Nalani's identification and development as a Hawaiian woman meant educating her on the accuracies of history, language, values, and behaviors of the Hawaiian culture. This would include "unlearning" other values and behaviors she had mistaken as cultural. For example, Malia observed that Nalani lacked good parenting skills, was often abrupt with her sons, and would make reference to the need for physical discipline.

Childcare and Parenting Skills

Prior to the birth of the twins, the Hawaii Department of Human Services permanently removed the oldest child from Nalani and Pohaku because they could not provide a safe environment. There had been reports of child neglect, and the family had been homeless and living in a tent for a year. Malia felt that Nalani was still dealing with her grief over the loss of her daughter. She stated to Malia that she really wants to learn to be a good mother to the other children, but it was apparent that her parenting skills needed improvement. Malia learned that she was not seeing her obstetrician on a regular basis for prenatal care, even though she was six months pregnant.

Marital Relationship

Nalani did not express any marital difficulties, suggesting that her relationship with Pohaku was fine. However, she indicated that she wished Pohaku could become more involved in parenting the twins. She said that Pohaku was ashamed of being a high school dropout and was afraid that he would fail a written examination for a refuse truck driving position. His present employment as a part-time maintenance person was not satisfying, and he hoped for full-time employment with the refuse department of the city and county.

Goal Planning: Working Together

Based on the problems and issues identified in Malia's work with Nalani, several goals were collaboratively established. Malia was careful to make sure the goals reflected the pertinent information obtained during the data collection and assessment phase and that they were acceptable to Nalani.

Self-Development

Nalani's struggle for personal development and growth was similar to struggles experienced by many Hawaiians in the 1990s. There was an increased awareness among Hawaiians regarding the historical devastation of their culture and traditions and a concurrent commitment to recapture the strengths of their cultural past. However, although many had an awareness of cultural loss, they were not fully cognizant of their traditional cultural values and norms. As was the case with Nalani, many did not know their cultural history, speak their native language, or practice cultural norms and behaviors. The search for one's Hawaiian-ness can be an intense experience, initiated by learning about Hawaiian values and norms and thereby strengthening an individual's own identity as well as the collective identity. Nalani's goals for self-development were:

- to learn about her genealogy and simultaneously apply for Hawaiian homestead land (a federal provision designating land entitlement for eligible Hawaiians);
- to learn to speak the Hawaiian language;
- to learn anger management skills and to specifically understand the perspective that Hawaiians adopted in disciplining their children; and
- to complete her graduate equivalency diploma (GED).

Childcare and Parenting Skills

The welfare of the children was central to the mission of the Horizons project, and goals related to childcare and parenting skills were an important part of the overall intervention with Nalani. Specifically, the goals for Nalani were (1) to deal with the grief resulting from her daughter's removal from her home, and (2) to develop and follow a prenatal care plan to assure a healthy pregnancy and birth.

Marital Relationship

Goals related to strengthening the marital relationship and supporting Pohaku's role as husband and father were also identified. These joint goals for Nalani and Pohaku included (1) learning about their joint responsibilities as parents, and (2) securing employment as a truck driver (Pohaku).

Intervention: Coordinating Care

As a care coordinator, Malia's primary responsibility was to link Nalani with appropriate community resources that would support her in getting her needs met. Secondary responsibilities included role modeling, counseling, and information sharing.

Malia promoted Nalani's search for her Hawaiian-ness in several ways. She helped connect Nalani to the state agencies where historical and archival information was available. At the same time, she encouraged Nalani to "discover" her family tree. She also continued to provide counseling on the cultural importance of family lineage and shared personal information on the value of knowing her own ancestors. Finally, Malia supported Nalani's application for Hawaiian homestead lands by picking up the forms and assisting her in filling them out. There were areas on the application that could be filled out only after Nalani went to the appropriate state offices and learned more about her ancestors. Nalani was able to negotiate this by herself.

In terms of language familiarity, Malia connected Nalani to an older Hawaiian woman (a Kupuna) who was a fluent native speaker and who lived in the same building complex as Nalani. The first meeting, spontaneous and casual, occurred as Nalani and the Kupuna collected their mail at the building complex mailboxes.

Malia: Aunty Kuuipo, this is the Hawaiian girl I was telling you about who wants to learn Hawaiian from you. This is Nalani Ethel.
Aunty: Aloha Nalani, pehea'oe? This is my mo'opuna nui (as aunty makes this statement, she simultaneously taps Nalani's stomach). Do you know what I said?
Nalani: No aunty, I don't understand.
Aunty: I said, "Hello, how are you?" I also said that this is my great grandchild—my mo'opuna nui.
Malia: Aunty, Nalani wants to learn how to speak Hawaiian. Would you be able to help her?

Aunty: (to Nalani) I live in the same building as you, come see me anytime.

Two important things occurred in this brief but positive interaction. First, Malia's use of the title "aunty" was deliberate and conveyed a sense of respect for "family." Second, Aunty Kuuipo acknowledged Nalani's unborn child to be her own grandchild even though the two women were biologically unrelated. This acknowledgment was made so that Nalani understood that Aunty Kuuipo would regard her with the same esteem she would a member of her family. This traditional idea suggested an important cultural value of family loyalty, thereby facilitating the relationship between Aunty and Nalani.

Malia had prepared both women for meeting each other but took the opportunity of introducing them to each other as the opportunity presented itself. The spontaneous interaction at the mailboxes was a positive one. Another meeting was set up, and an informal schedule was established to assist Nalani in learning the language.

Malia also provided Nalani with several learning resources, including a Hawaiian dictionary, pictures, and information on Hawaiian phrases. Finally, Malia continued to familiarize Nalani with the language by using words and phrases in their meetings together. For example, they would practice simple phrases such as good morning (aloha kakahiaka) and how are you (pehea'oe). In providing information to Nalani, Malia emphasized the cherished role of children in Hawaiian culture. Malia recognized the need to correct Nalani's misperception that physical discipline was a common practice in traditional Hawaiian culture. Malia also felt it important that Nalani and Pohaku learn alternative ways of caring for their children. For example, during one home visit, Malia was able to provide information on child rearing in Hawaiian culture. At one point during the visit, the twins were unintentionally disturbing their mother by racing back and forth down the hallway and laughing loudly.

Nalani: If my kids don't listen, I lick 'um (hit them).
(She called to the twins and as they approached her, she hit them with her slippers.)
Malia: You know, there is a myth that Hawaiians show love by beating their wives and children. Hawaiians love children. For many Hawaiians, the lei (flower garland) is a symbol of a child's arms wrapped around a parent's or grandparent's neck.
Nalani: I was abused when I was a kid because my father used to beat me all the time. Because of him, they took me away and put me in foster care. (pause) I don't want that to happen to my kids.
Malia: With what happened to you, and to Kahea, you don't want to place yourself in that position where the state may come in and take your twins.
Nalani: Oh yeah, I don't want to lose my two kids. I lost Kahea, I don't want to lose my two kids.

Shortly after this home visit, Malia referred Nalani to a parenting skills class called Malama Na Keiki (Taking Care of the Children), which teaches skills in anger management and positive child-rearing techniques. The timing was good, as Nalani was intent on learning alternative ways to manage the children. This was, in part, motivated by her wanting to keep her family together and avoid removal of the children by Child Protective Services.

The achievement of goals established for childcare and the marital relationship continued. Malia counseled Nalani on the loss of her oldest child and reinforced her resolve to "be a good mother" to the other children. Malia also counseled Nalani on the importance of prenatal care as a form of "good mothering," and Nalani obtained adequate prenatal care. Efforts were also made to secure a tutor for both Nalani and Pohaku to assist them in working toward a graduate equivalency diploma.

Evaluation: A Culture-Sensitive Approach

Throughout the social work process, from engagement to evaluation, Malia tried to be sensitive to the influence of culture on Nalani as well as considering the entire case situation. For example, Malia used a cultural style of discussion called "talk story," in which personal themes were shared in an informal and relaxed way. Talk story emphasizes the mutual exchange of information between participants and minimizes the question-answer format sometimes adopted by social workers. Cultural activities, such as genealogy explorations, language lessons, and teaching Hawaiian values and mores related to child-rearing, were the predominant points of intervention for Malia. It is believed that the infusion of cultural sensitivity into work with Nalani contributed to the ongoing positive nature of the relationship and the outcome of this case.

Accomplishment of the identified goals proceeded in stages, indicative of the ongoing nature of the relationship. Achievement of some goals may lead to termination of the relationship or to establishment of other goals and issues. Clients of the Horizons project are voluntary, and Nalani's choice was to maintain contact with Malia. Outcomes include:

- Nalani's ability to understand and speak Hawaiian words and phrases;
- an understanding of Nalani's familial lineage and completion of a Hawaiian homestead lands application;
- weekly participation in a parenting class and learning anger management skills;
- increased acceptance of the loss of her daughter and increased motivation to "be a good mother" to the other children;
- regular visitations to her obstetrician for prenatal care;

- participation by Nalani and Pohaku in counseling sessions with Malia on parenting responsibilities; and
- locating a tutor for Nalani and Pohaku.

Achievement of several outcomes indicates some measure of success, yet issues in life are continuous. Nalani expressed a desire to continue to work with Malia on several issues, old and new. For example, Nalani wanted to learn more about budgeting and financial planning, and Malia planned this as another area for exploration. The work between Malia and Nalani continued.

Readings

Arsenault, D. J. (2000). The modification of Ho'oponopono as group therapy in a male adolescent residential group home setting. *Journal of Child and Adolescent Group Therapy, 10*(1), 29–46.

Hurdle, D. E. (2002). Native Hawaiian traditional healing: Culturally based interventions for social work practice. *Social Work, 47*(2), 183–193.

McLaughlin, L. A., & Braun, K. L. (1998). Asian and Pacific Islander cultural values: Considerations for health care decision making. *Health and Social Work, 23*(2), 116–126.

Discussion Questions

1. What were some of the culturally appropriate behaviors Malia used to establish the legitimacy of her Hawaiian-ness and initiate a working relationship with Nalani?

2. According to Malia's assessment, what was Nalani's primary issue during their first home visit meeting?

3. What other culturally appropriate resources could have been explored and used in this case?

4. Is it always essential to match the cultural/ethnic background of client and worker as was done in this case? Why or why not?

5. Why was it critical that the goals were established collaboratively between Malia and Nalani?

6. Linking Nalani with community resources was one of Malia's primary responsibilities. Which social work role does this best represent?

7. How was self-disclosure by the worker used in this case?

8. What systems were potential targets for intervention in this case? Why was most of the attention devoted to Nalani?

5

Saundra Santiago

Diane Strock-Lynskey
Theresa Gil

Presenting Problem

Sitting in her friend Maria's kitchen and staring blankly ahead, Saundra sighed as she rubbed her bruised right arm. "All I wanted to do last night was go clothes shopping with my girlfriend from work." Maria exclaimed in exasperation, "Saundra, you know he'll never change. How can you stand his jealousy? He'll just keep hurting you." Saundra remained silent. Maria asked, "Do you still have that number I gave you for the Domestic Violence Hotline?" Saundra nodded, as she looked down at the floor, remaining silent and looking sad.

Maria walked across the room, picked up the phone, dialed the number to the hotline, and silently handed the phone to Saundra. As she listened to the phone ringing, Saundra thought to herself, "How can I do this? He's my only family. He's all I've got." She thought about the first time she met Erik and about all the good times they had together. She felt the ache of her bruises and remembered the reality of her life with him.

Judy Ridgeway had an hour left on her overnight shift at the Safe Haven Shelter. The telephone interrupted her morning routine of helping residents get up and get started with breakfast. She thought to herself, "How am I going to deal with another call and still complete my morning duties? We have to get some more volunteers to help out here!" She picked up the receiver and answered, "Domestic Violence Hotline, Judy speaking. How can I help you?" There was no answer from Saundra, only a short period of silence and then the connection was broken. Uncompleted phone calls to the hotline were routine, and Judy understood this as owing to the tremendous ambivalence her clients felt about leaving their abusers. She mused, "I hope whoever called can try again."

Saundra cried. Maria put her arm around her and patted her on the shoulder. She said, "You don't risk anything by talking to them. Find out what they think about your situation and if they can help. Try again, Saundra, I'll stay with you."

This time Saundra dialed the number herself, and Judy again answered. Saundra explained that she wanted to talk to someone about being physically abused by her boyfriend. Judy suggested that if Saundra wanted, they could meet at the agency office and talk for a while. Saundra agreed to meet that morning.

Data Collection: Saundra's Story

As Saundra approached the office of the Safe Haven Shelter, she hesitated and wondered if she was doing the right thing. She worried that if she left Erik she would feel alone, and that was a feeling she did not want to experience again. Twice during the past year she had actually left and stayed with a friend, but she returned both times. Although Erik had beaten her on these occasions, she did not notify the police because she felt the arguments were her fault. She thought to herself as she entered the agency, "If I could just keep my big mouth shut and let things go, I wouldn't have these problems."

Judy was waiting for Saundra at the office. She greeted her warmly and asked her to make herself comfortable. Judy explained some of the services offered by Safe Haven and explained her role as social worker for the shelter. After a while, Saundra said, "I guess you hear stories like mine all the time?" Saundra stared at the floor, and turned slightly to the side.

Judy wondered what she could say to Saundra to help her overcome her initial concerns about being there. Saundra looked up and said, "I don't know where to begin. I'm not sure what I can do about my situation, and I'm not sure there's anything that can be done." Judy helped out by saying, "Saundra, everyone has their own story and deserves to be heard. Why don't you tell me your story, and I'll promise to listen."

Saundra seemed to relax a bit, and she began her story. "I'm here because my girlfriend Maria told me you would help me. I'm living with my boyfriend Erik, who is 21. I'm 20, and Erik and I have been together since I was 17. We argue a lot, and sometimes he hurts me. A lot of times he gets angry at me, sometimes for no reason at all. Sometimes he gets jealous of other guys, and sometimes he gets drunk. When he gets like that, he hits me."

When questioned more specifically, she described Erik's behavior as slapping, punching, choking, knocking her down, and using a belt on her. In addition, she noted that Erik would verbally abuse her, using derogatory and demeaning words and phrases. She repeated, "He is very possessive and jealous. He hates for me to see any of my friends and constantly checks up on me."

Saundra indicated that although she had numerous bruises and bumps, she never sought medical care. Judy noted, "It looks to me that you have bruises on your right arm, left leg, and face." Saundra explained, "This time I called the shelter because he threatened me with a knife. He threatened to kill me if I ever leave the apartment again at night without his permission. I feel like a prisoner in my own place."

Judy asked if she had told anyone else about Erik's behavior. Saundra said that her friend Maria knew about Erik. She was the one who convinced her to call the hotline. "Other people know about Erik," she added. "Once my sister was there when he threw a chair at me. Another time he came to my job and yelled and screamed at me in front of my boss and everybody." She admitted that she has never really discussed her situation in detail with anyone and that no one, including her sister, ever raised it with her. She added, "I guess they really don't want to know what's going on."

Saundra stated that her life, so far, had been "hell" and that it will always be "hell." She recalled to Judy: "My mother was 17 when she got pregnant with me, and she didn't really want me. She never paid much attention to me except to tell me what I was doing wrong or to punish me. As I recall, my real father beat up my mom and called her bad names. I remember being in my bedroom when I was little and hearing him hit and push my mom while he called her names. When I was 14, I loaded my stepfather's double-barreled shotgun and went to my parents' bedroom in the middle of the night with the intention of killing them and possibly myself. I now wish I had killed them. (long silence) I wish I'd killed them because I could have stopped them from abusing my younger sister. (long silence) My stepbrother molested me, and when I told my mom she told my stepfather. They both called me a liar and a whore. They beat me until I bled. I never mentioned it again, and my stepbrother kept doing what he wanted.

"After that I started using drugs, and eventually I ran away and traveled from New York to Florida. I was involved in a couple of relationships during that time. When I was 15, I was placed by the Florida court in a group home and lived there until I was 17. I used to drink a lot, but stopped using drugs and alcohol three years ago, after going through a rehab program. That's where I met Erik."

Judy wondered what Saundra wanted to do about her situation and asked how Safe Haven might help. Saundra said, "I have been wanting to leave Erik, but I'm afraid what he would do if I left him. He always tries to solve his problems by becoming violent. Sometimes I get in his way, and I get hurt."

Judy outlined the types of services offered by Safe Haven: "We can offer you emergency shelter. We can also help you get on your feet financially by referring you to the Social Services Department for Emergency Assistance. We can also help you look for a more permanent place to live. We have an excellent counseling program and support group that also might help. Do you want to consider any of these options?" After some thought, Saundra asked to be admitted to the Safe Haven emergency shelter while she tried to get her life together. She again noted that she was concerned about how Erik would take it but added that she couldn't continue to live with someone who abused her. Judy made arrangements with Saundra to get some of her clothes and personal belongings while Erik was gone from their apartment. Judy admitted Saundra to the emergency shelter and left her in the care of the shelter workers.

Data Collection: Shelter Notes

On the night Saundra arrived at the shelter she was greeted by Joan, one of the shelter workers. Joan explained that her job was to assist Saundra to adjust to living in the shelter and keep track of her progress toward reaching her personal goals. She told Saundra that eventually each person who stayed at the shelter worked with all of the staff in formulating personal goals. After her initial few days at the shelter, Saundra would be asked to participate in this process. "In the meantime," said Joan, "we get a chance to get to know you and help however we can." Judy visited Saundra for the next few days, discussing her adjustment at the shelter and her plans for the future.

Part of Judy's job was to prepare a comprehensive assessment of each shelter resident, and she knew she would soon be asked to do an assessment of Saundra. To get a more complete picture of Saundra's situation, Judy studied the shelter workers' entries in the daily log kept at the shelter. The following entries concerning Saundra were found.

> Saundra arrived today. She seemed scared and quiet. She told me she had just come from her apartment with Judy. She and her boyfriend Erik have lived there for the past 18 months. I spoke with Saundra about her situation. She related that she has been on her own since the age of 15. Despite this, she finished high school and continued her education in the Job Corps. Although this is the first time she has sought the shelter's services, in the past she has been verbally, physically, and emotionally abused by her boyfriend.

> After three nights at the shelter, Saundra appears to be adjusting well. Sometimes she seems to seek out attention from everyone, and if she doesn't receive it, she goes off to her room and refuses to come out. She seems to miss Erik and has had very little contact with anyone except the guests at the shelter. She made a phone call to her sister during her second night at the shelter, but she has not received nor made any other phone calls thus far.

> Saundra currently works a part-time job and receives no financial support from her family. The money from her part-time job, however, is not enough to allow her to live independently. She refuses to seek any other financial help and currently has no medical coverage. She does not want to follow up with the Department of Social Services to get financial assistance or medical coverage.

Intellectually, Saundra seems to be functioning at an average level of intelligence. She does, however, seem to have trouble with spelling and expressing her thoughts verbally. Socially, she seems "immature," often appearing shy and awkward when conversing with others. At one point, Saundra stated to one of the shelter workers that she wished "someone would pay me a compliment. That's what I like about men. They pay attention to me."

Saundra is five feet two inches tall and weighs about 90 pounds. During the five nights she has been here, she has refused to eat dinner three times saying, "90 pounds is too much to weigh anyhow. My boyfriend likes me real skinny." Saundra says that her health is good and she doesn't have any health problems except as she describes "once and awhile I have these terrible headaches," which she attributes to "nerves." In a long conversation with Saundra, I learned that she is not sure what she wants to do to resolve her situation. She keeps talking about going back to her boyfriend but doesn't seem to be doing anything to contact him. Her sister said that Erik was looking for her and was angry that she had left.

On a positive note, one of Saundra's strengths appears to be her ability to express herself on paper. She loves to write poetry and keeps a journal of every poem she has ever written. She shared some of her poems with me, and they seemed to describe her feelings very well, especially about what has been going on in her life.

Although she indicates she is of the Catholic faith and has been involved with the church in the past, Saundra announced today, "I have lost my faith because I don't see life as ever getting any better." Some of the other residents questioned her about this, and I learned that she is really quite religious. She disclosed that the only way she has gotten through her life so far, especially with Erik's abuse, is through her faith. She seems deeply spiritual, yet in an unobtrusive and self-confident way.

When I asked what she wanted for herself as a goal, she stated, "I just want someone to love me. I wish I could be born again so that I would not make all of the same mistakes I've made in the past."

Data Collection: Other Sources

Judy also collected information from several other sources. Detailed information about Saundra's family situation was disclosed at group meetings in the shelter where residents were encouraged to discuss their home and family situations. Saundra revealed the following important details of her background and current situation.

Saundra reported that she was the middle child of seven in a family of Puerto Rican descent. Her family did not know she had entered the shelter. Her family liked Erik, and he was especially good to her mother, brothers, and sisters. She recalled that on one occasion her family needed money for food and Erik had given her mother his last $10. She suggested that her family knows only this side of Erik, not his violent one.

She did try to tell her family about Erik's violent episodes, but she received little sympathy. When Saundra told her mother that Erik had beaten her, her mother asked her what she had done wrong to get him upset. Saundra said that her mother thought she would not be able to make a good wife and that was why Erik was often upset with her. Saundra summed up by saying, "All my life, my family has told me that I wasn't good enough, that I always botch things up and that I demand too much. They even said they would feel sorry for anyone who would get stuck with me. Anytime anything goes wrong, my mother's voice echoes in my head." Saundra recalled several other comments her family made to her that made her feel small and unloved.

During group meetings at the shelter, Saundra recalled other incidents with Erik. He once blamed her for talking about him, screaming, "If you don't straighten out, I'll get another girlfriend!" In another instance, Erik became enraged and beat her when he found out she was using birth control without his knowledge. She recalled that he yelled, "What kind of woman are you? How dare you do this behind my back! You must be messing around when you go out with your girlfriend."

Staff was concerned because after disclosing these issues at the group meetings, Saundra seemed withdrawn and stayed in her room a lot. She hadn't had much interaction with staff or guests at the shelter, and she pretty much kept to herself, although she had complied with all the shelter rules and completed her house duties. Staff was also concerned that she might be contemplating a return to Erik.

Data Collection: Shelter Interviews

After a few more days, Judy interviewed Saundra to see how she was adjusting and to obtain additional information. Judy was in the staff office when she greeted Saundra.

Judy: Hi, Saundra, come in. I just wanted to check in with you and see how things were going.
Saundra: (looking at the floor) I'm OK.
Judy: Saundra, I've been concerned because I have heard from some of the other staff that you spend a lot of time in your room and have been pretty quiet for the last few days. Sometimes you haven't been eating dinner?
Saundra: Yes.
Judy: Would you like to tell me more about that?
Saundra: Well, I don't feel like I belong here.
Judy: And why is that?
Saundra: Because the other women seem to have it worse than me. (she pauses)
Judy: So the others seem to have it worse than you; tell me more about what you are feeling about this.
Saundra: Well, they are more bruised than me; I'm not like them. Erik never did to me what their husbands did to them; he never broke my nose or ribs. (she becomes

more agitated and angry) He never put a gun to my head or threatened to kill me or my family. If we had children, I know Erik would never hurt them. He would never do that, he loves children. He is not a monster.

Judy: Did you get the impression or did you hear any of us say he was a monster?

Saundra: No, but for you to think that I belong here, and that I am a battered woman like the others, you must also think that my Erik is similar to the men who are abusing these other women . . . and they sound like monsters.

Judy: It sounds like being here at the shelter, leaving Erik, and listening to the other women have all been a little overwhelming for you. It sounds like things are going too fast. It sounds like you miss Erik.

Saundra: That's right; he is a good man. He has been my only friend and family. I am not going to talk bad about him anymore to these women. That's why I've been quiet; I don't want to betray him.

Judy: Not all men who batter are monsters. Sometimes men who batter have a good side, and it makes people's situations pretty complicated. If they were all bad, the issue would be clear. Men who batter can also be very kind and giving. It is that side that makes it confusing. Saundra, I'm concerned for you. Maybe you have not had a gun put to your head, but it's not OK that Erik hits you, threatens you and tries to control your behavior.

Saundra: (after a long silence) I guess I am still confused. I really don't think he is so bad.

Judy: Saundra, there is a lot you need to know about domestic violence. You might benefit from having some more information about this and by getting some objective feedback about your relationship with Erik.

After lunch we are having a group training session about domestic violence. I strongly encourage you to go. But more than that, I encourage you to talk seriously with other members of the shelter group here and ask them for some feedback about what they think about your situation.

Saundra: I don't know how other guests in the shelter can help me and my situation. They're in the same situation as I am.

Judy: Right, but they're capable of helping each other. It's called "mutual aid," which means we all have the ability to give help as well as get it.

Saundra attended the group training session that day. Although initially she was very quiet, eventually she was able to discuss her situation briefly with other members of the group. Later in the evening, she approached Judy in the office. Saundra was obviously tearful as she sat down to chat.

Judy: Saundra, you look like you have been crying. What's going on?

Saundra: I am crying because for the first time I saw myself. I saw me and Erik and our relationship together. It feels like too much, and I'm scared. I don't know what to do, or where to go. I have nobody, no family, no friends. Erik was all I had; he loved me. I believe that even though he hit me he still loved me and that some love is better than no love at all. I'm so scared, I don't know what to do.

Judy: It sounds to me like you are doing something real positive right now. You seem to be opening up and trying to talk about where you are at this point. I think you are also admitting how hard it has been. You are sharing with others about how scared you are, and you are attending meetings and group sessions. You are doing the right things for now. And soon, when you have more clarity and are less scared, and when you begin to trust the support around you here, you will be in a better position to decide what steps you need to take. But for now, you are doing just fine.

Saundra: (still crying) Erik has tried to control my life. At first I thought it was love and that was why he wanted me with him and why he wanted to know where I was all the time. When he would call me several times a day at work and he would be waiting on the steps for me to come home, I was always happy. I thought he was a guy who really cared about me. No one else had ever shown me that kind of attention. My family is crazy; they fight and drink. (long pause) Erik showed me that he cared.

Judy: So he showed you a lot of attention by calling and waiting for you. What happened to change how that felt for you?

Saundra: I started to get in trouble at work. They said he was calling me too much, and I was spending too much time on the phone with him. When I told that to Erik, it didn't make a difference. He kept on calling. I felt so torn, like I was in the middle. I was risking losing my job and being yelled at, and Erik wouldn't stop the calls. I begged him, and he told me it didn't matter, I could get another job. He told me my bosses were too controlling and he didn't want me working for those kinds of people. I believed him, but now I know he was the one who was too controlling. I liked that job, but I got fired. I was always a little angry with Erik for that, but I never told him. I kept it to myself because I didn't want to have another senseless fight.

Judy: What do you mean by another senseless fight?

Saundra: We would get into arguments that would last for hours, sometimes early into the morning. It would start about one thing, and by the end of the night, I would forget what we were originally fighting about. It got out of control. We would stop just because we were too exhausted or because we were repeating ourselves.

Judy: Were you ever afraid that these arguments would end in physical violence?

Saundra: No, he would only hit me when he was high or when he was drinking. I knew not to argue with him if he had been drinking. I knew to just be quiet and not be noticed. He didn't drink much anyway, so I didn't get abused much.

Judy: Yes, but don't forget, Saundra, abuse is not just physical. Earlier you described other ways in which he had tried to control your life and your feelings. You felt a lot of tension at your job and had to leave because of Erik. You held back on your anger toward him because you didn't want to make trouble. That's a lot of pressure to experience.

Saundra: (long silence) Yeah, maybe.

Judy: You don't have to live under that pressure. That's a lot of emotional tension to bear.

Saundra: (long silence) Maybe.

Judy: Did I lose you, Saundra? What are you thinking?

Saundra: I don't want to talk about it. (She looks down and begins crying again.)

Judy: What don't you want to talk about?

Saundra: (looking up at the ceiling, with a crooked smile on her face)

Judy: I know that's a trick question. It's just that you look like you're deep in thought, and we were no longer on the same wavelength.

Saundra: We weren't on the same wavelength.

Judy: Where did I lose you?

Saundra: I don't want to talk about it.

Judy: If you talk about it, what are you afraid will happen?

Saundra: I'm afraid it will become real.

Judy: Talking about things doesn't make them real or unreal, it just allows you to get support and not have to do all the thinking and figuring on your own. Why don't you try telling me a bit?

Saundra: I didn't get my period. I'm not sure if I'm pregnant.

Judy: How do you feel about that?

Saundra: I don't know how to feel about it. If it was a week ago, I would have been happy. But now I'm in a shelter. I don't know where Erik is, and I don't even know if he hates me for leaving or if he is so mad that he'll kill me. I don't think he'll kill me, he only says that when he is drunk. I think if he knew I was pregnant it might change everything around. I think I screwed up by coming here. I don't know what to do.

Judy: What do you mean, "it might change everything around?"

Saundra: Well, he might love me again and take me back. If he knew I was having his child and he was going to be a father, he would mature, if not for me at least for the baby. He might get a job and stop drinking . . . he might stop hitting me.

Judy: Well, the first thing we need to do is to find out if you are pregnant.

Judy promised to make arrangements for Saundra to go to the clinic on the next day to have a pregnancy test. As Judy left the shelter to go home that evening, she wondered just what Saundra would do. She seemed so ambivalent, torn by her desire to make her relationship with Erik work and, at the same time, frustrated and depressed by his control, threats, and abuse.

As Judy prepared to retire for the evening, she received a call from Kathy, one of the workers at the shelter. Kathy informed her that Saundra had taken her things and left but had refused to say where she was going. Judy called Saundra's apartment, but there was no answer. Judy wondered what Saundra was going to do.

Readings

Abel, E. M. (2000). Psychosocial treatments for battered women: A review of empirical research. *Research on Social Work Practice, 10*(1), 55–78.

Krishnan, S. P., Hilbert, J. C., & VanLeeuwen, D. (2001). Domestic violence and help-seeking behaviors among rural women: Results from a shelter-based study. *Family & Community Health, 24*(1), 28–39.

Parsons, R. J. (2001). Specific practice strategies for empowerment-based practice with women: A study of two groups. *Affilia, 16*(2), 159–180.

Discussion Questions

1. *Is Saundra's action of leaving the shelter atypical? Why or why not?*

2. *What do you think is the most likely outcome of Saundra's leaving?*

3. *What is the purpose of having the wide array of "solutions" available, such as emergency shelter, financial aid, support groups, and so forth? Would not shelter be sufficient?*

4. *What factors typically contribute to the difficulty so many victims of domestic violence have when it comes to actually leaving their abusers?*

5. *From what you know of abusers, how common was Erik's behavior in not letting the victim spend any time with her friends?*

6. *What is the result of this prohibition about spending time with friends?*

7. *To what extent do you consider Saundra's mother an accomplice in her daughter's sexual abuse at the hands of her stepfather? What might explain why the mother would not believe Saundra and allowed the behavior to continue?*

8. *What social work value was Judy displaying when she presented the options to Saundra and allowed her to select the ones with which she was most comfortable?*

9. *In your assessment of Saundra, what strengths do you believe are evident?*

10. *The term* mutual aid *was used to describe what happens when group members help others who have similar problems. How is it possible for one victim of domestic abuse to really help another victim?*

6

The Case of Mrs. Miller: A Long Engagement

Earlie M. Washington

The Referral

Susan and Jeff came to the drug treatment unit of the local community mental health center (CMHC) requesting drug abuse counseling for their 55-year-old mother, Mrs. Miller. For the past year, Susan, a registered nurse, and Jeff, a prominent attorney, had been concerned about their mother's mental health. During the initial meeting with Maggie, their social worker, Susan stated, "Our mother is drug dependent and depressed. She seems to have lost her will to live, and she spends all of her time in bed at the personal care home where she lives."

As Maggie sat listening to Susan, she thought that this must be difficult for these two people. Maggie acknowledged Susan's and Jeff's feelings of frustration and distress regarding their mother's behavior and living situation by saying, "It must be frustrating and painful to watch your mother lose her will to live. How do you think I might help?" As Maggie listened, she noted tears in Susan's eyes. Jeff seemed to be avoiding eye contact as he slumped in his chair. "It is especially hard on Susan," said Jeff, "because she had assumed primary responsibility for our mother." Susan responded by saying, "Maggie, we have been affected by our mother's problems for a long time. Our parents divorced when we were in our late teens, and mother was awarded custody. Shortly after the divorce, mother began to abuse prescription drugs and lost her nursing license. She also exhibited violent mood swings and suicidal behavior. Consequently, she was hospitalized several times in the state psychiatric hospital." Maggie noticed that Jeff had been nodding his head in agreement. Jeff contributed by saying, "Mother was hospitalized once in a private hospital, but because of her erratic employment and lack of medical insurance, we were forced to find a public hospital that would admit her. Over the years, the financial strain of caring for mother has become a burden we can no longer bear."

Susan and Jeff went on to describe how they felt angry, abandoned, confused, fearful, and guilty following their parents' divorce. Maggie added, "Even as adults, you are still struggling with the consequences of your mother's illness. I can understand your feelings of frustration and despair. You have been trying unsuccessfully to get your mother to do something about her condition, and it must feel like you have been working on this forever."

As Maggie listened to Susan and Jeff, she learned that both were young professionals with job and family responsibilities. Caring for their mother left them feeling overwhelmed and frustrated. She wondered how it felt to be part of the "sandwich generation," caught between caring for children and a parent at the same time. She could somewhat identify with their struggles, having often wondered about her own capacity to be a caregiver for her aging mother. After all, she was just a few years younger than they were. Maggie realized that it was early in her career, and she was full of idealism, often throwing herself headlong into her cases. She wondered how she would feel if she were in Susan's and Jeff's position. The resounding question in Maggie's mind was, "How can I help Susan and Jeff?"

Maggie felt she had two options. She could work with Susan and Jeff, providing support, advice, and encouragement, or she could begin by visiting Mrs. Miller in the personal care home. Maggie debated with herself over this, recognizing that Susan and Jeff were defining their problem as their mother's behavior—that Mrs. Miller refused to come to the CMHC. The question remained, did Mrs. Miller see her own behavior as problematic?

Engagement: The First Attempt

Maggie decided to visit Mrs. Miller at the personal care home. She cautioned Susan and Jeff that since Mrs. Miller had not consented to complete an intake interview and register for services with the agency, she could not yet be defined as a client. Consequently, she would have to agree to receive services first. Maggie explained that she would visit Mrs. Miller to inform her of the services offered by the CMHC and to make an effort to encourage her to use them.

On her lunch break the next day, Maggie visited Mrs. Miller. She arrived at the personal care home to discover Mrs. Miller in bed. She greeted her by saying, "Hello, Mrs. Miller. My name is Maggie, and I am a social worker from the CMHC. Your daughter and son came to see me at the center yesterday to express their concerns about how you are doing. May I sit down and talk with you for a few minutes?" Maggie was greeted with a silence that seemed unbearable and interminable. Several thoughts raced through Maggie's mind. "Why won't Mrs. Miller look at me? What can I do to get her to respond? I feel so inadequate! What would my practice teacher, Mrs. Golden, suggest that I do in this case? Didn't she say in class that we should interpret the meaning of silence and try to understand what it means? Is it depression, resistance, a social skills' deficit, or is it that she simply feels I am intruding and doesn't want to talk with me? Before I can interpret Mrs. Miller's failure to respond, I guess I have to learn more about her."

As Maggie engaged in her internal dialogue, she noticed the squalid conditions in which Mrs. Miller lived. Her room was bare, and paint was peeling from the ceiling where water had seeped through. A single light bulb illuminated the room. A grimy window obscured the view of a vacant lot outside, where Maggie heard the voices of young boys shouting at each other. Maggie thought, "This facility is nothing more than an old tenement; it is dark, impersonal, and filled with deinstitutionalized psychiatric patients who are left to wander aimlessly with little or no supervision. There are no structured activities, and it appears the residents' only recreational activity is watching an old black and white TV in the front room."

Maggie shuddered as she recalled her initial feelings of apprehension when approaching the personal care home situated among gutted buildings and vacant, litter-strewn lots. She thought to herself, "There is a prevailing sense of despair and gloom here. Certainly this environment is not conducive to good mental health. Just the thought of living here could make a person depressed. I wonder how much of Mrs. Miller's depression could be attributed to her environment and lack of social stimulation?"

Although Mrs. Miller continued to be unresponsive, Maggie decided to stay and proceeded with her plan to present the services available at the CMHC. As Maggie described the services, she said to herself, "I'm engaging in an endless monologue. What is the use of this? Mrs. Miller does not appear to be interested. I wonder whether she even hears me. I feel like I am just talking to myself. But I made a commitment to Susan and Jeff."

She continued, "Mrs. Miller, please consider coming into the center for an intake interview. I don't expect you to make a decision this moment. So what I will do is come back later to get your decision. I'll be leaving now to see another client. Here is my card in the event you wish to call me before I return." As Maggie handed Mrs. Miller the card, she thought to herself, "I am glad that's over with."

Feeling like a failure, Maggie returned to the center. She honestly thought that going to see Mrs. Miller would increase her motivation to receive counseling. Processing what had happened, Maggie asked herself, "What could I have done differently? What prevented Mrs. Miller from at least acknowledging me? Is she really refusing treatment, or is she unable to accept help because she feels hopeless about her situation?"

Maggie remembered some advice from a former field instructor of hers, "It is important to start where the client is. You may have an agenda or a plan when you first meet someone, but remember, your client has his or her own thoughts on why you are there." Maggie realized that she had failed to abide by this rule. She had visited Mrs. Miller with some preconceived notions; namely, that Mrs. Miller would accept counseling after she met her. After all, Maggie was a social worker, trained to help people like Mrs. Miller. Why wouldn't she want to be helped to make her situation better? Maggie realized that she did not take into consideration how Mrs. Miller's depression and past experiences might have affected her ability to accept help.

Supervision

On the way to the center, Maggie decided that she needed to talk with her supervisor, Wendy. Once at the center, Maggie scheduled an appointment to meet with her. As she arrived at Wendy's office, Maggie said, "I need to discuss a referral with you." She briefly presented the members of the client system and the presenting problems. Wendy responded, "Maggie, I am impressed with your motivation and sensitivity with Mrs. Miller and her family. I want to remind you, however, that Mrs. Miller is not an agency client, whereas Susan and Jeff are. Therefore, I suggest you work with them and teach them to manage their mother's problem behaviors."

Maggie responded by saying, "This is a crisis situation. Before Susan and Jeff can benefit from counseling, we must succeed in alleviating Mrs. Miller's depression." Wendy replied, "If this is your evaluation of the case, then I suggest you talk with Susan and Jeff about recommending hospitalization for their mother."

Engagement: The Second Attempt

Maggie dreaded speaking to Jeff and Susan. She thought to herself, "I should have had more success than they had. After all, I'm the trained one." She decided to call Susan since she seemed to be carrying most of the responsibility for caring for Mrs. Miller. Maggie discussed hospitalization for Mrs. Miller, but Susan pointed out that her mother had been denied Social Security Disability and had no hospitalization benefits. Furthermore, past hospitalizations had not proven to be beneficial over the long term. Susan was against sending her mother back to the state institution. She also shared with Maggie how her mother had asked her to promise never to hospitalize her again in a state facility. After some encouragement, however, Susan at least agreed to discuss this recommendation with Jeff and contact Maggie later in the week.

Feeling confused, Maggie was having difficulty following her clinical intuition. She was feeling a lot of pressure from others. Wendy believed that Mrs. Miller needed to be hospitalized. Susan and Jeff thought their mother needed outpatient drug counseling. Maggie felt that Mrs. Miller needed a sense of hope for herself and needed to change her lifestyle and environment.

After pondering her options, Maggie decided to again visit Mrs. Miller, this time using an approach addressing her immediate needs for socialization. Maggie began the conversation through the use of self-disclosure and open-ended questions, reminding herself that Mrs. Miller's failure to respond might be more of a symptom of her depression and isolation. Maggie left an hour later, feeling that she was on the right track. Although Mrs. Miller did not speak, she made brief eye contact with Maggie, as if to say, "Why are you so determined to get me to talk to you?"

Supervision

In her next supervision session, Maggie reported to Wendy that she continued to visit Mrs. Miller. She expressed both her frustration and encouragement, stating, "There has been no significant progress, Wendy. Mrs. Miller did make brief eye contact with me on one occasion. I feel encouraged by this. I also spoke with Susan regarding hospitalization. She is very reluctant to do this. She promised her mother she would never have her committed to a state institution again. She did agree to discuss this with Jeff."

"I understand that you feel encouraged, Maggie," replied Wendy, "but our primary concern is Mrs. Miller's welfare. Based on what you told me, she is depressed and requires more intensive care and supervision than we are able to provide through your outreach efforts. Further, Mrs. Miller's history of depression suggests she may be at risk for suicide. Since she is unwilling to voluntarily seek treatment, I believe it is best to take a more conservative approach." Maggie answered, "I'm also concerned about Mrs. Miller's potential for self-destructive behavior. Are there any other options for treatment in a less restrictive setting?" Wendy suggested, "Our partial hospitalization program may be an option. I hesitated to mention this earlier because of Mrs. Miller's inability to communicate and become involved in structured program activities."

Wendy believed that Maggie was spending too much time working with Mrs. Miller, since she was not in the agency system and did not have substance abuse as a primary problem. In contrast to other agency units, drug treatment program revenues were based on the number of billable client contact hours (defined as a 30- to 50-minute office session). This information was kept through the intake and registration process. Since Mrs. Miller was not a registered client, the program was unable to bill for services rendered. Wendy also pointed out that the program did not sanction the relationship, and therefore no official records were being kept.

Maggie realized that Mrs. Miller was referred to the wrong unit. The drug treatment unit did not address Mrs. Miller's need for structured, supervised daily activities. A day hospital program would meet these criteria. Thus, Maggie called the partial hospitalization program to discuss the case.

The intake worker agreed with Maggie that Mrs. Miller was a suitable candidate for partial hospitalization, providing she would attend. In this unit, she could participate in structured daily activities, recreational therapy, and receive resocialization and counseling, vocational rehabilitation, medication maintenance, housing assistance, and financial advocacy.

Maggie suggested to the intake worker that she continue to provide individual counseling for Mrs. Miller, given her involvement in the case and Mrs. Miller's current mental state (that is, apathy and depression). Maggie argued that a change of worker would be contraindicated at this time.

Collaborating with the partial hospitalization program was successful. The challenges facing Maggie were to gain Wendy's support for the plan and motivate Mrs. Miller to participate. Maggie mused, "Gaining Wendy's support will not be too difficult. I certainly can make a cogent argument for Mrs. Miller's participation in the partial hospitalization program, but motivating Mrs. Miller will require all the skills I have, and then some!"

Maggie started the session by announcing, "Wendy, I took the initiative to consult with the intake worker at the partial hospitalization program. She believes that Mrs. Miller is appropriate for their services and would benefit from the program." Wendy replied, "How are you going to get Mrs. Miller to participate in the program when she will not respond verbally to any of your overtures?" Maggie noted, "I've given this a lot of thought. My plan is this: I will continue to visit Mrs. Miller daily for a period of one week. During this time, I will validate her as a worthwhile individual by reflecting on her achievements. To accomplish this, I will ask Susan to bring me a family photo album that will help me structure my 'monologue' with her and elicit responses. When appropriate, I'll self-disclose some of my own feelings. I will enthusiastically share with her information about the partial hospital program and how it may benefit her." Although the drug treatment unit had not been actively involved with the partial hospitalization program before, Wendy agreed to support the collaborative effort on a trial basis.

Engagement: The Third Attempt

Susan called to say that she and Jeff agreed to have their mother committed to the state psychiatric institution. They didn't feel good about this decision but realized they were unable to provide enough care to their mother to help her change her situation. Since Mrs. Miller was unwilling to receive help, they felt an involuntary commitment might be necessary. Maggie told Susan about the possible referral to the partial hospitalization program as an alternative to hospitalization, provided Mrs. Miller would be willing to participate. Maggie added that she had been visiting Mrs. Miller for the past few days and that their mother maintained brief periods of eye contact during their visits. Although Maggie did not consider this to be a major breakthrough, she believed progress was being made. She also told Susan she planned to visit Mrs. Miller again today, and she would call to report how the visit went.

Maggie arrived at the personal care home to find Mrs. Miller lying on her bed as usual. Nevertheless, Maggie felt confident that Mrs. Miller would respond today. Through their visits, Maggie had been validating Mrs. Miller as an individual rather than as a person in need of counseling (something she failed to do during the first visit). The use of the family album proved to be particularly helpful, at least in eliciting and maintaining Mrs. Miller's attention. Maggie's revised approach acknowledged Mrs. Miller as having roles other than that of patient. This was an important consideration for Maggie who wanted to recognize and build upon Mrs. Miller's strengths. Particularly, Maggie stressed that Mrs. Miller was a mother who had reared two children who were successful and that she would soon be a grandmother. Also, Maggie purposefully self-disclosed about herself to demonstrate that she was a real person and to help Mrs. Miller feel safe about sharing her feelings.

Maggie was Mrs. Miller's only real contact with the outside world. Susan and Jeff were so upset by their mother's condition that they could no longer bring themselves to visit her. Maggie figured that by now Mrs. Miller probably realized this. She hoped that her regular visits might demonstrate that she cared and was interested in Mrs. Miller's situation.

As usual, Maggie sat down and began to talk with Mrs. Miller. Suddenly, Mrs. Miller looked directly into Maggie's eyes and said, "Don't you have anything better to do?" Maggie responded, "No, Mrs. Miller. I am concerned about you. You seem not to be interested much in things going on in your life. You seem so isolated here. I've learned a lot about you through visiting and reviewing your family album. Susan and Jeff have helped too." In response, Mrs. Miller said, "I'm nothing but a burden to my children. I've ruined their lives, and I would be better off dead." Maggie responded, "It's true that your illness has created somewhat of a burden for your children, but this has not ruined their lives. Susan and Jeff are concerned about you and want you to seek treatment. Participating in treatment will not only help you but will also alleviate some of the stress they are experiencing."

Encouraged by her response, Maggie told Mrs. Miller about the partial hospitalization program. Mrs. Miller expressed some reluctance, noting she had no means of getting to and from the center. Maggie reassured her that a van would pick her up in the mornings and return her in the afternoons. Mrs. Miller replied, "I don't want to go . . . I don't want to be bothered." Maggie negotiated with Mrs. Miller until she agreed to try the program for a few days.

Supervision

Maggie discussed her breakthrough with Mrs. Miller. Wendy commented that Mrs. Miller's engagement was due, in large part, to Maggie's persistence and resourcefulness. She ended saying, "I admire your persistence, Maggie. You acted a little bit like my dog Zippy. When she gets a hold on something, like my slippers, she doesn't let go. You took Mrs. Miller's initial reaction to you as a personal and professional challenge. You didn't let go either!" Maggie responded, "This is just a first step, but it's a promising one."

Evaluation

Mrs. Miller became involved in the partial hospitalization program and received services for several years. Although the CMHC changed its structure, it continued to support Mrs. Miller and her children. They continue to see one of the social workers in the agency. Mrs. Miller now receives Social Security Disability and subsidized housing. She takes medication to control her depression and has avoided further hospitalization. She enjoys a satisfying relationship with her children and grandchildren. Susan and Jeff participated in Mrs. Miller's overall treatment and continue to be supportive of her treatment plan.

Readings

Kissman, K., & Maurer, L. (2002). East meets West: Therapeutic aspects of spirituality in health, mental health and addiction recovery. *International Social Work, 45*(1), 35–43.

Rogers, A., & Barusch, A. (2000). Mental health service utilization among frail, low-income elders: Perceptions of home service providers and elders in the community. *Journal of Gerontological Social Work, 34*(2), 23–38.

Stromwall, L. K. (2002). Is social work's door open to people recovering from psychiatric disabilities? *Social Work, 47*(1), 75–84.

Discussion Questions

1. *How did Maggie engage Mrs. Miller in a treatment program?*

2. *Should Maggie have continued to engage in outreach efforts with Mrs. Miller, or should she have discontinued her activity? At what point would discontinuing outreach be indicated? If outreach were discontinued, what steps should Maggie take to ensure that Mrs. Miller received needed services? What resources in your own community would you bring to bear on Mrs. Miller's situation?*

3. *What specific agency policies were barriers to initial service delivery? How did the worker remove the barriers? Assuming that agency policy prevented Maggie from extended outreach in the engagement phase, what might Maggie have done to ensure Mrs. Miller was engaged in another helping system? How would you change the agency policy that prevents workers in the drug treatment unit from doing outreach with clients who are not actively abusing drugs or alcohol?*

4. *What was Maggie's definition of Mrs. Miller's problem? How did the family define the problem? How did Mrs. Miller define the problem? How did the agency define the problem?*

5. *What factors contributed to the success of this case?*

6. *The worker's comment to Susan and Jeff, "It must be frustrating and painful to watch your mother lose her will to live," is an example of what kind of response?*

7. *What did Maggie mean when she said patients at the home were "disinstitutionalized psychiatric patients"? Why are such patients not provided care in formal settings such as private or public mental hospitals?*

8. *Which of Maggie's actions or behaviors would you consider evidence of "professional use of self"?*

9. *Initially, at least, Maggie seems to have a conflict between her sense of obligation to her agency and her belief that the client needs service even though the agency does not consider her a "paying" client. In your judgment, which of these obligations must take precedence and why?*

10. *Was it ethical for Maggie to talk Mrs. Miller into trying the partial hospitalization program when she initially expressed reluctance to participate? Was Maggie unduly influencing Mrs. Miller?*

7

Late Night with Bea Rosen

Kay Hoffman
Mary Alice St. Clair

Dear Gretchen,

I am writing this letter to you for several reasons. I don't have much time left, and I want to get this off my mind and move on with my life. I know this letter has a strange beginning, but bear with me, I think you will find it helpful.

I am writing this in my dorm room. It's 1:30 in the morning, and I've had too many cups of coffee, too many final exams and papers, and too little time to be concerned with convention. A year from now, you'll probably more fully understand this condition; believe me, it will pass.

Dr. David, our field coordinator, told me you would be assigned to Jewish Family Service for your field placement next year, and the folks at JFS tell me you will be taking over for me with the case of Bea Rosen. This makes me incredibly happy, since I have been working with her during this year and I want her to get the best services possible.

I may or may not be over-involved with the Bea Rosen case. Since this is the last week of my field placement, I am in the final phase of "terminating" with her, and it has been very difficult for me. I'm told by my professors at school, as well as by my colleagues at JFS, that having intense feelings during termination is sometimes normal for students and workers alike. However, I figured writing this letter and giving you my best insights on the case of Bea Rosen would be a good way for me to deal with my feelings, and perhaps, do some good for Bea at the same time.

You should know that I obtained permission from Bea to write this letter to you. To not do this would have violated her privacy and confidentiality. I also obtained permission from JFS and from school, so I think I'm all squared away with necessary permissions. Please remember that this material is very personal, both for Bea and for me, and it should be treated as confidential within the guidelines of JFS and the NASW Code of Ethics.

Having said this, I want to proceed with Bea's story. Attached you will find my collected insights, "for what it's worth." I hope it will be helpful to you and to Bea. I did make several entries in Bea's case record while I was at the agency. I also wrote a closing summary in the record this week, but it was so brief that it left me with an unsatisfying feeling. And so, I write to you . . .
Kathleen

Introduction

Bea Rosen is a 76-year-old, recently widowed woman. Her husband, Barry, died in November of last year after experiencing heart problems for 22 years. Bea and Barry were extremely close and dependent on one another. While both had heart problems, Bea was Barry's primary caregiver for the last ten years of his life. Bea now lives alone in the apartment she and Barry shared for 25 years. The apartment, a second floor walk-up, is part of an independent complex that offers no senior services. Bea's only child, Lenny, lives in the northern suburbs. He visits his mother every week and takes her grocery shopping.

I became involved with the Rosens as part of my field placement at Jewish Family Service (JFS). As their social worker, I spent time with the Rosens every other week. I became aware of the extent of Barry's decline when he was placed in a nursing home, and I visited the couple there. Barry died a week later. After that, I started visiting Bea every week.

I visited Bea in her apartment. She was usually dressed in slacks and a blouse or sweater, often with a little jewelry. She wears a wig and makeup, and her nails always look nice. Bea worked in a women's clothing store for years and has good fashion sense and always wants to look presentable.

My role as a social worker was to provide company and support for Bea as she coped with her transition. I offered her empathic listening, social support, and referrals to other community services as needed. I also served as eyes and ears for JFS, assessing Bea's situation at home, and watching for any dangerous or unhealthy situations that might develop because of her health and social situation. As part of Senior Support Services at JFS, I helped provide services and support to seniors to enable them to remain living independently. These services included homemakers, respite workers, shoppers, transportation, supportive counseling, and limited economic assistance.

Presenting Problem and Assessment

The loss of Barry has been particularly difficult for Bea. She and Barry were very close and dependent on one another throughout their marriage. Barry died just six weeks before their 50th wedding anniversary. The care of Barry dominated Bea's life for so many years that his death was a tremendous role loss for Bea. In my opinion, she kept him well and functioning far beyond the expectations for a man with his health problems. It was her constant, patient care and her coaxing that kept Barry going. Bea surrendered Barry to a nursing home placement only when it became impossible to care for him. He had become more confused, lapsed in and out of awareness, and finally sat down on the floor in the hall and couldn't get up. He was hardly aware of his circumstances.

Emotionally, placing Barry in the nursing home was very rough on Bea. Barry complained that he felt like he was in jail. Bea felt that she was abandoning him, even though she managed to care for him at the nursing home all day. The care Barry received at the facility was poor. He developed pneumonia and was transferred to the hospital. Bea knew the pneumonia would probably be fatal, and she was with him several days later when he died in his sleep.

In the days following Barry's death, Bea experienced profound grief, loss of energy, disrupted sleep, and many episodes of thinking Barry was there in the apartment with her. These episodes were disturbing to her for two reasons. Finding Barry was not really there with her shocked her out of the denial of his death (an early phase of grieving according to Kübler-Ross, 1969), and she was afraid she was losing her grip on reality. Some of the intervention work I did was to reassure her that these experiences and feelings were normal under the circumstances.

Health Status

Bea has multiple health problems: hearing loss in both ears (she wears hearing aids), gallbladder problems, and heart problems. She had a heart attack ten years ago and bypass surgery four years ago. She lives with a coronary aneurysm that affects her stamina and threatens the health of her heart. Her heart problems affect her strength to such an extent that going up and down the stairs is an effort and doing laundry in the basement of the apartment an impossibility. She receives homemaker services through JFS to clean and do the laundry. She no longer drives and uses several different means of transportation, including rides from neighbors, her son, the Senior bus (provided by the city of Southfield), and JFS transportation services. Bea tries to get out to walk a little in the apartment complex every day, but bad weather is often an obstacle. Shopping is available directly across the street from her apartment complex, but because of her decreased stamina, Bea is unable to walk to the stores and must depend on someone for a ride.

Mental Status

Bea is living alone for the first time in her life. She shared with me that she is afraid to be alone, especially at night. She disclosed that she had a "nervous breakdown" as a young woman and had received psychiatric treatment for her anxieties. She has been reluctant to be more specific about her past problems and about how they are affecting her now. She did say that she was a young mother at the time of her breakdown and that with treatment and the support of her loving husband she was able to run the household, raise a family, and work in a dress shop.

She also told me that sometimes, when she is upset, she annoys her son with frequent calls. She said the nights are the worst for her, when she can't sleep and just keeps on thinking. Because of her reluctance to be more specific, it has been hard for me to assess the depth and seriousness of her anxiety problems. She doesn't want to pay a lot of attention to them at this point in time. During this bereavement period, it seemed more important to her to just get through the day.

Bea's mental functioning is clear; she has no significant memory losses or inconsistencies, is not confused, shows proper judgment, and is reality-oriented. She does have a problem with anxiety about being alone, which may be paranoia, and I have been unable to assess this problem because of her unwillingness to get very specific about it. It has seemed inappropriate for me to question her extensively about her fears and possible phobias, since I am inexperienced in the field. My main purpose has been to support her in these early stages of acute bereavement.

In my latest session, Bea described some behavior that may border on the obsessive—for example, not trusting that she locked the door, checking it over and over again, or worrying that she has not turned off the stove. She said she doesn't trust her memory; she will check the door or the stove and then walk away and wonder if she checked it well enough. I got the impression that this behavior has been increasing. I plan to discuss these behaviors with my supervisor and alert another clinical therapist who is going to visit Bea to invite her to be in a seniors' therapy group.

At the present time, Bea is experiencing mild depression, mood swings, low motivation, and low energy. These are normal to the grieving process. In our sessions, she often talked about her losses, crying at times, and discussing the ways she was trying to cope with the situation. The past few months have been extremely difficult for her. Whenever I saw successful coping patterns, I talked about them with her and gave her encouragement that she was finding ways to get through the days and keep going. I emphasized her strengths and her resiliency.

Only once, very early in bereavement, did she suggest that maybe all her efforts weren't worth it and that living wasn't worth it. Later in that same session she said she did have a lot to live for, and she has continued to work toward a better quality of life for herself since that time. Her motto at present is, "If you want to make it, you've got to take it," exhibiting the survival quality she experiences in her life at the moment.

At 76 years old, Bea is experiencing very old age. She is hard of hearing, which is intrinsic to the aging process. She has heart and gallbladder problems that are disease states more common in the elderly than in any other age group. Psychosocially, she is facing the crisis of integrity versus despair, according to Erikson, or immortality versus extinction according to Newman & Newman. Bea exhibits efforts to achieve integrity as she reminisces about her life, especially her life with Barry. Most of the work I did with Bea and Barry this past fall involved reminiscing, which they found to be a very enjoyable and fruitful exercise.

Coping Patterns

Six weeks after Barry's death, Bea made a concerted effort to sort through his old clothes and give them away and to start to clean out the spare bedroom so she could rent it out. Sorting through Barry's belongings was physically and emotionally exhausting for Bea, but she considered the job her obligation as part of her religion. It was also necessary to get on with her life and to rent out the room.

When Bea had a rough day, she would force herself to get out of the house. On one such day, she asked a neighbor for a ride to a large department store, where she spent part of the afternoon looking around and visiting in the snack bar. She said it didn't help to take away the loneliness when she got home, but it did help her feel better while she was out. Part of what I did for Bea was to point out her coping methods and give her credit for the progress she made in creating a life for herself without Barry. When I think of Bea, I think of endurance. Even though she is physically frail and emotionally grieving, she possesses a special fortitude and endurance. It is shown in the way she cared for Barry through his years of hardship and her own physical problems, coaxing him to keep on living while she kept on loving him. It is shown in the way she hasn't given up on herself and has tried to regain a balance in her life, despite her numerous losses. Again, her motto is, "If you want to make it, you've got to take it." I guess we can all learn from that!

Bea is pretty insightful about herself and others. She is in touch with her emotions and feelings, and her emotions are generally congruent with the situation. She shows strong motivation to improve her situation, seeks help when appropriate, and doesn't want to be dependent on others. She has friends, a supportive family, and good relationships with everyone.

The limitations Bea faces are mainly attributable to her age and health problems. Her heart problems limit her energy level. Her finances limit the choices she has in housing and help. Her housing limits her mobility, finances, and other options. In federally subsidized senior housing, her rent would be lower and she would have access to meals, services and more socializing. Her lack of transportation makes her dependent on friends and community-based transportation services. Bea's problems with anxiety have limited her ability to envision herself successfully living on her own and have added to the trauma of losing Barry.

Financial Status

Bea is facing financial problems. Now that she is the single member of her household, she receives only her Social Security check and a very small pension. When Barry was living, their income was $979 per month. Since his death, her income is just $516 per month, and she has to pay monthly rent of $485. Financially, she says she's OK for the time being. I expect she may have some life insurance from Barry that is helping her out temporarily. JFS is helping by providing FEMA of $30 per month for six months. This will end soon but can be extended further if she still needs the help.

Bea would like to find a young woman to rent her second bedroom. This would provide both income and companionship for her. I have notified several workers at JFS that she is looking for a roommate, and she has advertised in the Jewish News.

Family and Social Status

Because now she is alone and has only one child, Bea worries about where she will live and who will take care of her when her health fails. This is a common fear for older women who have outlived their husbands, siblings, and sometimes their children. Middle-aged women (the sandwich generation) are the most likely caretakers of older family members. For Bea, this option is unavailable, because Lenny's wife, Darlene, is battling multiple sclerosis. Bea fears institutionalization, especially after she observed the substandard care Barry received at the nursing home.

Bea is doing her best to cope with the loss of Barry. When she has a bad day, she gets discouraged, but even on bad days, she makes an effort to raise her spirits. Bea tries to keep busy. This usually means visiting with friends, taking short walks around her building, going on short shopping trips, and generally trying to get out of the house. Bea's decreased energy and stamina, magnified by her health problems, combined with her lack of easy transportation limit her outside activities considerably. At home, Bea crochets, makes little stuffed animals, and visits with her friends Jan and Doris in the building.

Bea and I completed her eco-map during one of our sessions (see Figure 2). She wasn't sure how to begin, or what it signified. I put her name in the middle, and her son in one of the surrounding circles. As I asked her to tell me the other important people in her life, she broke into tears and told me I needed to put Barry on the map because he was still so much a part of her life. I put Barry in a circle touching Bea's.

Lenny has a strong relationship with his mother, although it is sometimes stressful when she makes too many demands on him. He sees her weekly and takes her shopping. Several times a month, she goes to his home for dinner, often bringing some of her friends. She also cooks meals for Lenny and Darlene to take home. This is her

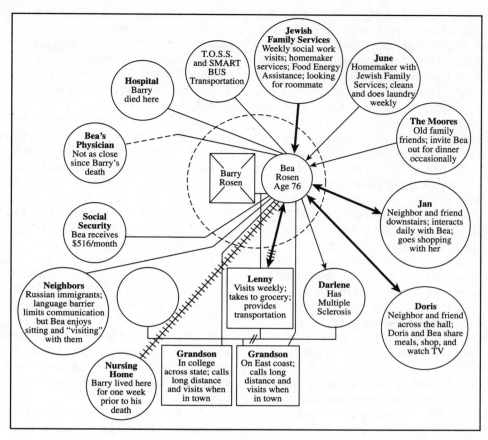

Figure 2
Bea Rosen's eco-map. *Source:* Courtesy of Jackie E. Pray, Ph.D.

way of helping them and giving back a little of what they give her. She says it also gives her something to do.

Lenny has two sons from a previous marriage. Both are in college—one across the state, the other on the East Coast. The grandsons both keep in touch with Bea, calling her long distance, visiting, and going shopping with her when they are in town. She is very proud of them both and loves them deeply. Their relationships seem mutually fulfilling.

Jan is a lively widow in her seventies who lives downstairs from Bea. Jan is more active and is able to walk to the stores, including the mall, one mile away. Jan's nature is bright, bubbly, and talkative. She and Bea shop together, check on one another, and socialize on a daily basis. Doris lives across the hall from Bea, is also widowed, and often shares meals and shopping with Bea. Doris and Bea frequently watch television together in the evenings. Bea's relationships with these two friends appear strong, with balanced energy flow in both directions.

The Moores are old family friends of the Rosens and continue to invite Bea out for dinner occasionally. Bea says she feels a little awkward with them, because she and Barry used to do so many things with the Moores as a

foursome. She does appreciate their efforts to socialize and show they care, but going out with the Moores sometimes makes Bea miss Barry all the more. At this time, I think the energy flow is more toward Bea than balanced.

Bea has other neighbors she is friendly with as well. There are quite a few older Russian immigrants in the apartment complex, and Bea enjoys walking with them, sitting with them on the benches, and exchanging the few words of conversation they are able to mutually understand.

With her and Barry's health problems, Bea has built a long-term supportive relationship with her doctor. She and Barry considered him a family friend. Since Barry's decline and death, the doctor hasn't been quite as warm and outgoing with Bea. He continues to supervise Bea's medical care and oversee her physical well-being with a watchful eye. I have indicated the energy flow toward Bea, and it is a bit tenuous.

Bea relies on Jewish Family Service for four services. A homemaker named June comes every week to clean and do laundry. June became very close to the Rosens, attended Barry's funeral, and suffered the loss of Barry along with Bea. Bea pays a reduced rate for the services, supplemented by Area Agency on Aging. During the last few months Barry was living, the Rosens received respite services once a week through JFS. Because of her extremely tight finances since Barry's death, Bea depends on JFS's transportation department when she is unable to arrange transportation through the Southfield Senior bus or the Smart Bus. Finally, I visited her once a week, for companionship and support through her bereavement.

Bea has indicated some interest in joining a seniors' therapy group at JFS, and the social workers leading the group will meet with Bea in a few weeks to discuss the group with her. I have indicated the energy flow as strong and toward Bea from JFS.

Bea and Barry did not have an affiliation with a Temple or Synagogue. This source of social support is therefore not available to Bea, although she could benefit from it greatly at this time. She has not had much contact with the Jewish Community Center near her, although I did tell her about a bereavement group that meets there.

Bea's Viewpoint

Bea views her problem realistically as one of loss and adjustment. She has tried to cope with getting through each day and to adjust to her loss emotionally, physically, and financially. She sees her first task as coping emotionally with her loss. She also knows that eventually she will need to make some decisions about housing, if she is unable to find a suitable roommate. She doesn't want to burden her son with her problems and instead, she has shared her concerns and hurt with me. She knows there are a lot of decisions ahead for her and is frightened that she may not be able to make good decisions for herself because of her emotional and mental problems. At the same time, she does not want to dwell on these deficits for fear she will become overwhelmed by them or become too self-involved.

Some Value and Ethical Dilemmas

Bea's case posed several value issues and ethical dilemmas for me. I had to wrestle with my own feelings about our encounters, and at the same time, confront ethical issues related to client confidentiality and self-determination. Given the complicated nature of Bea's situation, these issues were difficult.

I experienced the loss of Barry very personally. Barry loved to sing and was one of the most loving and lovable people I have ever met. On my first visit with the Rosens, Barry sang to me, "Just let a smile be your umbrella, on a cloudy, cloudy day. Just let a smile be your umbrella . . . " The song was his theme of life, and everyone who met him was touched by his sweetness and love. When someone at JFS suggested that my purpose with the Rosens was to give them someone to reminisce with in preparation for Barry's death, I had to gradually shake off the denial of his condition and the fact that he would probably

die soon. I was very sad for Bea and Barry when he went into the nursing home. As I watched him decline there I knew he wouldn't last long. Still, it was a shock to me to call Bea to confirm an appointment and hear that Barry had died. I would have gone to the funeral if I had known in time. I kept thinking, "Why did someone as wonderful as Barry have to die?"

When Bea talked about looking for a roommate, I thought of a friend who might be appropriate. I knew I couldn't talk to my friend without getting Bea's permission to give her name and number. I mentioned to Bea that I knew a woman who might be interested, and she gave me permission to contact her. As it turned out, the friend had found another good living situation so I didn't need to divulge Bea's name, but I knew ethically that I could not do so without her permission.

Several times Bea had mentioned her mental problems of anxiety and possible phobias. She had been reluctant to go into detail. I was concerned and curious but hesitant to push for details when she seemed uncomfortable doing so. I asked appropriate questions at times, and she opened up to tell me she had had a nervous breakdown. Because I was inexperienced with mental problems and because I respected Bea's desire to not put a lot of energy toward the topic, I stayed away from in-depth questioning on the subject.

When I heard the seniors' support group at JFS was restructuring and would begin again soon, I contacted the leader and spoke to her about my concerns for Bea. I wanted Bea to get involved with the group for three reasons: (1) for her mental problems, (2) to get her involved with other supportive people, and (3) to be able to transfer her case to another worker so our termination process will be eased. Bea, however, was not sure she wanted to be in a group where people talk about their problems. She was afraid she would feel dragged down by everybody else's problems as well as her own. She wanted to socialize with people who were looking at the bright side of life, not the dark side. As much as I wanted her to be in the group, I knew I could not force or coerce her into it.

Finally, Bea consented to meet with the leader of the group. I think she understood I was not trying to pressure her into something if she didn't want to do it.

Intervention Strategies

During my first visits with Bea after Barry's death, I was at a loss for anything I could say that would take away some of her pain. I knew I couldn't change the pain of her loss. All I could offer was my presence, my acknowledgment of her feelings, and, indeed, my own pain at losing Barry. Sometimes my validation of her feelings came in words, but at other times I responded with silence and a touch of her hand instead.

My earlier sessions with Bea and Barry were spent reminiscing about their lives together. We talked about how they met, how long they courted, what they thought about each other, their son Lenny, their jobs, their families, and some of their social activities. Since Barry's death, reminiscing with Bea has been marked with Bea's emotions and tears. I always let Bea lead the conversation. At times Bea willingly talked about her grief and loss. At other times, she preferred to talk about less stressful topics such as shopping or the neighbors.

Bea often mentioned she felt comfortable sharing her pain and tears with me but didn't feel comfortable doing so with her son or close friends. Even so, sometimes the pain was so great that she didn't want to acknowledge it, and I was timid about saying something that would bring on the tears. Even though I intellectually understood that experiencing strong emotions helped her progress in the grieving process, I was hesitant to stimulate these. I think my hesitancy originated from respecting her right to progress at her own speed and from my own inexperience with clients expressing strong emotions during the grieving process.

In the beginning days of her bereavement, when Bea experienced hallucinations of Barry in the apartment or in bed next to her she was very frightened that she was losing her mind. One of the first things I did was reassure her that these experiences were normal, as were her fatigue and depression. She continued to feel Barry's presence in the home from time to time, but she was not so alarmed by these occurrences. At other times, she wasn't able to believe he was really dead. I assured her that these feelings were also normal for the grieving process.

As Bea was faced with the financial strain of her very limited income, she was challenged to either keep her apartment or move to a seniors' apartment complex. She doesn't want to move from her home of 25 years and is still trying to find a single woman to rent her second bedroom. I helped Bea consider her choices in housing and also helped her brainstorm about finding a roommate. The issue of housing has always been Bea's to bring up when she needs to talk about it. As much as I see a need for seniors' housing and for other services in the near future, I didn't push my ideas on her. The same applied for support groups. I would like to have seen Bea get involved with a bereavement support group or the seniors' therapy group at JFS, but since she didn't want to, I accepted the choices she made for herself. I tried to help her find options in the challenges she faced.

Bea fits the description of a high-risk widow because of her physical and mental health problems. To the best of my knowledge, she has not suffered from any significant illnesses since her bereavement nor developed more emotional problems beyond the normal emotional state of grief. It is my hope that I have helped to lessen the pressures of acute grief for Bea, that I have had a positive impact on her grieving process, and that I have helped connect her with other service options.

Evaluation

In my practice with Bea, we regularly evaluated our goals together. All evaluations have been somewhat subjective. The goal of our relationship, though unspoken, was for me to support Bea in her grieving process. To accomplish this, we both had responsibilities. I needed to remain open to her loss, be empathic, and encourage her feelings and reminiscing. She needed to perceive my openness, express her feelings, reminisce, and acknowledge her loss.

In my opinion, we both fulfilled our responsibilities in this regard. I supported her to the best of my ability, and she responded with many feelings associated with her grief. In a recent session with her, I asked her for feedback about my help and participation in her grieving process. She shared that she has been grateful for my presence and that she doesn't really have any idea if it's helped or not. She said that sometimes she feels "lighter" after I depart, and sometimes she feels worse. She did say that I am usually the only person with whom she shares her feelings of acute grief, because she doesn't want to burden her friends or her son. She wasn't sure if experiencing her feelings, to the extent that she does with me, was healthy for her. I replied that from what I understood, it was very helpful to feel the feelings and experience the release they provide and that this was an integral part of the grieving and adjustment process.

Given the fact that I was the only person she openly grieved with, and the fact that she hasn't yet experienced an acute health crisis related to her bereavement, I think my presence and support during her grieving process have been very helpful. On her own, Bea wouldn't have sought out help in her bereavement process, but because I was already part of her support system, she was able to use my presence and skills to her best advantage.

In looking at outcomes, I am impressed at the level of adjustment Bea has made to her loss. At five months, she still experiences acute grief, but she appears a little more able to deal with it. With the advent of warmer weather, she gets out more and is more socially active than she was the first few months. She has gradually increased the distance she is able to walk, and this has had a great impact on the amount of socializing she does. I am sure this greater endurance has had a beneficial effect on her overall health as well.

Bea uses her social network for support and companionship. During her bereavement period, this support has been invaluable, and it is to Bea's credit that she has kept up these ties of friendship through times when she didn't feel she had much to offer besides grief. Given my observation of these positive outcomes, combined with positive feedback from Bea, I think my evaluation of her situation is accurate and appropriate.

Summary

Bea is a member of several at-risk population groups. She is an older woman, a widow, and a heart patient. She suffers from anxiety and phobias and is in the early stages of bereavement. The loss of her spouse is considered to be her most stressful life event and has led to a major role change for her. The transition to widowhood has raised her existing depression to a higher level and has had a negative impact on her social support networks.

Bea Rosen faces the challenge of adjusting to the loss of her dear husband after sharing life with him for half a century. Her age and health problems have complicated her bereavement process to some extent, and she faces life alone now without an extensive social support system. Bea is impacted both positively and negatively by government policies regarding the aged and has made use of several helpful services offered through JFS and other agencies. JFS will continue its outreach efforts to involve her in other appropriate services.

Bea is experiencing the ongoing process of bereavement, of which I have had a small part. She will continue to experience the loss of Barry for years to come, long after I have terminated my relationship with her.

Dear Gretchen,
Well, here it is 5:30 in the morning. I know I have gone on forever here, but I wanted you to have as much information as I could provide. I somehow know that, at this point in your social work education, you don't quite understand what you are getting into, but believe me, it's worth it.

My work with Bea has been both challenging and rewarding. I entered the relationship quite unaware of Barry's frailty and his approaching decline. I learned a lot reading up on bereavement counseling to help Bea to the best of my ability, and I experienced bereavement firsthand, right along with her. My experience with Bea has shown me how central the relationship between the client and the practitioner is to the helping process, and how even my simple presence can make a difference.

This has been my first experience with death and bereavement, and I experienced it right along with my client. It hasn't been easy for me, and I think I really haven't recognized how difficult it has been for me until now as I write and analyze the situation. I didn't know much about bereavement counseling at first, but I would just go and sit with Bea and let her talk, letting her know anything she needed to talk about was OK with me. It turns out that this was the most appropriate approach to take anyway. In bereavement situations, the social worker is often grieving right along with the client. It's a very human situation.
Goodbye,
Kathleen

Readings

Fischer, C., & Hegge, M. (2000). The elderly woman at risk. *American Journal of Nursing, 100*(6), 54–58.

Roff, S. (2001). Suicide and the Elderly: Issues for Clinical Practice. *Journal of Gerontological Social Work, 35*(2), 21–37.

Schoenber, N. E., Coward, R. T., & Albrecht, S. L. (2001). Attitudes of older adults about community-based services: emergent themes from in-depth interviews. *Journal of Gerontological Social Work, 35*(4), 3–19.

Discussion Questions

1. The worker indicates she believes it is inappropriate for her to question the client extensively about her fears and possible phobias and bases this reluctance on her own inexperience. Is her reluctance reasonable under the circumstances?

2. The worker sometimes seems to be focusing her efforts on reinforcing coping activities of the client and downplaying possible problems. Is this a potential problem?

3. The worker indicates Bea has income of $516 per month and pays rent of $485, yet has not inquired specifically about how the client is making ends meet on this limited income. Would it be appropriate for her to pursue this matter rather than glossing over it or assuming that the client had other sources of income?

4. Does the worker's statement that she had strong feelings of loss when Barry died indicate she was over-involved in this case?

5. What do you see as the strengths that Bea Rosen has exhibited to the worker?

6. *Based on the limited information available about Bea's husband, what do you think may have caused the behavior that preceded his move to the nursing home?*

7. *Do you think the reactions to Barry's death that Bea displayed were "normal"? Why or why not?*

8. *What does the worker mean when she says Bea's emotions are usually congruent with the situation? What might it mean if this were not the case?*

9. *What is meant by the term* sandwich generation*?*

10. *How does the Eco-map in this case assist Kathleen and Bea?*

8

Substance Abuse as Problem or Symptom: The Smith Family

Robert E. Weiler

Engagement and Presenting Problem

Mrs. Smith contacted the County Council on Substance Abuse by telephone to arrange an evaluation and possible outpatient services for her 16-year-old son, Gary. At the time of her contact, Mrs. Smith reported that Gary had recently been ticketed by the local police for illegal possession of alcohol. The Smiths were referred to the County Council by their local police department. The closest office of the Council was 15 miles from the Smith residence. Gary's individual intake session was scheduled for an evening appointment with Mr. O'Hare, a social worker.

Gary arrived for this appointment accompanied by his mother. Unbeknownst to the Smith family, Mr. O'Hare was originally from the same small town as Gary and had relatives living in the same neighborhood as the Smiths. This fact was not revealed to the Smith family at first, due to the fact that Mr. O'Hare was not familiar with the Smiths. Through the course of Gary's involvement with the County Council, however, Mr. O'Hare revealed to Gary and his family that he had come from their community. As it turned out, the Smiths were marginally acquainted with Mr. O'Hare's relatives.

Data Collection

Gary and his mother completed the agency intake forms prior to Gary's being called into Mr. O'Hare's office for his first session. Included among these forms were a sociodemographic profile, a detailed alcohol and drug use history, and a Children of Alcoholics Screening Test (CAST). Mr. O'Hare met alone with Gary initially and then requested that Gary's mother come in to corroborate information Gary had provided. Through the course of this and subsequent individual sessions with Gary, a psychosocial history was completed. This history revealed an abundance of information about Gary and the Smith family that cast additional light on his presenting problem.

The Smith family adopted Gary as an infant after they believed that they could not conceive. Subsequent to Gary's adoption, Mrs. Smith gave birth to Thomas, one year younger than Gary; David, three years younger than Gary; and Kimberly, four years younger than Gary. Thus, Gary was the oldest of four children in the family and the only adopted child.

Gary had known of his adoption for several years and was aware of the fact that at his birth, his mother placed him with Catholic Charities adoption services in a nearby city. Gary had no other information about either of his birth parents. At the time of his involvement with the County Council, Gary appeared to have little interest in finding out anything more about his birth parents.

The Smiths were Roman Catholic, with roots in their rural community that could be traced back through multiple generations. Gary's father, originally from a farm family, worked in a local retail business after downsizing occurred in the industry in which he was formerly employed. Gary's mother was an elementary school teacher. At the time of his initial session, neither Gary nor his mother voiced concern about the use of alcohol or other drugs by anyone else in the family.

In addition to using alcohol, Gary had experimented with marijuana on a few occasions. He denied use of any other mood-altering drugs. At about the time Gary entered high school, he began to display behaviors that increasingly caused concern for his parents and siblings. He displayed a severe and unpredictable temper and often took his anger out by being verbally or physically aggressive toward his younger siblings, by punching doors or walls with his fist, or by verbally threatening his mother. His temper seemed to flare with greater frequency and intensity when he consumed alcohol.

A little more than a year before his initial session with the County Council, Gary had been in a serious automobile accident. He was in a coma for several days after this accident and sustained a head injury, resulting in a prominent scar on one temple. This accident prevented him from playing sports, one of the major activities that motivated him to attend school.

Gary received special education services from the school district related to a mild learning disability and behavioral problems. His school attendance and academic performance had been marginal, at best, throughout much of his high school career. At the time of intake, he was at risk for not graduating on time. Gary openly derided his younger siblings for their academic achievements and for their participation in any nonsport school activities.

Gary had self-administered tattoos on the backs of both hands. Some of these, he told Mr. O'Hare, were gang-related and he claimed to be a member of a well-known street gang. Gary substantiated his claim of gang affiliation by presenting Mr. O'Hare with a number of handwritten papers containing the gang's creed and various gang symbols and their definitions. Gary stated that his first exposure to gang activity was during his extended hospital stay in a nearby metropolitan area, following his automobile accident. He had difficulty articulating just what purpose gang affiliation served for him. When pressed, he conveyed a certain degree of ambivalence about continued involvement in the gang, but he seemed reluctant to renounce his gang connection. He contended that he would eventually become too old to be in the gang.

At one point during Gary's involvement with Mr. O'Hare, Gary was hospitalized on an adolescent mental health unit in a nearby city following a weekend episode of alcohol consumption, verbal threats toward family members, and physical aggression taken out on the walls and door of his bedroom. Although the County Council had a 24-hour crisis line, the Smith family did not utilize this service during this episode. Mr. O'Hare learned of Gary's hospitalization when Mrs. Smith called to cancel Gary's individual appointment for that week. Gary spent several weeks, including a major holiday, receiving inpatient treatment on this unit. Mr. O'Hare made arrangements to attend Gary's discharge planning meeting on the unit, which seemed to surprise and please Gary. Upon his discharge and return to the County Council for continued outpatient services, he was taking Lithium Carbonate, a medication that had been prescribed for symptoms of bipolar disorder (manic depression). Gary expressed his disdain for having to take prescribed medication but generally followed the regimen associated with the medication.

Assessment

The County Council held clinical team meetings weekly to participate in case conferences and assist the clinical staff in their treatment and discharge planning. A consulting physician served on this team and was charged with assigning a DSM-IV diagnosis to each client. Based on the results of his intake and case discussion at the clinical team meeting, Gary was given a diagnosis of alcohol abuse. This diagnosis was related primarily to the problems that alcohol consumption had caused in Gary's life (e.g., family, legal).

As was often the case in working with families affected by substance abuse, Mr. O'Hare realized that the concerns and needs of the Smith family were more complex than the presenting problem suggested. Taking into consideration Gary's psychosocial history, information gathered through individual sessions with Gary, and observations of family interaction during initial sessions with the entire Smith family, Mr. O'Hare's observations were as follows.

1. Gary's abuse of alcohol had caused life difficulties in and of itself. However, Gary also used alcohol as a means of asserting his individuality and of venting anger, resentment, and fear, possibly associated with his identity as an adopted child.
2. Gary's continued abuse of alcohol, given such factors as his age, developmental concerns, unpredictable and volatile behavior, and ambivalence toward his adoption, posed a significant threat to Gary and his family.
3. Gary was angry with his birth mother for "giving him up" for adoption and often took this anger out on his adoptive mother. On the other hand, Gary had respect for, and a certain fear of, his adoptive father and seldom crossed him.
4. Gary sensed that his parents would not have adopted him if they had known that they would be able to conceive children of their own. This might explain, in part, his aggression toward his parents and younger siblings.
5. Gary relied on gang affiliation to establish and maintain an identity that was in sharp contrast to the qualities of the family into which he was adopted. In a sense, gang affiliation provided Gary with a "family" of his own choosing. Consciously giving up gang affiliation would have represented a significant loss of security and identity for Gary.
6. Gary had assumed the role of the family troublemaker (i.e., the scapegoat), drawing focus away from family dynamics and problems being experienced by other family members.
7. Gary responded more favorably to intervention efforts in the absence of other family members, especially as he moved toward young adulthood. Family sessions often ended with one or another sibling in tears or with Gary's storming out of the office, refusing to continue the session.

The Smith family often engaged in detrimental, entrenched patterns of verbal and nonverbal interaction during family sessions, and these often seemed to heighten Gary's anxiety and reinforce his belief that he was an outcast within the family. In light of this and considering Gary's potential for volatile behavior under such conditions, Mr. O'Hare decided to work primarily on an individual basis with Gary. Family sessions were scheduled on a monthly basis and focused on developing and reinforcing adaptive interaction patterns among family members. However, due to conflicting work, school, and activity schedules of various family members, it was difficult to bring all family members together on a consistent basis.

Goal Planning and Intervention

Any use of alcohol on Gary's part carried a potential for dire consequences, including legal problems, risk for physical and psychological harm, and increasingly strained family relationships. Gary's ascribed role as troublemaker in the family reinforced his self-perceptions of worthlessness and failure. He was in need of an advocate who could accept him unconditionally and help him find new and more constructive ways of viewing himself and his social environment. As part of an empowering strategy, Mr. O'Hare engaged Gary in the mutual process of developing an intervention plan of feasible goals and objectives, eliciting Gary's agreement and commitment to working toward these. Included in this plan were specific strategies for achieving the specified goals.

A primary goal for Gary, consistent with the mission of the agency, was to achieve abstinence from alcohol and other mood-altering substances. This goal was desirable not only because of the potential consequences of substance abuse for Gary, but also because of the agency's stand against underage drinking and the use of illegal drugs for any client.

A second goal for Gary was to explore what purpose alcohol use served in his life and to examine the potentially unfavorable outcomes of continued alcohol use.

A third goal was to discuss his feelings about having been adopted and to begin to understand and modify the ways in which he acted upon these feelings with significant others.

In order to achieve these goals, several objectives and strategies were undertaken. Gary was scheduled to attend weekly one-to-one sessions with Mr. O'Hare. During these sessions, they discussed Gary's activities of the previous week, his interactions with others, any problems that had occurred, and measurable progress toward achieving mutually agreed-upon goals.

In addition to Gary's weekly individual sessions, the entire Smith family was asked to attend monthly family sessions with Mr. O'Hare. Gary's behavior and the progression of events that precipitated his becoming a client of the Council could be fully understood only when family roles, dynamics, and patterns of interaction were revealed and modified.

Gary agreed to pursue abstinence from alcohol and other mood-altering drugs as an ongoing goal of receiving services. Mr. O'Hare, understanding that many substance abuse clients fall short of the ideal of abstinence, secured Gary's commitment to honestly report any incidents of alcohol or drug use so that circumstances around such use could be discussed and preventive measures could be taken. Mr. O'Hare explained to Gary that his parents might well be expected to discipline him with regard to alcohol or drug consumption. In order for Gary to understand the causes, conditions, and consequences of his alcohol and drug use, an early focus of individual sessions was to determine and discuss the purposes alcohol use served in Gary's life and to outline and discuss ways in which alcohol or other drugs had negatively affected or could affect his well-being. This insight, it was hoped, would serve to help motivate Gary to make more constructive choices as time went on.

A significant aspect of Gary's treatment related to his having been adopted. Mr. O'Hare suspected that many of the problems Gary was experiencing could be traced back and linked to his ambivalence surrounding the adoption, his birth parents, and his adoptive family (the only family he had ever known). Accordingly, a great deal of work was done on exploring, in depth, Gary's feelings toward his adoption, toward his birth parents, and toward each member of his adoptive family. Given that affiliation with a notorious street gang represented a surrogate "family" for Gary, Mr. O'Hare encouraged Gary to examine and discuss his involvement in the gang and explore its meaning for him. Gary was asked to identify any negative correlates of his gang participation and to brainstorm and rehearse ways in which he could have his needs for identity, belonging, and connection with others met in ways that were more to his advantage.

Gary was nearly 17 years of age when he began working with Mr. O'Hare and was preparing to enter his final year in high school. Regardless of his conflicts with his parents and his attempts to assert his independence and individuality, Gary remained quite immature and behind his peers developmentally. With Gary's adulthood approaching, it became increasingly essential that he take responsibility for his own actions and their consequences.

Moreover, practical planning for an adult life beyond his parents' care and supervision took on an increasing sense of urgency. A primary goal for Gary related to achieving independence from his parents was to take all necessary measures to graduate from high school.

Evaluation and Termination

Gary had been a client of the County Council for more than two years when Mr. O'Hare received a job offer from an organization in another city. Mr. O'Hare told Gary and his parents of his impending departure one month prior to the effective date of his resignation. Based on the duration of Gary's involvement with the agency and the level of progress toward his treatment goals, the family decided to terminate services with the agency rather than have Gary transferred to another worker. The remaining few individual sessions were devoted to reviewing Gary's progress and to planning for retaining the gains he had made. Gary reported few incidents (less than a half-dozen) of alcohol consumption throughout the time that he was receiving services. Two of those incidents resulted in intoxication to such a degree that Gary became verbally aggressive with his mother and physically aggressive with one of his younger brothers. One of these incidents resulted in Gary being hospitalized in an adolescent psychiatric unit (see Data Collection).

As time unfolded and he drastically curtailed his alcohol use, alcohol consumption became less and less a focal point of Gary's individual sessions. Interestingly, Gary's younger brother had begun to experience some legal consequences of his own alcohol use by the time Gary's case was closed.

Gary was entirely willing to own up to any alcohol use throughout his involvement with the County Council, and he seemed to enjoy being able to confide in Mr. O'Hare in an atmosphere of acceptance and challenge. He also appeared to appreciate the seriousness of the problems that alcohol use had caused, or could cause, in his life.

Gary demonstrated a moderate level of strength and capacity to link his emotional and behavioral difficulties in the present with the tentative feelings he entertained regarding his adoption. He admitted being resentful toward his birth mother for placing him for adoption. Nonetheless, at the time of termination Gary reported that he was getting along better with his parents and younger siblings. In separate consultation, Gary's parents confirmed that this was true.

Mr. O'Hare suspected that his focus on Gary as the primary client actually bolstered Gary's self-concept at least to the degree that he didn't see himself as the only problem facing the Smith family. Gary was less likely to be as willful with his mother or to instigate arguments and fights with his younger siblings.

Gary had also established a relationship with a young woman his age in the months prior to his discharge. He referred to this young woman as his girlfriend and spent an increasing amount of time with her. His parents welcomed her into their home, stating that she had a calming effect on Gary.

Although Gary remained reluctant to denounce his gang affiliation entirely, he did demonstrate a willingness to decrease his level of conspicuousness with regard to gang identity. For example, when Mr. O'Hare suggested that Gary not wear colors associated with the gang to his sessions at the Council, Gary obliged.

Reflecting successful completion of one aspect of Gary's contract with Mr. O'Hare, Gary graduated from high school with his class. Mr. O'Hare had offered Gary the incentive of a gift certificate for Gary and his girlfriend to the restaurant of their choice, upon Gary's graduation. Gary happily collected on this offer, sending an unexpected thank you note to Mr. O'Hare afterward.

Gary appeared to genuinely enjoy this moment of personal accomplishment and seeing Mr. O'Hare follow through on the promised reinforcement.

Readings

Bray, J. H., Adams, G. J., Getz, J. G., & Stovall, T. (2001). Interactive effects of individuation, family factors, and stress on adolescent alcohol use. *American Journal of Orthopsychiatry, 71*(4), 436–450.

Brown, S. A., D'Amico, E. J., McCarthy, D. M., & Tapert, S. F. (2001). Four-year outcomes from adolescent alcohol and drug treatment. *Journal of Studies on Alcohol, 62*(3), 381–389.

Brown, T. L., Parks, G. S., Zimmerman, R. S., & Phillips, C. M. (2001). The role of religion in predicting adolescent alcohol use and problem drinking. *Journal of Studies on Alcohol, 62*(5), 696–706.

Discussion Questions

1. *What ethical considerations might arise for a social worker practicing in a small community or within the social worker's own hometown?*

2. *What are some limitations of assessing an individual's substance use based solely on the amount and frequency of use and consequences associated with use?*

3. *How might various developmental issues of adolescence interplay with an adolescent's relationship with alcohol and other drugs?*

4. *Which has more impact on an individual's self-concept and behavior—the circumstances surrounding the individual's adoption or the family into which the individual is adopted? Explain your answer.*

5. *What special challenges do street gang infiltration and ganglike behavior present to nonurban communities?*

6. *How might a social worker help an adolescent who claims to be a gang member find acceptance and identity in more adaptive ways? In light of a social worker's concerns for a client's well-being and right to self-determination, should the worker encourage a client to "get out" of a gang? Why or why not?*

7. *How might Mr. O'Hare have included the Smith family to a greater degree in Gary's treatment, taking into account his adoption and the complex and challenging dynamics of the family's interaction?*

8. *What responsibilities does the social worker have toward ensuring the physical safety and emotional well-being of other members of an individual client's family? Use this case as an example.*

9. *How would you determine the degree of success of Mr. O'Hare's intervention with Gary and with the Smith family? What baseline and criteria for success would you use?*

9

Una Rosa

Richard Furman

This case is based on the work of one of my students. It is an example of how one person can make a difference by using multilevel system intervention.

Social Agency

After graduating with my BSW from a Midwestern university, I traveled to Guatemala to improve my Spanish. As it turned out, I worked for two years as a social worker for a Suisse nonprofit agency in Antigua, Guatemala. For several months, I volunteered for this nongovernmental organization, providing many types of social work services to expatriates living in the area as well as to local Guatemalans. The director of the program was able to secure funding to pay me a small salary that allowed me to live very simply.

My role was to provide all levels of social work services to those in the community who had no access to other resources. In truth, this represented the majority of people living in the area. While there were many nongovernmental organizations, very few provided direct social work services. Many were social development programs that provided important community development services. However, persons who suffered from individual problems rarely had access to services. Most helping professionals in Guatemala were psychologists who followed a western model of psychoanalytic practice that many found out of touch with the realities of the people in Guatemala.

Early in my work, I was assigned to visit a patient in a local hospital and offer my services to her. All I knew about her was that she was soon to be released and the director of my organization had been asked to assign a social worker to follow up with her after she was discharged. A hospital worker contacted the nongovernment organization that I work for and asked if we could evaluate Rose. I was told to visit the hospital and begin to establish a working relationship with someone who needed me.

When I first met Rose, she was polite but distant. She never looked me in the eyes as we spoke. The hospital staff reported that she spent most of her time staring out into space. They reported that she had been placed in the hospital after a suicide attempt. When asked why she cut herself, she said that she was a shame to all those who knew her and that she did not deserve to live.

I eventually learned some information from her during those initial hospital visits. Rose was a 25-year-old Guatemalan woman living in Antigua, Guatemala. She was born and spent her formative years in a small village in the western highlands. Her family members were farmers who tended to a small plot of land in which they grew tubers and vegetables. The market where they sold their goods was only 25 miles away but took nearly two hours to get to by bus.

I learned that when Rose was 15 years old, she witnessed the brutal murder of her mother and father at the hands of masked paramilitary troops. Her father was shot, and her mother was raped and subsequently hacked to death with a machete. Rose was also raped, as was her 13-year-old sister. After the death of her parents, Rose moved in with her aunt and uncle and their children in Antigua, nearly 40 miles away. Now 25, Rose's trauma became reactivated as she became close to a man who was interested in marrying her. She subsequently became consumed with depression, guilt, and shame, and attempted to kill herself. Rose was hospitalized for nearly a week.

Engagement and Presenting Problem

Rose agreed to come see me twice a week once she got out of the hospital. I was fairly surprised, as several clear barriers existed that could have prevented her from contracting with me for services. First, I am a man from the country that has supported the government that was responsible for her suffering. I was not certain if this would be a barrier or not, yet I wondered how it could not be. Second, seeing a professional for personal problems is stigmatized in Guatemalan culture, in part due to mistrust of the help of Anglos, but also because the individual is seen as a less important social unit than is the family. Although this is also common in ethnic communities in the United States, it is even more intense in this country with so little history of social work and mental health services. Also, I am not sure how artful I was during our two meetings at the hospital. I was nervous and perhaps asked too many questions. I saw Rose's willingness to meet with me not as a sign of my good work, but as being indicative of her strength and desire for help. I was not really sure what to call our sessions at first, and I was not certain I knew my role. I knew that in many ways I was not equipped to deal with such intense psychological trauma. I also believed that I could rely on good, basic social work skills and hopefully that would help. I reasoned that I would be better than what she would otherwise have—nothing.

I think I made several mistakes early on in working with her. When she asked if I could help her, I told her

57

that I would help her to help herself. To this she laughed and wondered out loud what I would then be good for. Also, I was trained in my BSW program not to give advice, but instead to help clients come to their own decisions. This incensed Rose, for she thought I was being evasive. I learned quickly that she wanted me to be more directive in my helping approach. Although this was not my style, I pushed myself to be more active and less reflective. It is always important to start where the client is.

Prior to seeking services, Rose had never discussed what happened to her and her family. She worked hard blocking out her pains by focusing on work. She also had become very involved in the Catholic Church. Until recently, she had never dated or expressed romantic interest. The month prior to her hospitalization, a young man from her church asked her out. Rose agreed, and they went to the movies. After a few dates, Rose began to have romantic feelings for her new friend, which seemed to trigger waves of memories and feelings that she had spent years attempting to ignore. As she contemplated a marriage and a sexual relationship (she stated she wants children), memories of her rape and the murder of her parents flooded her mind. She became racked with guilt and shame, and she told the man that she would never see him again. The next day, Rose attempted to kill herself at work by cutting her wrists with a machete. A customer found her, and she was taken to a nearby hospital. The lone mental health professional associated with the hospital called me, and I visited her the next day.

Social History

Rose reported her early childhood experiences as happy and normal. Like many Guatemalan indigenous children, she had dual responsibilities of school and helping her family. I think she saw on my face that I was surprised at the amount of work she actually had to do. She informed me that long days at work and school were normal for Guatemalan children, whose families wanted them to advance but had pressing financial concerns. Rose reported doing fairly well in school. She especially loved reading Spanish literature, and she was proud to tell me that she was the best reader in her school by the time she was finished eighth grade. Rose stopped attending school for two years when she was 14. She helped her family on their farm.

Increasingly, tensions grew between many of the men in the village and the soldiers who frequently arrived in town looking for guerrilla activity. Rose informed me that while her father was sympathetic to the struggles of the guerrillas, he mistrusted them as much as he did the army. One evening, army officers came to the house to talk to her father. Outside, she heard arguing and heard a loud thump. A soldier had hit her father during an argument.

The following evening, men with masks broke into her home. Rose witnessed the beating and killing of her mother and father, and the rape of her sister, and was subsequently raped herself. Rose then moved to Antigua to live with her aunt and uncle. For the first several months, she did not speak. She ate very little, cried frequently, and had nightmares. She never spoke to anyone about the trauma. Over time, she worked hard at pushing the event out of her mind, and she started to work at her uncle's grocery store.

Social Context

Guatemala is a country of nearly eight million people located south of Mexico on the Central American isthmus. With the exception of Bolivia, Guatemala has the highest concentration of indigenous persons in the Western Hemisphere. From the late 1950s to the early 1990s, the people of Guatemala were a population under siege. In 1954, a democratically elected government, which had worked toward land reform and progressive social welfare, was overthrown by right-wing factions supported by the Central Intelligence Agency and others within the American government. Since then, right-wing paramilitary "death squads" have systematically tortured and killed 200,000 people. The term *disappeared* began to be used as a verb for what happened to people who were never heard from again.

Although many of those who were tortured and killed were college professors, labor leaders, and other activists, the vast majority were innocent farmers of Mayan descent, many of whom were not in the least bit politically active. Many simply lived in areas where there were high concentrations of revolutionary activity. The "scorched earth" policy of the government, consisting of terror, intimidation, and the destruction of whole villages, sought to isolate revolutionaries and prevent them from receiving help. This reign of terror merely exacerbated the poverty and struggles of an already poor population that have had little access to heath care and education.

Assessment

Rose possessed many strengths that could be directly utilized in the intervention phase of work. Perhaps her most apparent strength was her ability to survive and overcome trauma. Although she clearly had not dealt with her trauma sufficiently to prevent her current crisis, she had managed to create a meaningful and productive life for herself. Many in her circumstances would not have been able to go on with their lives after the tragedy.

Rose's religious faith was also an important strength and resource. She was able to keep her present life in perspective through the belief that God would not have let her suffer so in vain. Although she was not able to currently see how her experiences could help others, she was convinced that one day she would help others heal from similar traumas.

In a country of great poverty and unemployment, Rose managed to carve out a career for herself working in stores that serve the tourist industry. She was employed in the same store for the last four years, working as the salesperson selling woven goods to tourists. She had learned enough English and French to be able to help many customers more effectively. The owner of the store regarded her as a major asset and paid her well by Guatemalan standards. Her work also served as an important source of social relationships. She was responsible for buying from indigenous women in the area, thus enabling her to maintain connections to those communities.

I learned that it was important to assess the strengths of all clients, but it is especially important for social workers working with historically oppressed clients. Failing to do so places the social worker at risk of replicating patterns of neo-imperialism: treating indigenous people as inferiors in need of fixing, civilizing, or "advancing."

Intervention Strategies

Developing an intervention plan with Rose was a lesson in cultural helping. At Rose's insistence, it was essential that native healers and religious supports be integrated into the helping process. With encouragement, Rose agreed to meet with her parish priest. The priest was supportive of her and told her that God would forgive her attempting to take her own life. He told her that God understood what a burden it was for her to carry her pain with her for so long and that perhaps her suicide attempt was, in an odd way, God's way of getting her help. The priest also told her that there was no shame in seeking help from professionals, that he himself received counseling through the church for some personal problems years ago. As a descendant of Mayan peoples himself, the priest asked if she wanted to seek the help of a Mayan priest who could, in addition to himself, say prayers and blessing for her.

Rose agreed and decided to go to a nearby town to see a Mayan healer who was a distant relative. He provided his healing outside the shrine of San Simon of Maximon, a local "saint" who represented a fusion of Mayan and Catholic beliefs. She brought offerings of grain alcohol and cooked chicken and asked for her pain to be released and for her heart to be opened to her friendship. The healer said prayers for her and engaged her in healing rituals.

Perhaps one of the most important interventions was connecting Rose to an advocacy group fighting for the rights of indigenous women who had experienced trauma similar to Rose's. The group sought to empower women who have been historically oppressed and disempowered and who suffered further through losses and abuse at the hands of the military and death squads. Rose and I went to the capital to meet with one of the group leaders. The leader explained to Rose that she could become involved in many ways. She could attend a support group that met once a month. She could also call members any time she desired support. If she chose, she could get involved in the political process of advocacy. The leader explained the options for involvement, the risks, and the potential benefits. Rose asked me what I thought she should do. I told her that I thought she needed to trust her own opinion, which I trusted very much. Rose smiled and said that since Antigua was a tourist center, perhaps she could help educate tourists and the international community about the plight of women such as herself. She asked me if I would help her plan such activities, which I told her I most certainly would.

After 12 weeks of working with Rose, several changes became evident. First, she began to tell me the story of her trauma. At first, she was vague and apologetic. Utilizing a technique from narrative work, I helped her work on re-authoring her story from one of a helpless victim to one of an empowered, proud woman fighting for what was right and true. I made certain to use concepts that were culturally important such as *argullo* (pride) and *respeto* (respect). Although she made some gains in reframing her tragedy, I wondered if she had spent enough time on it. I reasoned that in using a strength and empowerment approach, it was most important to maximize her abilities and move toward other ways of healing. I began to wonder if talk therapy, as we often prefer in the west, was not indeed overrated.

I helped Rose organize a monthly discussion group where she would discuss the plight of Guatemala's women with westerners. Since Antigua is a center of Spanish-language study, we went to language schools and asked for their support. Several schools promoted the events to their students. Several of the directors of the schools saw it as an opportunity for their students to learn about Guatemala, as well as practice their Spanish. At first, only a few people showed up for Rose's group. After three months, however, she was being utilized as an important resource to the community. Rose began to see herself in a new light. She saw how her experiences could benefit others and be of some good.

I realized that my intervention plan with Rose used a multilevel systems approach. Although I was able to work with Rose as an individual, I was also able to assist her to be part of several important primary groups. Her group work not only assisted her in meeting her own needs, but also allowed her to become part of a system of mutual aid among the groups' members. Connecting Rose to these groups also set the stage for linking her to the community.

Her work as a community interpreter with the language school groups not only provided her with an important opportunity to help "the larger system" but also gave her additional strength and status as a survivor.

Termination and Ethical Issues

After five months of meeting twice a week, Rose said that she thought she was better and would not need to meet with me further. She stated that she would like to keep in touch with me socially and remain friends. I felt a combination of feelings that I was not prepared for: abandonment, fear, excitement, and satisfaction. So many thoughts swam through my head. Although she was certainly feeling better and doing wonderful things, we had talked so little directly about her trauma. I wondered if she had just been repressing some of her feelings as she had done previously. I also felt as if I did not want our sessions to end. She had become such an important part of my life. I also was both excited and perplexed at the idea of being her friend. This clearly seemed to be the type of dual relationship that I had been taught to avoid. But to what degree did the NASW code of ethics apply to me here, in this town so far away, with this client? In contemplating my relationship with Rose and how it might change, I wondered if a friendship with her would be appropriate. Was it the culturally appropriate way of supporting a client, or was I rationalizing my desire to remain in contact with a person whom I had grown to admire and respect? Was I overly involved? Now, keep in mind that all this occurred in my head in a matter of a few seconds. What I kept coming back to was how she might respond if I had told her that we could not be friends. I thought she would have had one of two responses. One, she would have told me I was being a silly American and that is not what is done in Guatemala. Or two, she would have been deeply hurt by someone whom she had grown to trust and respect. I told Rose that I would be glad to be her friend, and that I was glad that she was feeling like she no longer needed my help.

Over the next several months, I would see Rose every week or so for coffee or at her education group. I think that maintaining contact helped her feel safe and secure while she continued her recovery. Rose seemed to intuitively understand that our friendship should be more casual than perhaps she would have liked. I did not have to worry about setting boundaries. In six months time, I returned to the United States to begin the application process for graduate school in social work. For several years, Rose and I exchanged cards on holidays. She has become an important member of her community and an inspiration to women who have been abused and victimized.

Readings

Billups, J. O. (Ed.). (2002). *Faithful angels: Portraits of international social work notables*. Washington, DC: NASW Press.

Garcia, J. G., & Zea, M. C. (1997). *Psychological interventions and research with Latino populations*. Needham Heights, MA: Allyn & Bacon.

Greene, R. R. (Ed.). (2002). *Resiliency*. Washington, DC: NASW Press.

Discussion Questions

1. *Should the worker have shared his concern with Rose about not having sufficiently dealt with her trauma?*

2. *What would you have done differently in regard to the termination of the case?*

3. *Was the worker ethical in his decision to tell Rose he would be her friend?*

4. *What part does the context of the case play when deciding upon whether or not the worker was ethical?*

5. *How might the worker have evaluated his practice in this case?*

6. *What macro interventions might be used to help improve mental health services in the community?*

II

Mezzo Practice:
Families and Groups

We use the term *mezzo practice* to signify that the generalist social worker must often confront a practice situation by carrying out the problem-solving process with middle-range systems, specifically families and groups. Working with individuals in their environments is always a focus for social work, but there are times when the "target system" for intervention is more appropriately the system in which the individual experiences the identified problem. In addition, families and groups can be a great source of support and strength for individuals experiencing problems, and these "action systems" can be brought to bear on the client's situation to resolve problems and empower the client. Consequently, families and groups are two very important systems for all individuals.

We begin this section with a personal account of a worker who must confront his "otherness" by working in an environment with which he is unfamiliar. In *Personal Growth and Self-Esteem through Cultural Spiritualism: A Native American Experience*, James Wahlberg documents work done with a Native American family living on a reservation. His approach to working with this family involves using the strengths of Native American culture and the access to cultural healing provided by the reservation community. Spirituality is an important factor in intervention, and this case demonstrates how this often-neglected aspect of social work can have an empowering effect on individuals and on the family system. Though not discussed in this case, Jim became an experienced practitioner in several Native American communities. I had the privilege of following his path on the same reservation cited in this case (RFR).

Lettie L. Lockhart and Alicia R. Issac tell the story of a highly religious African American family struggling with a rebellious teenager. *In the Best Interest of the Child* stresses work with the teenager and her family in the context of a child welfare situation. The case also illustrates the influence of religion and spirituality in generalist practice situations.

Between Two Worlds, by Rupa Gupta, is an in-depth look at a college student's adjustment to the demands of two cultures. Many wonderful issues are illustrated here, including the concept of culture shock, cultural definitions of illness, and the use of both traditional and nontraditional means of treating physical and mental crises among the Hmong culture. Readers are certain to learn a great deal about this culture and the role of the family, the extended family, and the clan in the lives of this population at risk.

Chuck Young contributes *Sally's Saga*, the story of a worker in a probation setting who must face a less than supportive climate from her colleagues and deal with a Native American couple experiencing marital discord. Again, the role of culturally appropriate resources is illustrated. The reader is confronted with several ethical dilemmas that will provide lively class discussions. In another probation setting, the story of *Brad: Consequences of a Dysfunctional Family* is documented by H. Wayne Johnson. This account follows a social worker through the court process as he engages a teenager in trouble. Family assessment and the placement process are discussed in this case.

Jody and Linda Gottlieb describe work with an Appalachian family from rural West Virginia. Problems faced by the family that are common to the region include unemployment and poverty. The case illustrates some of the strengths, problems, and characteristics of families living in this geographical area and provides the reader with a tremendously interesting cultural experience. The last three cases in this section contribute to learning about groups and group work. A number of issues are brought up in these cases, including effective planning for groups, group dynamics and the stages of group development, and the role of the worker in providing leadership for the group.

Cynthia Duncan writes about a social worker who helps two rival groups of Latino teens settle their differences through creative programming and group work. *No Mad Dog Looks: Group Work and Mediating Differences* stresses planning and intervention as well as many other aspects of group work. Again, culturally appropriate techniques are discussed in this case. Jannah Hurn Mather and Robert F. Rivas provide the account of an empathic worker who seeks "to explore new worlds" and start her first group in a drug rehabilitation center. In *Deanna's Dilemma*, the reader will travel with the group through its stages of development and learn about group planning, contracting, and intervention from the standpoint of the worker. Issues of confidentiality and self-determination are stressed, as is the group as a client system.

James Bembry and Betsy Vourlekis document a creative intergenerational group experience in *Ari and Simone: Notes from the Group*. This case provides a good example of how the group worker intervenes with the individual within the group, with the group as a system, and with the environment in which the group functions.

There is much to be learned from these middle-system cases from the standpoint of the family or the group as well as how workers intervene with individuals within each system.

10

Personal Growth and Self-Esteem through Cultural Spiritualism: A Native American Experience

James Wahlberg

Introduction: My First Impressions

This was my first trip to the reservation under these new circumstances. I had traveled through on a number of occasions but only to "get someplace else." After earning my MSW degree, I came to live among Native Americans and have been practicing social work there ever since.

Due to a restructuring of the regional human service network, I became responsible for a satellite clinic located adjacent to the reservation. The clinic was part of a regional service center located in both the urban and rural parts of the state. Several Indian reservations are part of these regional operations. In an effort to provide services in the most rural environments of the state, satellite centers such as mine were staffed mostly by local people.

As I approached the reservation, I was struck by an apparent oversensitivity to the different stimuli I was receiving. Perhaps this was partly attributable to a generalized fear I identified within myself. I was very concerned about being so clearly "white" and so obviously "different" from the population I was approaching. I had considerable exposure to academic content relative to cultural diversity and the Native American experience, and I had been studying the spiritual lessons of the culture with a Native American mentor. I had worked with Native Americans in urban areas, but this seemed somehow quite different, inasmuch as I was going to them rather than they were coming to me. I clearly remember my first impressions as I arrived at the reservation border on a rather crisp February morning. The trip took about two hours. The temperature was ten degrees below zero, without the wind-chill factor. A recently fallen three-inch blanket of snow covered the landscape. As I approached the reservation, I was struck by the beauty of the rolling forested area with its heavenly blanket of snow. I noticed a herd of buffalo, unfenced and roving to my right, and I was struck by the historical impact buffalo herds had in this region. Adjacent to the buffalo range was a modern-looking industrial complex with hundreds of camouflage-covered gas, water, and oil tankers manufactured for use in the Gulf War. The corporation responsible for these survived primarily through government contracts and was a major employer of Native Americans.

As I proceeded further onto the reservation, I was impressed with the extremely colorful grounds of a local Catholic cemetery immediately to my left. Although it was the dead of winter, the plastic flowers and other ornamentation provided a colorful contrast to the white environment. This colorful symbolism exemplifies the paradox of religious syncretism involving Native American spirituality and white Christendom.

The reservation was characterized by a wide diversity of housing types, ranging from modern, beautiful, new homes to Bureau of Indian Affairs (BIA) housing projects similar to public housing projects in urban areas. I was impressed with the variety of buildings associated with the properties. Stereotypical or not, many properties had sheds, lumber, additional vehicles, and horse trailers adjacent to the dwellings. I also noticed the evidence of domestic and farm animals, as dogs, cats, horses, and cattle seemed attentive to my visit.

It was difficult to define the borders of the "city" or to describe "downtown." There were a number of gas stations, convenience stores, fast-food outlets, as well as a tiny mall. In addition to the dwellings, a community college and other government buildings dominated the city landscape. If the structures that were government-connected were removed from this landscape, there would be few major buildings in this community.

Engagement: Mapping the Environment

It was not difficult to assume where the offices might be located, since I spotted a large (obviously government) complex between a convenience store and the mini-mall. After parking my car and walking toward the entrance, it became obvious that people were staring at me. I expected to be viewed as a newcomer but was unaware of how communications about my coming had been transmitted throughout the community. I was later informed that almost immediately the local police had verified my identity by checking my license plate with the state Department of Motor Vehicles. This had become a regular procedure because of the increase in drug trafficking on the reservation. I also learned that since many people on the reservation own scanners to monitor law enforcement and other communications, my arrival had been duly noted. Approaching a new job situation is at best uncomfortable and sometimes traumatic. Recalling that I was a white person moving into the Native American community, issues of comfort, ethnocentrism, and stereotypes came to mind. Perhaps my thoughts and feelings were similar to those of minority persons functioning in the environment of a majority. Most of the individuals working in the office were Native Americans, since the Bureau of Indian Affairs, Public Health Service (PHS), and other government agencies had instituted policies of recruiting underrepresented populations, especially Native Americans. I wondered how I would be viewed and whether my authority and legitimacy would be questioned because I might be seen as another "white" person intruding on "their territory."

There were many new issues to settle. I had to set up an office, hire a secretary, check out the cafeteria, arrange for coffee, locate restrooms, and attend to countless other details to get started. I also had to carry out other activities on my first day, including meeting my colleagues, reading policy manuals, and finding housing for myself. The satellite operation was new and would suffer growing pains, as any new operation might. Developing and maintaining relationships with the tribe and the tribal government, with other governmental units, and with members of the service delivery network would certainly keep me busy. I learned that many of these agencies had a history of serving at cross-purposes, and this would make my job more challenging.

I was looking forward to my first contacts with clients. As I began to familiarize myself with information about my clients, a colleague gave me several books. I was encouraged to do some reading to help me understand the context of the people I would be serving. My literary benefactor cautioned me that, while many Native Americans have some characteristics in common, there are often more differences than similarities among people of differing tribes.

In my orientation to the reservation, I met several interesting people. It was suggested that I spend some time with the tribal police to better understand some of the problems experienced by people on the reservation. A visit to the Tribal Law Enforcement Center might otherwise have been somewhat threatening. However, as part of my orientation to the reservation, I was able to connect with people who knew other people who knew people with the tribal police. I was authorized to participate in a "ride-along" program, riding with law enforcement officers as they patrolled the reservation. Participating with the officers on a day-to-day basis provided considerable insight into not only their personalities but also the personality of the whole community. The awareness and understanding the law enforcement officers had was enhanced by their roots in the community, especially through family, extended family, and clan. Because of the size of the reservation community, it was not unusual for law enforcement officers to know almost everyone on the reservation. They knew about various situations and the social problems people were experiencing, and they seemed particularly wise when it came to predicting people's behaviors such as child neglect and abuse, spouse abuse, unemployment, and alcoholism.

On one particular Friday evening ride-along, the law enforcement officer I was with really didn't do any "law enforcement." Rather, he was mostly involved in a series of domestic events, spending his full shift working with individuals and personal problems. In essence, he used some of the same skills I use as a social worker. He used the strength of his personal relationship with his clients, and this seemed to be appreciated by those with whom he worked that night. I realized there was a lot to learn about relating to people on the reservation, including the importance of noninterference, avoidance of manipulation and coercion, and the values of mutual respect, consideration, and sharing. I appreciated the lessons I learned on my ride-alongs.

Data Collection: My First Case

I received a referral from the Tribal Law Enforcement Center concerning a 27-year-old man who was in custody for suspected spouse abuse. The report indicated that John Red Fox was drinking and had apparently threatened his wife. The law enforcement authorities were called to investigate, and it was discovered that John had been drinking and was verbally abusive, although there was no evidence of his physically attacking his wife or children. It was decided that he should be incarcerated for his own protection. Although the incident took place two days prior to receiving this referral, John was still in jail. It was decided that a visit to the correctional facility would be an appropriate plan.

I knew the officer who made the arrest and was able to talk to him prior to entering the cell to talk to John. Apparently, John Red Fox was recently discharged from the state hospital for alcohol treatment and had started drinking just prior to his arrest. It was reported that he had been fighting with his wife, but there was no evidence of physical abuse.

As I entered the cell, I was surprised to see a very handsome, well-built young man with braided long black hair. He was wearing blue jeans, tennis shoes, a red and black flannel shirt, and a beautiful beaded necklace. John seemed rather subdued and sullen and volunteered little information. His expression was almost blank, and his voice expressed little inflection or affect. He seldom looked up while we communicated and spoke rather softly. John was aware of the referral to my agency and, consequently, did not question my approaching him. Although I needed to prompt him with specific questioning, John was able to provide a good deal of information.

John told me he was 27 years old and had dropped out of high school when he was 14. He and his wife Mary, age 22, have three children. Two of the children, aged 7 and 5, are from two different fathers, and the couple have a 3-year-old son from their two-and-a-half-year marriage. Mary also dropped out of high school at a young age. John and Mary survive by getting part-time jobs on the reservation. They are also involved in seasonal work. John admitted to having a drinking problem, and he described his most recent admission to the state hospital for alcoholism.

John's mother and father were alive and also lived on the reservation. John has six brothers and three sisters. In general, Mary's mother takes primary responsibility for caring for John and Mary's children because Mary also has a problem with alcohol.

John suggested that there were serious troubles with the children. He described all three children as being unmanageable, easily distracted, hyperactive, and difficult to communicate with, even under the best of circumstances. John said that both he and Mary had been drinking since their teens. I wondered if fetal alcohol syndrome (FAS) might play some part in the children's behaviors.

When I asked him why he had dropped out of school, John said he didn't particularly dislike school but that studying was difficult for him. He often found it difficult to concentrate, and, consequently, he got poor grades. He said he was never tested for any learning disabilities but admitted to having difficulty transferring numbers and letters. He also finds it difficult to read basic material. He did say he was interested in sports and enjoyed playing baseball and basketball in grade school and junior high. He also admitted to being involved in a peer group that did not complete high school and was involved in parties, drinking, smoking, and some petty theft. At the time he quit school, there were good-paying jobs on the reservation, mostly in construction of BIA-funded housing projects. The money he earned from these jobs helped him support himself and contribute to his family. He considered taking care of himself and helping his family as more important than the frustrating experience of completing high school.

When we discussed the event leading to this arrest, John related that a brother and a friend who were living in Minneapolis had recently returned to the reservation. The brother had just lost his job but had considerable money and decided to move in with John and Mary. While Mary was disappointed about this decision, she accepted John's brother as a matter of tradition and respect for John's family. Since John's brother had the necessary money, the three were able to party almost day and night for about a week. John had been released from the state hospital about three weeks prior to this and had remained sober. However, this latest incident of drinking had an immediate effect on his functioning. Mary became more and more agitated about John and experienced difficulty with the children. As a result, a fight broke out between the two, causing the police to get involved. John admitted to being very angry and threatening, but he denied striking Mary or the children.

Both John and Mary had been involved in periodic counseling since their marriage. Although Mary did not participate often, both were involved in counseling while John was in treatment at the state hospital. It was recommended that John and Mary become involved in Alcoholics Anonymous and Al-Anon, but they participated only sporadically. The reservation community provided little support for individuals struggling with maintaining sobriety. The amount of alcohol consumption and its visibility and acceptance on the reservation were strong motivators for individuals to abuse alcohol.

After my discussion with John, I thought it might be important to talk with Mary, with the children, and with members of the extended family. Perhaps they would add their insights about the overall situation with John. The family didn't have a telephone, and because of the urgency of the situation, I made an unscheduled home visit.

The family lived three miles north of the agency on a rural, unmarked gravel road. I had to ask for directions from some of the neighbors, but I finally found it. When I arrived, I was curious about the scene I viewed. The residence included three dwellings, two of which were connected, suggesting that the living arrangement had been built in sections over time. There were a number of exposed roof areas—shingles had apparently blown off. Tarpaper was visible through the siding, most of the windows had no screens, and a few windows were broken. Four automobiles in various stages of repair and disrepair were in the front yard. There were two dogs, three horses, chickens, ducks, geese, and goats around the living area. Outside the home were a number of old appliances. There were also some fallen trees and firewood stacked in neat rows. In addition, I saw a number of tools and other woodworking items. I was somewhat surprised at the overall appearance of John and Mary's home.

I was surprised again as I entered their home. An elderly woman answered the door and invited me in without hesitation. I was impressed with the colorful wallpaper, drapes, fixtures, and furniture in the home. There were some beautiful Native American arts and crafts throughout the home, and overall it appeared orderly and tidy. I was impressed with the small size of the quarters relative to the number of people living there.

I identified myself, and the woman responded by saying, "I figured someone would be out. I suppose you want to see Mary?" Mary came from a back bedroom, and after I introduced myself we settled at the kitchen table. Mary was an attractive young woman with features distinct to her tribal heritage. She had long dark hair, a pleasant smile, and intense dark eyes.

Mary was gracious and hospitable during the visit. She said that she knew the reasons for my visit and appeared interested in volunteering information about her husband. Throughout the interview, Mary's three children and four other children were continually in and out of the kitchen. Although not specifically disruptive, their presence was obvious. They jumped on and off Mary's lap, and eventually they paid attention to me, climbing on my lap and looking through my attaché case and other effects. They appeared curious about our conversation but would appear and disappear frequently. Mary volunteered a good deal of information about herself. She described her childhood as difficult. She faced a lot of pressure as a teenager and had difficulties attending and performing in school. She mentioned, "I became a mother way too early." When I asked her to clarify her statement, she said she had gotten pregnant at a young age. She also said that she was the second oldest of four children and had to care for her brothers and sisters in her parents' absence. According to Mary, her father disappeared from the family when she was rather young. Her mother spent considerable time away from home participating in part-time and seasonal work, and she had a drinking problem. Mary described a series of unstable relationships she had with boyfriends, and she said that her parents sent her away to an Indian boarding school. Mary said she dropped out of high school because she became pregnant and had difficulty making good grades.

Mary told me that she and John had been having problems with their marriage. She felt that her relationship with John was made difficult by their mutual drinking problems, but she felt that their relationship was salvageable. In general, the information she provided was similar to the information John and others had provided.

I appreciated Mary's spontaneity. However, when I asked her about her children, she was much more guarded. Although she said that each of the children had different fathers, she refused to talk any more about her children's behaviors. It appeared that Mary was motivated and willing to be further involved in some form of counseling relationship, although I was unsure of what that might be. In retrospect, I wondered if Mary "had all the right things to say," since she had been in and out of counseling with multiple human service providers for many years. In addition, I wondered if she said what she thought I might want to hear so I would leave her, her children, and her relatives alone.

About a week after John's arrest, he was released and returned to Mary. Knowing this, I decided to review their situation more closely by examining their existing case records and making contact with other providers who had been involved with this family over time. Having received written permission from John and Mary to obtain information from other service providers, I discovered that as a child Mary had apparently been abused by her older stepbrother and had possibly been physically and sexually abused by her stepfather. In addition, there was some suspicion raised by the school system relative to sexual abuse of Mary's two oldest children, ironically, by that same stepbrother. Having obtained this new information, I realized why Mary might have been reluctant to share information about herself and her children.

Assessment: Defining the Issues

It seemed important to me to review all the information I had in this case to establish some priorities and possible intervention plans and strategies. It was obvious that the Red Fox family had multiple problems. John and Mary, and both of their parents and grandparents, had continuously lived on the reservation. There was a history of unemployment, alcoholism, divorce, desertion, and parent-child relationship issues throughout both families. Most family members had survived by taking odd jobs and seasonal work, using the food allotment and subsidy received through Tribal Social Services, and benefiting from monies distributed from treaty renegotiation resettlement for enrolled tribal members. Several family members had been involved with various counseling services that were arranged by Public Health Service workers. Although the Red Fox clan had benefited from several programs to which they were entitled, such as medical and dental services, most of the counseling services to which they were referred were deemed ineffective.

I decided to sort out the different components of the Red Fox situation. My preliminary assessment led to identifying the following problems:

1. John's drinking and threatening behavior to Mary and the children often brought the family into crisis.
2. Mary's drinking contributed to the overall instability of the family situation. Mary also had a family history in which she might have experienced physical and sexual abuse as a child.
3. Lack of employment opportunities on the reservation made the family at risk for poverty. This was exacerbated by John and Mary's lack of educational credentials and employment skills.
4. John and Mary suffered frequent marital discord. This was due, in part, to their inability to deal with their children and their difficulties resulting from alcohol abuse.
5. There were significant issues with the children's behavior, perhaps owing to fetal alcohol syndrome and

physical or sexual abuse. The children were hyperactive and could have learning deficits or disabilities.

6. Although living arrangements were not identified as being unusual, the family's ability to access services, such as employment and education, was limited. The distance from the reservation and the family's lack of adequate transportation contributed to the isolating experience of living on the reservation.

While I was able to identify a number of interrelated problems in the Red Fox case, I was somewhat pessimistic about whether I could help John and Mary solve any of them. I thought of all the services available to them, both on and off the reservation, and realized that these traditional services had all been tried, with little success. I was not sure whether the ineffectiveness of the services was due to the Red Foxes' lack of motivation or whether the services themselves were ineffective or culturally inappropriate. It seemed obvious that I was going to have to be pretty creative to involve John and Mary in any kind of treatment plan.

Goal Planning: Finding a Point of Intervention

As I sat alone in my office, I tried to decide how to reach the Red Fox family. Work had been done before with John and Mary, and more of the same didn't seem appropriate. I thought that if only I could reach the children and explore their situation, a point of intervention might present itself.

As luck would have it, I remembered a staff presentation I had attended during my first week at the agency. A number of individuals from Montana, Arizona, and New Mexico had presented a program about efforts to revitalize traditional Indian beliefs and culture. There were several social workers involved in the presentation, and this rather impressed me. The presentation, entitled "The Red Road," had to do with the traditional Native American spiritual orientation, which stressed a holistic unification of people and the environment. As I thought back to the presentation, I realized I had neglected to consider helping the Red Fox family with any strategy other than a traditional, agency-oriented intervention. As a social worker, I had been trained to think of the human condition in a holistic way but not in the same sense as is stressed in traditional Native American beliefs.

I made contact with a number of the presenters and intensified my study in this whole area. I decided to look up a friend who was also my Native American mentor, Frank Running Deer, and ask him how to connect with people like John and Mary. Frank, who held the honored tribal role of "Pipe Carrier," had been authorized by tribal leaders to conduct the Sweat Lodge ceremony, and I had been granted the privilege of learning and participating in this and other ceremonies since coming to the reservation. Although I didn't identify the Red Fox family by name, I discussed my concerns about engaging them and other families with traditional social services. Frank agreed to work with me on my concerns. As we shared intervention strategies and goal planning relative to my assessment of the family situation, we agreed that working with the children might be a good beginning.

Frank told me of a new program developed by private and public sponsorship, including religious groups, spiritual leaders, and a number of funding agencies. It was a unique combination of "white religion and native spiritualism" in which the traditional involvement of people in their cultural environment was stressed. I agreed to make an on-site visit to the program to assess its possibilities.

The program was located in beautiful surroundings halfway between the reservation and the city. It included, among other things, a lovely beach, canoes, and all associated water and outdoor camp activities. In addition, authentic Native American structures were constructed, including the traditional wigwam, teepee, and earth lodge, used for ceremonial and educational purposes by such tribes as the Ojibwa, Mandan, and Plains Apache. Children were instructed in Native culture and spiritualism, and they were able to sleep outdoors in a teepee. I was told by the camp staff that a critical part of the experience was involvement of the parents, which stressed their contribution to educating the children in Native American cultural ways. As I listened to the camp staff, I realized why Frank had suggested the program as an intervention. For one thing, by involving the children in this culturally appropriate activity, it was unnecessary to "label" the parents as the "identified patients." I also realized that the program might help identify the strengths I believed existed within this family, including the relationship between John and Mary. Frank and I later agreed that the program had possibilities that might help John and Mary use their innate capacities, which we believed were considerable.

Intervention: Using Culturally Appropriate Programming

I had some second thoughts about how to approach this situation. I realized that I had been doing a lot of planning without involving John and Mary, and they had the right to participate in the planning process. I also wondered about the ethical implications of "getting to" John and Mary by involving their children in programming, even though the program seemed innovative and worthwhile.

My strategy included asking the school system to refer all three children to the camp program. I worked with the staff and consulted with Frank Running Deer as I sought ways to encourage John and Mary to enroll the children in the program. Although they appeared hesitant at first, John and Mary agreed that the program would be appropriate for the children. They appeared to welcome the respite from the demands of the children and even expressed interest in participating in their children's experiences. I considered this to be my first victory and a marvelous point of entry into the helping relationship.

The children's experience with the program was quite positive. I discussed their progress with John and Mary, hoping to reinforce their involvement with their children's camp activities. I also worked with the camp director, urging him to write notes home with the children and asking him to seek ways to involve John and Mary. As I recalled my first contact with Mary, I remembered the beautiful Native American art projects she had completed and displayed in her home. I suggested to the camp director that Mary be invited to come to camp to help teach children some of the Native art. Although several of the camp activities were recreational, many had cultural implications. For example, children participated in Native dances and "talking circles" and were encouraged to study their heritage. I felt Mary's special talents would fit well with the mission of the camp, would increase her feelings of connection to her community, and could enhance her self-esteem.

After further discussion with the camp director, I learned that there was a continuous need for adults to supervise children as they designed and constructed authentic Indian dance outfits. This involved the traditional tanning of hides as well as making Indian costuming. Later, the children would learn to dance and would attend various powwows throughout the area. I suggested that the camp director contact Mary about involving her in these activities. Mary was delighted at the camp director's suggestion. She said she was interested in helping children with beadwork and especially with work in leather and birch bark. Her involvement in camp programming developed and increased over time.

My friend Frank Running Deer, who seemed to have a particular interest in this case, suggested that while we were encouraging Mary's involvement we should think of a way to ensure John's participation. He offered to help John become involved, suggesting that John and he might plan a children's powwow, including constructing a Sweat Lodge and other important components of the powwow. As luck would have it, John took up Frank's invitation. As we later found out, John was somewhat frustrated by Mary's increased involvement in the program and saw this as a good way to keep in touch with his family.

Mary, John, and the children remained involved with these activities through the summer months. There was no further indication of marital discord, abuse, or alcohol consumption, although I was not sure why, given their stormy history. As summer ended and fall neared, activities diminished on our rural, northern reservation. With the changing climate and the restrictions of winter, Frank and I were puzzled about how we might continue to work with this family. Frank suggested that at the closing ceremonies of the camp he and I should approach Mary and John to talk with them about their participation. He suggested that we stress their positive involvement and that they continue to stay involved in the future.

After the ceremony, there was an opportunity, though brief, for Frank and me and Mary and John to walk through the camp and chat about the experience. Frank was first to approach the subject and suggest there might be ways to continue involvement throughout the winter in anticipation of more involvement in next summer's program. Frank's way of broaching this suggestion to John and Mary was very nondirect, and I realized this was his cultural style of communicating. Although Frank's intent was clear, his way of making the suggestion seemed less judgmental and intrusive, allowing John and Mary to accept his suggestion by exercising their own self-determination. Frank also suggested that John and he needed to continue their activity with Native spiritualism, which included involvement with the Sweat Lodge. John and Mary seemed to hold Frank in very high regard, and they tended to follow his suggestions. I later found out that as a result of Frank's suggestion, both John and Mary rejoined Alcoholics Anonymous.

Frank and I continued to work with the family, and we were able to arrange for diagnostic services for the three children and educational testing for Mary and John. Because the family had become more involved in activities in town, they had more access to the available diagnostic services. I developed an excellent relationship with the school social worker who helped secure thorough medical, physical, and emotional exams for the children. In addition, Frank convinced John and Mary to check out the adult education program at the community college and to consider enrolling.

It would certainly be unrealistic and unfair to suggest that all was smooth throughout the process of my involvement with the Red Fox family. I was proud for them, since they seemed to find a way to help themselves. The goals that John and Mary eventually set for themselves included participating in the Sweat Lodge ceremony and the Sun Dance, which would help them reach their potential as individuals.

Evaluation

Throughout the process of working with this family, I attempted to define what might constitute success. It seemed to me that I evaluated the family, evaluated the effectiveness of the various treatment strategies that had been used with this family in the past, and evaluated my own efforts. From the beginning of my involvement with the Red Fox family, it was obvious that many others had tried to reach this family, so I wasn't very optimistic about my chances of reaching them.

I also evaluated the effect of the workshop on me and the others in attendance. Assessing and analyzing the outcome of that experience led me to believe that other interventions might be available. I concluded that I was not going to be able to reach this family, nor was I going to create an immediate link between the family and traditional social service agencies. Involving another person in the intervention helped engage this family and helped suggest a creative and culturally appropriate treatment plan.

The ending of this story is positive. John and Mary continue to participate. John has been involved in many Sweats. He is not yet a pipe carrier and has not yet been authorized to dance in this year's Sun Dance; however, he continues to struggle with his lessons to achieve that distinction, honor, and responsibility. Mary continues to work throughout the winter months and has worked with several children and parents to produce beautiful costumes for many of the traditional dances. She and John have been involved in several powwows.

Both John and Mary successfully completed their GED and are beginning college studies. Although the studies are very difficult and frustrating, they have received good support from the instructional and counseling staff at the community college. They remain living at home with their extended family, and while this continues to cause a certain degree of difficulty, it appears manageable. The children are less of a problem in school this year but will require continued observation and attention as we continue to learn more about fetal alcohol syndrome, its consequences, and its treatment.

I encountered some interesting variables in this situation: mapping the service terrain of the reservation, using traditional and nontraditional interventions, assessing and intervening in the "spiritual" aspects of people's lives, and a holistic understanding of people in their environment. In addition, working together with a "veteran" helped this to be a positive experience for me. The idea that my clients in this situation were somewhat "manipulated" into a process of "treatment" raised some ethical questions for me. I'm still not sure how to answer them.

Readings

Brave Heart, M. Y. H. (1999). Gender differences in the historical trauma response among Lakota. *Journal of Health and Social Policy, 10*(4), 1–21.

Canda, E. R., & Furman, L. D. (1999). *Spiritual diversity in social work practice: The heart of helping.* New York: Free Press.

Voss, R. W., Little Soldier, A., & Twiss, G. (1999). Tribal and shamanic-based social work practices: A Lakota perspective. *Social Work, 44*(3), 228–241.

Weaver, H. (1999). Indigenous people and the social work profession: Defining culturally competent services. *Social Work, 44*(3), 217–225.

Discussion Questions

1. *Are the worker's concerns about "manipulation" of the family justified? Why or why not?*

2. *What role did spirituality play in this case?*

3. *Why did John allow his brother to move in even though it increased the likelihood of further problems for him and his family?*

4. *What factors explain Frank Running Deer's influence with this family?*

5. *What is ethnocentrism, and how did it affect the worker in this case?*

6. *Why is the value of noninterference mentioned by the worker?*

7. *How might fetal alcohol syndrome play a role in the behavior of John and Mary's children?*

8. *What influence does spirituality have in traditional Native American culture? Are there any other cultures with strong spiritual components?*

9. *What limitations to confidentiality were evident in this case? Can you think of similar situations where confidentiality can be difficult to maintain?*

10. *Once Mary, John, and the children became involved in the camp program, the social worker said, "There were no further indications of marital discord, abuse, or alchohol consumption, although I was not sure why, given their stormy history." What might explain this dramatic change in family and individual behaviors?*

11

In the Best Interest of the Child

Lettie L. Lockhart
Alicia R. Issac

Engagement and Presenting Problem

Linda Dixon, a Danfield County Department of Family and Children's Services foster care worker, was having a particularly difficult time working with the Sutter family. The family had been referred to Linda from the agency's child protective services unit. The family court had determined that Jeannie, the 16-year-old daughter of Reverend and Mrs. Sutter, had been a physically abused child. It was alleged that Reverend Sutter had beaten Jeannie, leaving her with several bruises and a black eye. The court ordered that Jeannie be placed in a foster home for a temporary period until a satisfactory plan for her care was worked out with the family.

From the beginning of the agency's involvement with the family, Reverend Sutter asserted that he had done nothing wrong. He noted that Jeannie dressed in a manner forbidden by his church, and that her failure to obey his rules threatened to harm his reputation and his ability to lead his congregation. Linda remembered how frustrated she had become when she first interviewed Reverend Sutter. When she inquired into the apparent abuse charges, he had made some very strong statements.

> You and the Danfield County Department of Family and Children's Services need to respect my religious beliefs! What's wrong with kids today is that there aren't enough parents who discipline their kids, and the ones who do are persecuted! I have to be able to control my kids to be able to teach my congregation that it is God's law that they control their kids. It was not my intention to hurt Jeannie, but she must understand that she'll live by my rules and by God's rules. If she had just accepted my punishment and allowed me to scrub off all of her filthy makeup and wash her mouth out, she wouldn't have received those bruises or that black eye.

Reverend Sutter explained that his religious denomination was very conservative and strict. Women were forbidden to wear pants, makeup, or jewelry and were not allowed to participate in activities such as school dances, where there was "likely to be immoral behavior." He further explained that African American families like his raised their children in a different way, sometimes correcting their children's behavior by physical punishment when necessary. Reverend Sutter indicated he would try to cooperate with Linda, although he felt that "social workers could do a better job if they understood certain cultures and allowed parents to control their children."

Data Collection

Through interviews with the Sutter family, Linda began to put the pieces of the puzzle together. Reverend Sutter, age 42, seemed to be rigid and opinionated. His demeanor indicated that he needed to be in complete control of both his family and the other circumstances in his life. He asserted that he did not intend to make changes in his values or in how he ran his household. Mrs. Sutter was a quiet, passive woman, seemingly dominated by her husband and appearing older than her stated age of 41. She rarely spoke and, when questioned, allowed her husband to answer for her.

Reverend and Mrs. Sutter married young. She was 18 and he was 19 years old. Their five daughters were born early in their marriage and came relatively close together. Reverend Sutter entered the ministry at 22, having been groomed for this career by his father, also a minister.

The two older daughters were married and living away from home. The two younger daughters lived in the home but were somewhat invisible. They had no history of problems within the family and appeared to follow the rules established by Reverend Sutter. They attended a local elementary school and received good grades. They did not participate in school activities but were involved in youth groups established by their father's congregation. Both younger daughters seemed to care very much for Jeannie, but they voiced concern about her behavior, suggesting they just wanted Jeannie to behave, finish high school, and go away to college.

Jeannie, the middle child, appeared quiet and passive. She was a good student with aspirations of attending college. Attractive and articulate, she appeared popular among her peers at school. In her initial interview, she told Linda she only wanted to be a "normal teenager" and to be accepted by her school friends. She said her father's rules about her dress and behavior made her feel "out of place." She didn't feel she was doing anything wrong when she dressed as her friends at school did.

Linda knew it was her responsibility to assist the Sutter family to work out an acceptable plan for Jeannie's care but was very concerned about working with Reverend Sutter. Linda's assessment of the situation suggested that each member of the family played an important part in the family's functioning. However, Reverend Sutter appeared to be the pivotal player, and everyone but Jeannie allowed him this position without question. He had used physical force to attempt to regain his position of authority over Jeannie. Because Jeannie failed to comply with Reverend Sutter's rules, she was identified as the family's problem.

The protective services worker was concerned about how far Reverend Sutter would go to gain control over Jeannie. This constituted the primary reason for the court ordering Jeannie's six-month foster care placement. During Jeannie's placement, the Sutters were supposed to attend a parenting class for parents of adolescents and to work with the foster care worker. Linda was assigned to work with Jeannie and her parents to help prepare for Jeannie's return to her home.

Assessment

Linda thought about her contacts with the Sutter family and about her conversations with others involved in the situation. She organized her thoughts and made a list of her observations.

1. It was clear that physical abuse had occurred in this family and that Mrs. Sutter might not be able to prevent further abuse.
2. Jeannie's parents were complying with the court order by attending the educational group for parents of adolescents.
3. Although the family was somewhat cooperative, there were several problems in the family yet to be resolved.
4. There were cultural and religious factors that influenced the child rearing, disciplinary policy, and overall functioning of the family. It would be difficult to intervene without considering these issues.
5. Reverend Sutter felt he had done nothing wrong, seemed not to want to change his attitude about Jeannie, and appeared cooperative only to satisfy the court order rather than out of genuine concern for Jeannie.
6. Jeannie continued her desire to break from the religious and family traditions of the Sutters.

Linda knew that if a successful reunion between Jeannie and her family were to be accomplished, she would have to help the Sutters resolve some of these issues. Admittedly, Linda felt discouraged. There appeared to be no middle ground between the Sutters' demands and Jeannie's desires.

Goal Planning

Two factors influenced Linda's thinking about how to plan realistic goals with the Sutter family. First, she recognized that Reverend Sutter was quite set in his ways and did not want to change his child-rearing and discipline practices. These stemmed from a very powerful religious

value system that influenced his thinking on such matters. Second, Linda realized the legal system could mandate attendance at educational meetings as well as involvement with family and children's services, but if Reverend Sutter did not wish to change, he could merely attend without really becoming involved. Linda discussed this with the family, and Reverend Sutter said that he did not want further involvement from the court. He intended to stop going to the parenting classes when the six months were finished and Jeannie was returned to her home. Based on these factors, Linda felt three realistic goals were possible.

1. Mrs. Sutter and the children would support Jeannie during her weekend visits to the home, in hopes that Reverend Sutter would avoid resorting to physical punishment.
2. Reverend Sutter would agree to not use physical punishment on Jeannie.
3. Jeannie and her parents would begin to communicate in an attempt to reach a compromise regarding expectations for Jeannie's behavior and mode of dress.

Linda met with the Sutter family together and discussed these goals. Surprisingly, Jeannie's parents felt they could agree to the goals and stated that they would do all they could to help reunite the family. Mrs. Sutter noted that African Americans feel strongly about their abilities to take care of problems within their families, sometimes calling on members of the extended family to assist when help was needed. Linda noted this might be a possible source of support for the family and complimented Mrs. Sutter on her sense of family solidarity. Reverend Sutter also echoed this sentiment. He also suggested that the family and children's services agency should support him in his efforts to discipline his children. Jeannie, however, continued to be adamant in her desire to be a normal teenager and in her preference for foster care if things could not be worked out at home.

Intervention

Jeannie's foster care placement was going well. She made a satisfactory adjustment and was anxious to return home for a weekend visit. Reports from the parenting class instructors were less enthusiastic. Not much had happened to help Reverend Sutter see alternatives to physical discipline. Although many group members disagreed with him, he continued to believe that children should act and dress according to their parents' wishes.

Linda met with Jeannie on a frequent basis. Much of their work together was aimed at establishing a trusting relationship in which Jeannie could talk about how she could help make things better at home. Although Jeannie came to realize that she would probably have to compromise with her father, she was reluctant to do so without some indication from her father that he would be able to compromise as well.

As Jeannie's placement was approaching its fourth month, Linda arranged for her to have a weekend visit to her home. Soon, Linda would have to prepare a report for the court on the progress the family had made on their goals, and the weekend visit seemed to be a good way to observe whether any progress could be made. On Saturday morning of the first weekend visit, Linda received a telephone call from Mrs. Sutter stating that Jeannie had run away from home and returned to the foster home. Mrs. Sutter stated that Reverend Sutter had not hit Jeannie but had ordered her to stay in her room until she changed into a dress and removed her jewelry and makeup. In a later call, Reverend Sutter reminded Linda that he had been working on his court-ordered treatment plan and had not used physical discipline on his child. He noted that at the end of six months, and after he had done all that the court had required of him, Jeannie should be returned. He felt that the court would determine there was no longer a substantial risk of child abuse and that they (her parents) were able to care for Jeannie.

Later in the day, Linda met with Reverend and Mrs. Sutter and discussed Jeannie's situation. Linda tried to explain how important it was to Jeannie to be accepted by her friends at school. She tried to discuss some of what she knew to be "normal" adolescent behavior and described how Jeannie was trying to assert her independence. Linda also explained some of the pressures Jeannie felt when she was seen as "different" from other teens at school. The Reverend Sutter seemed to understand how his rules of behavior could make Jeannie feel different and somewhat softened his usual statements about child rearing. He ended his comments by becoming introspective about Jeannie's behavior and humorously stating that Jeannie had been "sent to test [his] commitment to God." Mrs. Sutter laughed and said she certainly agreed.

Later, Linda met with Jeannie at the foster home. The following is an excerpt from their conversation.

Linda: I know you love your parents and that this has not been particularly easy for you.

Jeannie: Ms. Dixon, four months ago I was so mad at my father that I didn't care if I ever went home again. But I do miss them. I just don't understand why he can't accept me for what I am. I am not a bad person. I get embarrassed sometimes when the kids at school call my family "The Holy Rollers." But I still love them.

Linda: Have you been able to tell this to your parents?

Jeannie: No, I never get the chance; he is always yelling at me. I have often wondered what it would be like if he wasn't a preacher at the church.

Linda: So his being a preacher makes his standards difficult to follow?

Jeannie: Some of my other friends at school have fathers who are ministers, and their fathers seem much happier and are always involved in the community. My father is always worried about sin taking over someone. I know my mom misses her old friends and some of her family, but she can't be around them because they are not "saved."

Linda: I guess it's tough for both you and your mom, not being around your friends and making your own choices.

Jeannie: I don't know what I'm going to do. I don't want to turn out like my sisters or those other girls in my church. I want to go to college, be an actress, and get away from this town. I'll never leave if I become the type of person my father wants me to be.

Linda: Jeannie, I'm glad you shared this with me. I understand a good deal more about your situation now, and this can help me work with you and your parents. Perhaps you and I can talk about your own plans for the future. Soon you will be able to make your own decisions and hopefully go away to college as you want. Perhaps we could talk to a career counselor friend of mine, get some ideas for where you want to be in a couple of years. In the meantime, we have to discuss what is going to happen next. The reality is that the court may order you to go home soon. How can we make that situation better?

Jeannie: If I go home, I think I can tone down my makeup and wear smaller earrings. And I won't wear shorts or tight jeans. Now Ms. Dixon, that's about all I can do. Oh, and since I'm such an embarrassment to him, I'll go to church by myself.

Linda: I think that is a reasonable beginning compromise, Jeannie. Let's talk to your parents about that.

Linda felt encouraged about her meetings with Jeannie and the Sutters. Finally, there appeared to be some common ground between Jeannie and her parents. Linda thought the key to further progress would be opening lines of communication between Jeannie and her parents and continuing the foster care placement until a solid agreement could be reached.

Evaluation and Ending

Despite several meetings with the family, further compromise was not possible. Linda felt her only course of action was to recommend to the family court that Jeannie's foster care placement be extended for another six months until Jeannie and her parents could reach agreement on expectations for Jeannie and on Jeannie's future. Also, Linda thought that individual work with Mrs. Sutter might be a way to influence Reverend Sutter's opinions about expectations for Jeannie.

On the day of the court hearing, Reverend and Mrs. Sutter arrived with an attorney who presented an eloquent argument on behalf of the Sutters. The central part of this presentation was that the state had no business taking care of an unruly child when the parents wanted to and were capable of taking care of that child. The attorney pointed out that the Sutters had satisfied every requirement of the treatment plan.

Linda presented her recommendation for an additional six-month foster care placement and gave details of her work with Jeannie and her family. Jeannie was allowed to voice her desires, which included her preference for foster care if she were not allowed to engage in what she considered "normal" behavior.

The family court judge noted that the Sutters had, in her opinion, satisfied the "letter of the law" in regard to the court's orders. However, the judge felt that Reverend Sutter needed to rethink his discipline practices. After some deliberation, the judge ordered that Jeannie be returned to the Sutter home and that the family remain under the supervision of the county family and children's services for an additional six-month period. The judge ordered that another report be submitted at the end of that period.

Two days later, Linda received a call from Mrs. Sutter reporting that Jeannie had not returned from school as told. She suspected that Jeannie was at a school football game. Jeannie was already on restriction since her return home, and Mrs. Sutter was worried about what might happen as a result of this latest incident. Linda and Mrs. Sutter spoke at length, attempting to arrive at a solution to the problem. Mrs. Sutter agreed to meet alone with Linda that afternoon to try to work in Jeannie's best interest.

Readings

Haight, W. L., Black, J. E., Workman, C., & Lakshmi, T. (2001). Parent-child interaction during foster care visits: Implications for practice. *Social Work, 46*(4), 325–340.

Hurn Mather, J., & Lager, P. B. (2000). *Child welfare: A unifying model of practice.* Pacific Grove, CA: Wadsworth.

Taylor, R. J., Ellison, C. G., Chatters, L. M., Levin, J. S., & Lincoln, K. D. (2000). Mental health services in faith communities: The role of clergy in black churches. *Social Work, 45*(1), 73–86.

Discussion Questions

1. *How might Linda have approached Reverend Sutter about discussing his child-rearing and discipline practices?*

2. *How could Linda have educated the Sutters about differentiating "normal" from "dysfunctional" adolescent behavior?*

3. *What role should an adolescent play in the decision-making process about foster care and returning to his or her own home?*

4. *What rights do parents and children have in determining choices about religious beliefs?*

5. *This case illustrates a clash between public policy and the religious and spiritual beliefs of a family. In your view, does the state have a right to interfere with the rights of parents to raise their children according to the dictates of their church? Explain your opinion.*

6. *What do you see as the strengths of Reverend Sutter and Jeannie?*

7. *Can you think of any way the worker might use these strengths to build a bridge between father and daughter?*

8. *How would you go about evaluating the success of the worker's intervention in this case? What might you use as a baseline? What criterion for success appears most logical?*

9. *Can you think of any community resources or individuals that might help in this situation? Compare this case to the earlier one involving Native Americans. What parallels are evident?*

12

Between Two Worlds

Rupa R. Gupta

Problem at Referral

Bea Xiong, a 22-year-old college freshman, had come to the University Health Services with a complaint of constant headaches and nausea. The attending physician had run several diagnostic tests to understand the causes of her ailments, but the results were negative. Although some medications had been prescribed for these symptoms, a referral was made to the counseling department because Bea was found to be under a great deal of stress.

Intake Summary

A social history done by the intake worker of the counseling department revealed that at the age of 12, Bea Xiong had immigrated to the United States with her family. Although originally from Laos (and a member of the Hmong culture), Bea remembered most of her childhood years as having been spent in a refugee camp in Thailand where her family had escaped after the Vietnam War. One of her older brothers had been killed during this flight, and Bea still had vivid memories of this event. The Xiong family had lived in the Thai camp for seven years until a Congregational Church sponsor was found for them in a small Midwestern town in the United States. Bea recalled her years in the camp as having been "happy" ones.

In the United States, Bea's parents, two brothers, and three sisters lived in a small town 150 miles from where Bea attended college. One of her married sisters lived in Michigan. Her older brother was also married, and he and his wife had lived with Bea's parents after their marriage. They both worked in a paper manufacturing plant. Her parents were unemployed and were receiving government assistance. Of all Bea's siblings, she was the only one who had ventured to go to the university.

As Bea's uncle (father's older brother) lived close to the university, Bea was sent to live with him while she attended college. Bea had been made to feel comfortable at her uncle's home. Her uncle had three sons, all of whom were younger than Bea. Bea was treated by her uncle and aunt as part of the family. She had to perform household chores, however, that sometimes became overwhelming in light of her other responsibilities.

The aunt and uncle were very traditional. They continually reminded Bea that she had passed the normal marriageable age and that she needed to settle down soon. They encouraged her to consider Chou, who was her aunt's brother's son, as a possible mate. Bea did not like Chou

but was afraid to openly reveal this to her uncle and aunt for fear of being disrespectful. The pressure mounted toward the end of the semester, not only with the increase in schoolwork, but also with the family's greater insistence on considering marriage. Whenever Bea called her parents at home, they agreed with the uncle and reminded her that it was her duty to respect and obey him.

Soon after that, Bea began complaining of severe headaches and nausea that rendered her unable to eat or hold down food. This situation caused a great deal of concern to the family, especially her uncle and aunt. Other clan members had also become involved in finding remedies and suggesting alternative means of treatment for Bea. Some of the remedies recommended giving Bea herbal mixtures to stop her vomiting, cupping (which is a suction technique of placing a cup on the patient's forehead, creating a vacuum, and then "sucking out the headache"), trying certain incantations to appease the "house spirits" that might have been offended, or calling in the shaman to conduct traditional rituals in an attempt to return Bea's soul to her body in case it had escaped.

After intake, the case was assigned to a female social worker, Stella Jones, at the university counseling center. Stella realized she needed to learn more about the Hmong culture since this would have direct bearing on how she would understand Bea's situation and provide appropriate services. Her initial work, therefore, involved reviewing literature on the Hmong and consulting with a bicultural worker who was a coordinator for minority students at the university. The following is a brief summary of the information Stella collected on the Hmong.

The Hmong were a tribal people in Laos. As they were an ethnic minority in that country, they essentially led an isolated existence, mostly farming, raising animals, and cultivating opium as a cash crop. In 1960, they were approached by the CIA to fight a "secret war" in Laos to halt the spread of communism westward in that region. As the United States involvement in Vietnam increased, so did the Hmong recruitment in the war. Consequently, the Hmong paid a high price in terms of the communist persecution that followed the Pathet-Lao takeover in Laos. They were compelled to flee their homeland as they saw their people decimated by the communists. They escaped to Thailand until a third-country sponsor was found to take them in.

Presently, there are more than 100,000 Hmong residents in the United States, mostly in states (listed in terms of their Hmong population density) such as California, Wisconsin, Minnesota, Michigan, Rhode Island, Colorado, Oregon, Illinois, and Washington. Because of a major shift from an agrarian to a technologically driven economy and the corresponding difference in the lifestyles, the Hmong have had to make tremendous adaptations in the United States. Their difficulties have been further exacerbated by differences in the two cultures with regard to family lifestyles, clan membership, marriage customs, and health care practices.

The Hmong family is of an extended type, and it is normal for the unmarried children, as well as married sons and their families, to continue living in the parental household. Daughters join their husband's families and clans upon marriage. Hmong families are closely tied by strong bonds of affection as well as obligations and responsibilities. Should a married son establish a separate household, he is still expected to recognize the patriarchal authority of the family elder.

Each family belongs to one of the 18 clans and bears the clan name. The clan serves as a second layer of the extended family. The Hmong believe that all members of a clan have descended from the same ancestors and are related as cousins. Marriages within the clan are therefore taboo, and marriages are essentially arranged between members of different clans. The "arranged marriage" is the most common form, and negotiations are conducted by the family and clan elders. Marriage is considered to be a sacred institution that marks the union not only of two individuals but of the two families and clans as well.

Clans serve as a source of support, belonging, and as a provider of social services. Clan members have a strong sense of obligation to each other and expect to take care of their own members. It is considered shameful to seek or accept help from another clan. Problems that defy solution within the confines of the family are handled by clan elders.

Important values support this system of the clan and the extended family. These include patriarchal decision making (where the eldest male has the most authority), respect for elders or "filial piety," humility and modesty in behavior, cooperation and sharing, high emphasis on awareness of and consideration of others' feelings, group orientation in problem solving versus an individualistic style, and shame as an important means of social control. A Hmong individual who behaves in a manner that reflects negatively on the family or the clan brings dishonor to the larger social group. How others evaluate an individual's actions is, therefore, often more important to a Hmong than how he or she feels about it.

The Hmong system of health care is unique in its perception of causation and treatment of illness. Both physical and mental illnesses are often thought to be caused by the "loss of soul." They believe that the soul has a tendency to wander outside the body, and if this happens for long, the person could become severely ill and die. The Hmong also believe in the existence of spirits. Should a spirit be offended, the person may become ill. Possible treatment in such cases involves communicating with the spirit to regain the soul, which may have been captured. These negotiations with the spirits are undertaken by trained shamans. Some shamanistic rituals last a whole day, during which an animal may be sacrificed and a feast held for the clan members. Other causes of illness may be organic and are treated by herbal potions mixed by women according to secret formulas handed down in the family through the generations. Illnesses resulting from "natural causes" are thought to occur because of an imbalance between humans and nature and are preventable.

While some Hmong do not practice indigenous medicine, most tend to combine western and Hmong approaches to treatment.

Stella realized that because of the vast cultural differences between herself and Bea, she would need to be particularly sensitive to Bea's cultural background. This would also mean that she would need to maintain a high level of self-awareness and avoid imposing her own values and value judgments in Bea's situation. She also recognized that there was a likelihood that she was being ethnocentric without being aware of it. Most important, she cautioned herself against overgeneralizing her understanding of the traditional Hmong culture to her client who could, quite possibly, be acculturated to mainstream U.S. culture. She would need to assess her client to see where she stood in terms of her cultural beliefs and practices.

The following information is taken from Stella's case notes. Hence, it is reported in the first person.

First Contact with Bea

On the morning of the scheduled interview, Bea called to inform me that she would not be able to meet with me. I indicated my disappointment and inquired about her health. Bea reported that she felt nauseated at times, but the medication had helped her a great deal. She was unable to eat anything, and she also continued to experience headaches. In general, she felt very weak.

I empathized with her and encouraged her to come to see me soon so we could explore possible ways of easing her situation. After a second's pause, Bea remarked that the nurse at the health service had told her that they needed to do further assessments and that the social worker at the counseling services would do some of those. The nurse had assured her that it would be helpful for Bea to meet with the social worker. Bea said she wondered, however, how I could really help her. I responded that I worked very closely with the health clinic nurses and doctors and received many referrals from them. I explained to her that we had learned from experience that many students who came with ailments were often under emotional stress and that when steps were taken to reduce some of this stress, treatment was more effective. This helped students recover faster. To this, Bea remarked that she was not sure if anyone could really help her with her problems. Since there were few other options, however, she would come once and meet with me.

Assessment

Bea's reluctance to meet with me was obvious. Since it was not uncommon for students to question a referral to counseling services when they were seeking treatment for a physical problem, Bea's resistance was understandable. In addition, given the Hmong pattern of seeking help, and given the idea that professional counseling from outside the clan might be discouraged, it must have taken a great deal of courage on Bea's part to agree to this first meeting. Bea impressed me as someone who was determined and motivated to take risks to do something about her problems.

Initial Goals

From the intake summary and my telephone conversation with Bea, my goals for working with Bea were to evaluate the causes of her emotional stress, which might be affecting her physical condition, and help her find ways of dealing with it. Because of Bea's reluctance to come to the counseling services and her unfamiliarity with social workers in general, I needed to maintain a friendly, informal, and accepting atmosphere that would allow her to feel comfortable in her interactions with me.

First Interview: Bea's Initial Concerns

This time, Bea came for the interview as scheduled. She was a small and attractive young woman, but she seemed weak and unwell. She held her books tightly through most of the interview, sitting on the edge of the chair and avoiding eye contact. Upon entering the room, Bea apologized for having canceled the earlier meeting. I responded that I could understand Bea's frustration about having to see so many people at the clinic and that I hoped our meeting today would help her look at options that might aid in reducing her stress.

After a short pause in which Bea did not respond, I remarked, "This must be an especially difficult time for you. I know term papers are usually due around this time, and final exams are close at hand." Bea interjected that papers and finals were part of the stress. She had done well, and better than most of her Hmong friends in school until now, and wanted to maintain at least an average of a B-minus in her courses. "But I am having a hard time concentrating on my work this semester, and I am afraid that my grades may drop," she said. She added, "I am very concerned about my history paper, which I haven't started yet; it's due next week. Although I attended high school in this country, I find U.S. history very difficult to understand."

We discussed her course load for the semester. Bea reported how overwhelmed she was with college, "I stay awake at nights worrying about my different courses and whether I will make it through college." I asked her, "Besides school, are there other things that seem to worry you at this time?" She replied, "I think the history paper is my main problem at this time. I feel so weak and tired, and my head hurts all the time. I am not able to read or study!

This frightens me very much." To my inquiry about seeking an incomplete grade in history, Bea indicated her ignorance of such possibilities in college. "I am not aware of this option, but I do not like to ask my professors for special favors," she indicated. I explained that the function of an incomplete was to help students overcome unforeseen difficulties that prevented them from completing their class work on time. Further, I told her that the incomplete would not affect her overall grade point average and that as a student I had once taken an incomplete.

"It is very difficult to be Hmong," she said. "Many students feel we get special treatment at the university. Sometimes they joke that you only have to be Hmong to qualify for a scholarship. This makes me feel like I am not capable of succeeding on my own." She added, "I am aware that the Hmong students do qualify for special minority scholarships, but I think the purpose of these scholarships is to enable good students to pursue higher education, and without financial aid, it might not be possible to do so." I asked, "Do you think the university would have accepted you had it not found you capable?" After reflection, Bea commented that it probably would not have, since she knew of some students who had been rejected. Bea returned to the issue of the incomplete, asking, "Do you think my history professor will believe me if I explain my difficulties to him?" She further asked if the clinic could provide her with a doctor's certificate that might be more convincing. I agreed that it might be a good idea to get a doctor's certificate and that it would not be a problem obtaining one. Toward the end of the interview, I remarked that Bea had mentioned to the intake worker about living with her uncle's family and having home responsibilities that interfered with her schoolwork. I reminded her that she had also talked about her family planning to arrange her marriage. I wondered how all this affected her and whether she would like to talk about it on her next visit.

Bea looked at me momentarily and smiled. She said, "I was not sure about meeting with you today, but I think I really enjoyed talking to you and would like to come back to see you." She indicated that she appreciated my suggestion about seeking an incomplete. For the first time, Bea laughed and remarked that she was not sure I would understand the Hmong way of life, which is quite different from the American way. She looked at me, and when I did not respond, she expressed shyly, "I am afraid you will find many of our customs strange." I responded, "I might find your customs different, but I wouldn't call them strange. I feel every culture has its own practices that have special meaning for its members. I have tried to learn a little about the Hmong culture myself, but I do not know a great deal. Maybe you can teach me and help me learn some of your customs." Bea repeated again that it was difficult to be Hmong in this society, because she found that most people did not understand her. "I can see that it must be frustrating," I empathized, and asked if that was the reason she did not wish to talk to me earlier. She looked a little embarrassed and said that she thought I was "quite different" and "very understanding." Bea set up another appointment to meet with me the following week.

Assessment

Bea appeared to be a bright, articulate client. Although she avoided making eye contact during most of the interview, she seemed very involved and attentive to what I was saying. She also came across as being a proud and independent young woman, asking numerous questions during the course of our first interview. I had the impression that she was evaluating me all along, testing to see how accepting I was of cultural differences. Although she seemed quite acculturated in her manner of dress and speech, I gathered from some of Bea's comments that she might be more traditional in other aspects of her personal life. It also seemed to me that Bea might be avoiding talking about her family or the marriage problem, which, besides her schoolwork, might be a major reason for her stress. Being aware of the Hmong value of "shame" and not bringing shame to one's family, Bea might be uncomfortable talking about these issues.

I also observed that Bea was experiencing some cross-cultural conflicts, from comments such as, "It is difficult to be Hmong in this society." She seemed to be receiving conflicting messages from her Hmong and non-Hmong environments. Her Hmong peers, and possibly her family, recognized her as a good student, but apparently, the messages received from other students tended to contradict that image, introducing a degree of self-doubt regarding her capabilities as a student. It will be important for me to maintain a "dual perspective" in my work with Bea and to recognize that her lack of self-confidence might also be a result of the university environment, which was not sensitive to her ethnicity and cultural differences.

Goals

Based on our first interview and the impressions I was able to form, the following goals seem appropriate for further contacts: (1) to evaluate how Bea feels in relation to talking about her personal and family problems and to respect her need for privacy if she is hesitant to discuss these issues, and (2) to help build Bea's self-esteem and to help her feel more comfortable about being "different" in a university environment that was essentially homogeneous.

Second Interview: Bea and Her Family

Bea arrived for the interview on time. She was smiling and looked happier than before. She told me she was feeling much better. She had been able to eat a little in the last few days and had slept well. "I also talked to my history professor, who was very understanding and has permitted me to take an incomplete," she said. "This will give me time to put more effort into writing my history paper and to raise my grade." I asked how things were going at home. Bea mentioned that her parents had visited the previous weekend and she had been happy to see them. They were worried about her health and had arranged for a shamanistic ceremony to ensure that she would get better. I asked her about the ceremony, to which she responded, "The shaman performed a ritual and several of my clan members were invited. Many of them had been concerned about my health. Some elderly women stopped later to talk to my mother and aunt, and they advised them to take my situation seriously and to make sure that I got enough rest." Bea laughed and said that her aunt later told her that she did not want to see Bea "around her" for a while and that she was not to "enter the kitchen" for a few weeks.

I inquired if Bea was normally expected to perform chores in the kitchen. Bea hesitated for a moment. She said that nobody had ever forced her to do anything. "My uncle and aunt are very affectionate and keep me well, but I feel that I need to help my aunt when I see her constantly working," she explained. "My uncle and cousins barely help at home. In the Hmong culture, housework is the woman's responsibility." She said that even when she lived at home her mother had expected all the sisters to help in the home, and they were scolded if they did not. In a Hmong family, it was the mother's responsibility to train a girl for household duties in preparation for marriage. If she could not perform these tasks after marriage, her in-laws could criticize her parents for not providing her with a proper upbringing.

I asked whether she thought her aunt might also think the same way if she did not help her. Bea responded that if she did not, it could reflect poorly on her mother. "I therefore feel a great deal of pressure to always be polite, obedient, and helpful in the house. However, since my aunt herself has prevented me from doing any work lately, it is much easier. I do not feel as guilty. I know my uncle and aunt have never attended school and are unable to understand my difficulties." Bea also shared that one of her "distant uncles," a clan member and leader she respected highly, had also attended the ceremony. He had children in college and was more familiar with American ways. Bea said that he had spoken to her family about how difficult college was. This seemed to have made her uncle and aunt, as well as her parents, a little more sensitive about her situation.

I remarked that the ceremony seemed to have helped Bea in many ways. Bea laughed awkwardly and said, "You must really wonder how a shaman could make anyone better by talking to the spirits. But the Hmong do believe that it can be helpful, especially if nothing else works." I remarked, "What is important is the faith you have in a certain treatment, because when you have faith, its effects are often positive. I see great value in a ceremony where there is so much support and concern. This must have made you feel good." Bea agreed, suggesting that I might want to witness such a ceremony myself someday.

I finally asked Bea about her marriage. Bea said that during her parents' visit her uncle had again referred to the marriage proposal from Chou's family. I asked her how she felt about that, and she said emphatically that she disliked Chou and she would not like to marry him. Her parents, however, tended to feel it would be a good arrangement. They and her uncle and aunt were of the opinion that if she did not accept this proposal, the possibility of finding other eligible men in the future was slim. Her parents had warned her that she would remain a spinster and people would think there was something wrong with her. At this point, Bea began to cry. "I know I want to get married sometime, but I do not like Chou," she sobbed. "I have talked to my brother and sister-in-law about my feelings, but they do not seem to understand me either. Right now my family has put the marriage issue on hold because of my health problems, but I know that once I feel better they will all get after me again. I am afraid that if something is not done soon, they will go ahead and negotiate the wedding arrangements. Once that happens, I cannot refuse because that would bring shame to my family and clan," she said.

Bea indicated that she felt very trapped. She explained, "It feels like I am being torn between two worlds. I want to study further, but I also know that I have to get married." I asked her if she had an opportunity to marry someone else, what would be her chances of being able to continue her education. She responded, "I don't know. Once I am married, I might not have much control. It would then depend on how my husband and my in-laws feel about my studying further. I could very well be asked to accept a job somewhere, if the family needs money." I recognized that this must be a very trying situation and wondered why Bea did not clearly explain to her parents how she felt about Chou. Bea said that she had tried to do so, but they had brushed off the matter saying she was being immature and she would eventually come to like him. She also felt very obligated to her uncle and aunt, who had been so kind to her, and she felt she should obey them since, after all, they were doing this in her best interest. She felt they had more experience and that maybe her parents were right when they said she was being immature. She said sometimes she wondered if she should just marry Chou and leave everything to fate. But she said that something told her it would not be a good marriage for her.

I asked her if there was anyone in the extended family or the clan who could help her. Bea replied that the only person who might possibly understand her and also be able to talk to her uncle was her distant relative, Mr. Tou Xiong, about whom she had spoken earlier. "However, it would not be very appropriate for me to talk to my elder about such a matter. Do you think you could speak to him on my behalf?" she asked me. I agreed to do so. We decided to meet in two weeks after I had a chance to meet with Mr. Xiong.

Assessment

After this interview, I was better able to understand some of the various pressures on Bea: her family's insistence that she consider marriage to Chou, the reality of being away from her own parents, her need to play the role of the "model daughter" to protect her mother's image, and her desire to succeed within a demanding university situation that had not been particularly accepting of her. These factors seemed to create a tremendous amount of stress. In this emotional struggle, Bea felt alone and misunderstood, paradoxically, in a "caring" and "supportive" family environment. Having been exposed to an American system of education, she found that her personal goals and aspirations clashed with the expectations of her family; namely, to tailor her decisions to traditional patterns of Hmong life. Within a system of hierarchical decision making where norms and traditions are often assigned greater importance over individual preferences and, given her bicultural socialization, Bea felt engulfed in a battle between two cultures. As this cross-cultural conflict ensued, Bea found few legitimate channels of communication and emotional expression within her family system. As a result, she tended to internalize her frustrations, and this affected her mental and physical well-being.

In the interview, Bea seemed to appreciate my help. It provided her with a means to explore practical solutions in a safe and accepting environment. Toward the end of the second interview, she almost tended to cling to me for security.

While this interview was difficult for Bea, it was also challenging for me. I found my own system of values tested to the core. Having lived in a society that places a high premium on independence and the ability to control one's own life decisions, I found it difficult to accept the fact that Bea should have little say about matters I believe to be so critical. I had to constantly remind myself that what I defined as "critical" may not be so for Bea in light of higher social priorities. Support and acceptance from her cultural group may be more important to her. I realized that Bea's social reality and the meaning it had for her needed to be perceived from her perspective. My role in this was to support her during her moment of crisis and to provide her a clarity of vision she needed to make decisions, which would enable her to live with dignity and pride in her own cultural environment.

I concluded that Bea had many strengths. Her motivation to explore alternatives and to take risks, her intelligence and practicality in searching for solutions, her independence, and her ability to express thoughts and feelings would all serve as assets in helping her bounce back to normal once her marriage issue was resolved.

Goals

There seem to be two major goals to guide my intervention at this point.

1. I should enlist Mr. Xiong's help, if possible, to obtain suggestions as to how Bea's situation might best be handled with her in a culturally sensitive way. This would also help me better understand Hmong marriage customs and practices and the values associated with them.
2. In my work with Bea, it would be important to provide her with emotional support, to validate her feelings, and to help her explore her options objectively so she could make decisions that would help her live comfortably in her cultural environment.

Meeting with Mr. Xiong

Mr. Xiong was very obliging and agreed to come to the counseling center. I explained Bea's situation to him. He commented that he was aware Bea was under pressure, having recently started college and being away from home. "No matter how good the extended family is, it is never the same as being with your own parents," he observed.

I explained the possibility of Bea's family negotiating her marriage with Chou Vang. Mr. Xiong indicated his surprise at this, saying that he knew Chou came from a good and a reputable family but he did not think he was very capable and that he would not, in his opinion, be a suitable husband for Bea. He realized that because of Bea's age, the family's options in finding eligible men might be limited.

In the Hmong custom, it was usually the boy's family that approached the girl's with a proposal. It is likely that not too many proposals had been received. He could very well understand Bea's reservations and feelings. He agreed to talk to Bea's uncle regarding this matter. He indicated that he would have to be very careful as to how he approached him, because her uncle had a reputation for being short-tempered. At the same time, he knew that talking to Bea's father would not help much, since he usually listened to his elder brother, whom he greatly respected.

Mr. Xiong talked further about Hmong marriage customs and practices for families who were in the United States. He shared that many Hmong families preferred to get their daughters married while they were still quite young for fear of having a smaller matrimonial selection at a later age. Besides, many Hmong did not yet value education for girls and were not aware of possible career choices available to women in this society. He had been greatly disturbed by this situation, since he believed that education was the only way for the Hmong to succeed.

He asked if the university could help him develop some programs to educate families about higher education. He was sure that he could obtain support from the other clan leaders in the community with regard to this matter. I told him that the person responsible for such activities was the minority students' coordinator, Jim Smith. However, I felt there was a good possibility of being able to do something about this situation since Jim Smith had also voiced similar frustrations in the past. I promised to talk to him and told Mr. Xiong that one of us would call him back regarding this matter in the near future.

Third Interview with Bea: Resolving Issues

Today, Bea looked brighter and happier. She indicated that she had almost recovered from her medical ailments and was feeling better. She looked like she had gained some weight, and she had received a good report from her recent medical examination.

Bea reported that Mr. Xiong had stopped to visit her uncle last weekend. He had been very tactful in not revealing his knowledge about the Vang family marriage proposal and had pretended to have stopped by for a chat.

In the course of the conversation, he mentioned that he knew about a young man in Seattle, Peng Lor, who was a school friend of his son-in-law. Peng was a senior at the university there and was expected to graduate soon. Since he was "highly educated," it had suddenly dawned on him that Peng would be a good match for Bea, who was also a good student. He had met Peng during his recent visit to Seattle when he was visiting his daughter. Peng had impressed him as being intelligent and hard working. He admitted, however, that he knew very little about his family background. He knew that Peng's father was deceased and that Peng lived with his older brother. The family, however, did not seem to be very illustrious or well known. He told Bea's uncle that if they were interested he could investigate further and pursue the matter through his son-in-law.

Bea related that her uncle had initially been reluctant to consider this proposal, since Peng was not from a well-known family. Her uncle had consulted with her parents about it. He had finally called Bea and spoken to her at length about the pros and cons of marrying into a reputable family versus one that was not very well known. He realized that Peng was better educated than Chou and asked Bea what her preference would be. At that time, Bea had felt comfortable to speak about her feelings. Her uncle had then decided that he would investigate Peng's family background further by contacting their clan members in Seattle. Bea felt hopeful about this proposal.

We talked a little about school. It appeared that things had stabilized for Bea and that she did not feel the need to see me again. After some discussion, we both decided to terminate our counseling relationship at that point.

Evaluation

I realized, for the first time, the impact of experiencing a cross-cultural conflict. Reading about it was not the same as witnessing it firsthand. It dawned on me that the Hmong youth must have the greatest difficulty as they became exposed to the new culture faster than their families. As a social institution, education provides a powerful influence on young people. Hmong youth must constantly live with the contradictions between the two cultures as they try to find meaning and unity in their lives "between two worlds." I was convinced of the value in working with Mr. Xiong and the Hmong community to maintain a proactive-preventive approach to these problems that could affect other Hmong students at the university.

Readings

Ino, S. M., & Glicken, M. D. (2002). Understanding and treating the ethnically Asian client: A collectivist approach. *Journal of Health and Social Policy, 14*(4), 37–48.

Schwartz, P. Y. (2002). Psychosocial considerations in working with the Chinese immigrant. *Journal of Immigrant and Refugee Services, 1*(1), 65–80.

Tuong, P. (2000). Investigating the use of services for Vietnamese with mental illness. *Journal of Community Health, 25*(5), 411–426.

Discussion Questions

1. *What levels of intervention (micro, mezzo, or macro) did the worker utilize in this case?*

2. *Cite some examples to show how the worker utilized the various steps in the problem-solving process.*

3. *What cultural differences did you see in this case that affected the client's problem-solving style?*

4. *What values and ethical principles are reflected in the worker's handling of this case?*

5. *What ethnic-sensitive techniques does the worker use to engage and effectively help the client?*

6. *What similarities and differences do you see between the traditions and customs of the Hmong described in this case and those of Latinos or Native Americans?*

7. To what might you attribute Bea's lack of eye contact noted in the first interview with the social worker?

8. What reasons might explain why Bea focused on her schoolwork and avoided talking about the family situation in the initial interview?

9. What does the worker mean when she says she must maintain a dual perspective in this case?

10. What did the worker mean when she said she wanted to avoid "overgeneralizing her understanding of the traditional Hmong culture to her client"?

13

Sally's Saga

Charles M. Young

Sally was excited and apprehensive as she began her field placement at the state probation office. She felt fortunate to have been assigned her first choice for a field setting. Having identified an interest in correctional social work early in her social work education, she was both eager to begin and determined to excel.

After a brief but rigorous orientation, Sally was given a small caseload, for which she would eventually assume primary responsibility. She eagerly began learning as much as she could about her clients. She read agency records and discussed them with her field instructor. She also went on home visits with the agency probation workers who had previously provided services to the people on her new caseload.

Some of Sally's initial enthusiasm diminished when she observed some of the agency's workers. Some of the probation workers seemed quite different from what Sally had anticipated, behaving in ways that ran counter to her personal, educational, and professional values and expectations. Some of her new colleagues seemed judgmental, bitter, and very pessimistic about their clients' abilities to change. Sally wondered if perhaps they might be experiencing a form of "burnout." Concerned, she expressed her observations to her faculty field placement advisor, who suggested she share her experiences with her peers at the next senior seminar.

During senior seminar, Sally shared her thoughts about the field experience with her peers. She learned that several of her classmates had somewhat similar experiences and concerns. After a spirited discussion, the class decided they should mentally "file this information away" and discuss it later in the semester when they had additional opportunities to observe their coworkers.

Engagement: Developing a Cultural and Family Perspective

Back at the Probation Office, Sally was introduced to Joe, a 21-year-old Native American on probation for possession of marijuana "with intent to sell." Joe had a history of drug abuse, grew up in a low-income family, and spent his early years in public housing specifically developed for his tribe. Although the community housing project was referred to as "the reservation," it was technically not part of one.

Initially, Sally had some difficulty engaging Joe in conversation. Her attempts at communicating with him to complete a social history presented a real challenge. Joe seemed reluctant to participate in the interview. She and Joe were about the same age, and Sally wondered if this made Joe a bit uncomfortable, especially since she was feeling this way herself.

In subsequent interviews, Joe was late for his appointments and seemed to have no need to explain his lateness. Sally expressed concern to her supervisor, wondering if Joe's behavior might show that he did not hold her in high regard or that he was resistive to the helping process. At her supervisor's suggestion, Sally did some research about Native American customs and culture. Among other things, she learned that the tribe Joe belonged to did not view time in the same way as the majority population. Joe's community tended to mark time by the passing of seasons or by movement of the sun or moon. They simply were not driven by the same time-consciousness that causes most of us to keep one eye on the clock. Sally developed a new perspective about Joe's lateness as well as a renewed enthusiasm to learn more about Joe and his culture.

Sally asked questions that allowed Joe to talk about his family. She learned that Joe was very devoted to his extended family. They had been experiencing some ongoing medical problems, and with only his car in working order, Joe provided transportation for the family when they needed to see a doctor. Sally gained a fuller appreciation of Joe's behavior (being late for appointments) as appropriate to his cultural value system, which stressed attending to family responsibility rather than less important matters. Based on her new understanding, their professional relationship grew. Sally became somewhat more sensitive, and Joe became somewhat more communicative.

Data Gathering: Further Information

During the balance of her first semester in field practicum, Sally developed a positive, helping, professional relationship with Joe. She learned that Joe dropped out of high school in his senior year so he could work to help his family financially. Although the small apartment Joe occupied with his wife Sue and their infant son Billy was some distance from his extended family, he continued to help them when needed, despite the considerable drive it involved.

Sally learned that Joe was an average to above-average student in high school and at one time had expressed a desire to go to college. Since dropping out of school, he had held a variety of low-paying, unrewarding, and menial jobs. He was fired several times, usually for tardiness or missing work. Some of his former employers believed that Joe's drug use was responsible for his history of missing work or being late. All agreed that he had a great deal of potential but seemed to lack motivation and drive. Joe's friends described him as devoted to his family, especially to his son.

Married life was problematic and full of crises for Joe and Sue. Pregnant at 16, Sue dropped out of high school and did not complete her secondary education. Joe and Sue were married shortly after Sue became pregnant, and Joe dropped out of high school to find work and support his family. Sue and Joe had frequent arguments, and both used alcohol and marijuana on a regular basis. During her fifth month of pregnancy, Sue lost the baby, and both Sue and Joe became severely depressed. Both tried to cope through continued drug use. Marital arguments escalated and, at times, became physically abusive.

Less than a year after the miscarriage of their first child, Billy was conceived. His birth brought peace and tranquility back to the relationship for a while. Joe and Sue both doted on their son, and Joe was especially proud and pleased when friends and family frequently remarked on how much Billy resembled his father. Marital stability, however, continued to be a problem.

Assessment: Priority of Problems

From the agency's standpoint, the focal problem in Joe's situation needed to be defined relative to his felony conviction. Sally recognized, however, that for optimum success her assessment and intervention plan had to consider other factors. After several family interviews and collateral contacts, the following problem prioritization was formulated.

1. Joe's conviction for possession of marijuana with intent to sell.
2. Marital strife, reflected by frequent arguments, physical and verbal abuse, often resulting in Joe's leaving home in anger. (This occurs on average three times per week.)
3. Underemployment and inadequate family income.
4. Lack of adequate educational preparation for both Joe and Sue.

Relative to problem number one, the probation department required that Joe follow a standard set of rules for probation, including reporting regularly to his probation officer, refraining from further drug use, and obeying all other laws.

Sally noted that in almost every instance, marital strife (problem number two) was precipitated by episodes of drinking alcohol, sometimes involving both of them. Both Joe and Sue denied using other drugs, and they somewhat minimized the role of alcohol in their disputes. Sally

recalled one interaction when, using her best probing technique, she asked, "Joe, can you help me understand what makes you so angry that you end up fighting with Sue?"

Joe was somewhat evasive and defensive, stating, "Well, it's not always my fault. Sue has a temper too."

Sue reacted defensively and with anger saying, "I'm tired of being blamed for everything all the time." Sally tried to pursue Sue's response, but without success. Joe became quiet and withholding. Sally continued to try to seek understanding of this dilemma, but to no avail. Subsequent interviews probing this area also proved fruitless. Sally realized that the couple had a serious problem that needed more professional skill than she currently possessed.

Problems three and four seemed to be related. Joe and Sue did not have many employment opportunities due to Joe's conviction and past employment record, as well as their lack of formal education. Joe had above-average ability, and Sue had been a good student prior to quitting high school. During their discussions with Sally, both expressed interest in obtaining their high school equivalency diplomas and perhaps trying to earn some college credits.

Planning and Intervention

Sally met regularly with Joe as required by the probation agreement. On two occasions Sally suspected that Joe might be using marijuana. She confronted him, and he denied any drug use. She learned that the relationship between Sue and Joe continued to be stormy, with many outbursts of anger. There seemed to be little progress being made in any of their identified problem areas.

Sally presented Joe's case at a case conference held at the agency. She sought input in two areas: (1) What might be the best way to make sure Joe was not in fact using drugs? and (2) What might be the best marriage counseling resource for Joe and Sue? During the case conference, one worker suggested that Sally arrange for random testing (urinalysis) for Joe. Sally graciously thanked the worker for the suggestion but wondered if that might not impair, if not destroy, the rapport she had worked so hard to establish. The worker, his voice heavy with sarcasm, wondered if Sally should be wasting her time establishing "rapport" with "druggies." Another worker suggested that Sally might be wasting her time and valuable resources on "dirtballs." Sally said she preferred to work with her clients in terms of their strengths as opposed to labeling or stereotyping them. She left the staffing feeling angry, frustrated, and hurt.

At her senior seminar back at college, Sally reintroduced her concerns about the unprofessional behavior of some of her colleagues at the agency. Although several of her peers had described similar experiences in their field agencies, no one other than Sally seemed to be experiencing ongoing difficulty at this time. Sally wondered how any social worker could behave as she had seen her agency workers behave. Discussion of the situation produced two helpful questions.

- were the agency workers professionally trained, and
- might the social work licensure law (which was pending before the legislature) provide clients with better protection regarding self-determination, confidentiality, and privacy?

Sally left the seminar feeling better. Although she hadn't solved the problem, she felt supported by her peers and faculty.

Sally met with Joe and Sue to discuss the possibility of marriage counseling. Both were resistive to seeking help to save their marriage. Sue was upset, and Joe was angry. Joe wanted no part of counseling and wanted out of the marriage. Sue agreed. Joe seemed surprised but quickly restated his desire to divorce. Sally suggested they think about the matter for a week, and both agreed this might be wise.

Three days later Sue called asking Sally to help her find a divorce attorney. Joe called the same day requesting the same help. It was a thoroughly confusing situation. Sally knew of an attorney who might be helpful. Peter Redcloud had spoken to a social work class, and Sally remembered that he was a BSW with social work experience prior to earning his law degree. After calling Joe and Sue for permission, she contacted Peter Redcloud and described the situation. Sally shared her feeling that neither party really seemed to want a divorce. She thought both might profit more from a marriage counselor, if only they could be convinced of the worth of such a resource. Sally thought Peter (who was from the same tribe as Joe and Sue) might be helpful in encouraging the couple to reconsider. Peter agreed to see the couple and subsequently met with them several times. Working conjointly, Sally and Peter were successful in referring the couple to a very skilled therapist for marriage counseling. Working in a case manager role, Sally obtained permission to provide the marriage therapist with important referral information.

She continued to maintain contact with Joe and Sue but now turned her attention to helping them advance their employment and educational opportunities. Both Sue and Joe agreed that their financial woes were due mainly to lack of adequate education or job training. As they developed plans to pursue their graduate equivalency diplomas, they spoke positively of their experience with the marriage therapist. Although both wanted to obtain the GED, it was mutually decided that Joe would begin his studies first, and as soon as possible. Sue would stay home to care for Billy for at least a year. Arrangements were made for Joe to attend classes at the local technical college to prepare for the GED.

On one of his trips home to provide transportation for his parents, Joe heard about a job opening at the area tribal gambling casino. Joe's father told him about the opening and spoke to one of the tribal officers on behalf of his son. Joe applied for and got the job, which paid much better than the minimum wage he had been earning.

Evaluation: Sally's Dilemma

The quality of life for Joe, Sue, and Billy was really improving, although several incidents proved that problems continued to occur. The marriage therapist reported that the couple was really making progress. Serious conflict had declined from three or four episodes to sometimes none per week. However, from time to time Joe missed work because he said he was ill. He was occasionally late to work due to car trouble, but all in all things seemed to be really improving. The GED studies were progressing nicely, and if all went as anticipated, Joe might be ready to take the exam in six more months. Sally noted that Joe had kept all of his appointments, was on time, and she seemed more optimistic than usual.

With mid-semester's arrival, Sally realized that in just eight more weeks she would be graduating. Although she had discussed termination at the beginning of her relationship with Joe and Sue, she initiated her planned termination by reviewing with them the progress they had made. They talked about the problems they had experienced, how they felt, what they had learned, and the many changes that had occurred for them. Caught up with the positive mood of the moment, Joe said, "Sally, I really appreciate what you have done for me and Sue. You know, I used to smoke a lid or two a week, and now I only smoke a joint or two a week!"

Sally now faced an ethical dilemma. Given this new information, it was clear that Joe had been violating his probation agreement by continuing to smoke marijuana. Clearly, Joe was required to obey the law, and smoking marijuana was illegal. She recalled that the NASW Code of Ethics indicates that social workers have responsibilities to the client, employer, community, profession, and their colleagues. She also recalled the section on confidentiality and wondered how this part of the Code of Ethics applied to her situation.

Violation of the probation agreement could mean revocation of probation and incarceration for Joe. Sally felt strongly that prison would do Joe more harm than good, yet agency policy reflected in the probation agreement seemed to call for revocation. Sally felt she was in somewhat of a "catch-22" situation. How could she honor her professional responsibilities to both her client and her agency when they seemed so diametrically opposed?

Sally decided that Joe had to be confronted. She felt that Joe needed to know there were consequences to all behaviors. She also felt he should have some choices and self-determination, so she offered him two alternatives: revocation of probation, which would result in a prison term, or a residential treatment program to treat his drug use.

Joe initially reacted defensively to the confrontation, minimizing his drug use and focusing his anger on Sally. Sally was firm and unwavering, yet supportive, helping Joe look at his self-defeating drug-using behavior. After his initial angry response, Joe shared that Ms. Smith, the therapist he and Sue were seeing, also had concerns about his drug use. He expressed concern that entering a treatment program at this time might jeopardize his employment. Sally offered to speak to Joe's employer with Joe to explain and confirm the need for residential treatment. Joe accepted Sally's offer, and the net result was that Joe did not lose his job and he successfully completed residential treatment for drug abuse.

Sally graduated in May while Joe was undergoing treatment. Sally's supervisor assumed responsibility for Joe's case and was caring enough to send Sally a graduation card with a note detailing Joe's progress and expressing his appreciation for the professional job she had done. Sally wondered if being a professional social worker meant that her work and her life would be full of difficult choices and value dilemmas.

Readings

Garrett, M. T., & Carroll, J. J. (2000). Mending the broken circle: Treatment of substance dependence among Native Americans. *Journal of Counseling & Development, 78*(4), 379–389.

Mattison, M. (2000). Ethical decision making: The person in the process. *Social Work, 45*(3), 201–212.

Reamer, F. G. (2002). How to practice ethically: Part II. *The New Social Worker, 9*(1), 18–20.

Discussion Questions

1. *The initial information obtained during the social history indicated that Joe and Sue had frequent arguments and that these escalated and became physically and verbally abusive. What services could you recommend relative to the physical spouse abuse?*

2. *Although it was not specified, what assumptions did you make about who was doing the physical abuse? Why?*

3. *When Joe self-disclosed about his marijuana use, what other alternatives could Sally have considered? Considering the progress made by Joe and Sue, could Sally have ignored Joe's self-disclosure or done something else?*

4. *What differences do you perceive between social work with "willing" clients and those who are forced to see the social worker, as is the case with Joe?*

5. *Social workers sometimes work in positions as "agents of social control," in which they enforce the rules and regulations of the larger society. Probation officers are a good example of this. What special challenges do workers in these positions face?*

6. *The negative reactions of Sally's coworkers to her efforts to help Joe were referred to as possible "burnout." What is burnout, and why might workers in this particular setting be more prone to this experience?*

7. *What possible motivations might Joe have had for disclosing the information on his drug use to Sally?*

14

Brad: Consequences of a Dysfunctional Family

H. Wayne Johnson

Like most probation officers, Robert had a large caseload and needed to set priorities for managing all his case responsibilities. One of his highest priorities was giving attention to all new cases in which youngsters were being held in the local detention center. He saw the institutional experience of detention as potentially damaging for some youngsters, particularly because of the overcrowded conditions prevalent in the Rock River County detention facility. Robert made it his practice to visit young people in detention as quickly as possible, interviewing them and obtaining information from staff and from the records to determine how each youngster was adjusting to the detention center environment.

As Robert drove to the detention center that morning, he mentally reviewed what the police had told him the night before. Jimmy, a police officer and personal friend of Robert's, had called him to report that Brad had been apprehended for stealing a car and had been placed in the detention center awaiting disposition of his case. Although Brad was unknown to Robert, Jimmy noted that Brad had been taken into custody on three other occasions for car theft and was currently on probation as a result of these offenses. Jimmy and the juvenile intake worker had determined that detention was appropriate for Brad because of the seriousness of the offense and the repetitive pattern of his behavior. The plan was for Brad to remain in detention until his hearing and final disposition.

Engagement and Data Collection

As Robert turned into the parking lot of the detention center, he wondered what Brad would be like. He also hoped he could gain some insights into Brad's behavior. He entered the center, greeted several of his friends who worked there, and asked for the case record on Brad. Robert settled back and scanned the record for some beginning information. The following information was recorded in the detention intake summary.

Brad Mercury, age 15, was referred to the juvenile court by the juvenile unit of the police department after being apprehended for taking a car. At his preliminary hearing, Brad was ordered returned to the juvenile detention facility where he was held after his arrest. Brad had been apprehended for car theft on three different occasions and was on probation since the first theft. Detention was seen by the police, the intake worker, and the judge as needed because of the repetition of the

car thefts while on probation and the seriousness of the offense. Preparation is being made for his final hearing on this offense and the disposition of his case. The case has been referred to county probation for assignment of a worker.
(J. Morrisey, Intake Worker)

Although Brad was currently on probation, his former worker, Ms. Elliot, had unexpectedly left the agency, so Robert had little personal information about him. Robert spoke with detention staff and learned that Brad related readily to adults and was well thought of by the staff. He got along satisfactorily with his peers in detention but appeared to be more comfortable with adult staff. He was not perceived as a troublemaker or security risk and didn't seem as "delinquent" as some of the other boys.

Robert made a quick call to Rick, the school social worker at Rock River High School, to obtain some information on Brad's school situation. Brad was enrolled in a regular academic program of study. Intelligence tests at school indicated that Brad's IQ was above average. However, he was expelled from one of his past high schools because of poor attendance, unfinished and unsatisfactory work, and conflict with school personnel. His attendance at Rock River High was regular, except for four days when he ran away from home. His academic achievement, as reflected in grades received for the last few marking periods, had deteriorated and was well below what would be expected, given his intelligence. His grades ranged from average in some classes to failure in others. He was not involved in extracurricular activities at school.

Robert considered this beginning information before he sought out Brad for an initial interview. As he entered the living area looking for Brad, he mused to himself about how such a young boy could get himself into such a pattern of dangerous behavior. He found Brad watching television with some other boys in the recreation room. He introduced himself and asked Brad to join him in one of the interview rooms for a few minutes.

In the initial interview, Brad appeared to be rather outgoing, verbal, personable, sensitive, and intelligent. However, he seemed unable to explain his illegal behavior and appeared puzzled about his conduct. Brad expressed remorse about the car theft both verbally and nonverbally, and he seemed very anxious. Robert noticed that Brad's nonverbals seemed to indicate a pervasive tone and sense of sadness. It appeared to Robert that Brad was taking his situation seriously.

In one part of the interview, when they were discussing the factors contributing to Brad's car thefts, Robert asked, "Why do you think you get into trouble?" Brad responded, "I don't have anything else to do. I don't have enough interests, and I'm not into sports." Brad's statement seemed to be said in a superficial way and without much conviction. Robert was reminded of the many times parents had given similar explanations of their children's delinquent behavior, and he wondered if Brad wasn't just repeating something he had heard at home.

Brad continued, "I used to do a lot of things, but my folks weren't interested in anything I liked."

"What did you like to do?" asked Robert.

Brad responded, "I was into coin collecting and car models, but Dad didn't go for those things. He doesn't seem to like anything I do." Robert noted that he would have to talk to Brad's father about this and see if this was a pattern of actual behavior or if this was just Brad's perception of his father's thinking.

Brad mentioned that his father and mother were divorced and that he had lived with his mother back East for a year. Brad said, "I thought I was getting along OK there with her. Then one day she told me that the next day I would be getting on a plane and returning to my dad's place to live."

Robert asked, "How did you feel about that?" Brad didn't respond, he just shook his head back and forth and looked downward. "Were you angry with her?" Robert questioned.

Brad replied, "I was then, but now I'm not so sure. Maybe I was too much for her."

"Too much?" reflected Robert.

"Yes, I don't think my stepfather wanted me there, and that put her in a bind."

It seemed to Robert that this had been a damaging experience for Brad—another type of rejection. It seemed that he had very mixed feelings about his mother. He was also not certain of her feelings toward him, and this might have contributed to his insecurity and anxiety. Later, Robert would learn that Brad had experienced rejection, or at least lack of emotional support, from all four of the most important adults in his life: his mother, stepfather, father, and stepmother.

Robert made arrangements to visit Brad's father and stepmother that evening. He wanted to get their perspective on Brad's behavior and see how he might involve them in planning for Brad. They lived in an attractive house in a pleasant, middle-class neighborhood. Mr. Mercury greeted Robert and apologized for Brad's behavior. Robert assured him that he was there to try to understand why Brad continued his pattern of dangerous behavior and asked if anyone in the family had any insights to contribute. Mr. Mercury was quick to begin, noting, "I don't think he has enough to do; he has no interests, and he is not into sports." Robert smiled a sad smile, recognizing the same words Brad had offered early in his first interview.

Robert learned, mostly from Mr. Mercury, something about Brad's background and the family history. Mr. Mercury worked as an office manager and earned a fairly substantial income. He and his present wife had a daughter 4 years old and a son who was 2.

Robert asked Mr. and Mrs. Mercury to share some details about Brad's early years. Mr. Mercury, a verbal person, did most of the talking.

Mr. M.: Brad was born in Memphis a year after I married my first wife. I was in the army for Brad's first two years, and he was with my wife. After three years of marriage, when Brad was 2, we were divorced, and I got custody.

Robert: How did it happen that you got custody?

Mr. M.: My first wife was fast and loose and didn't care about Brad. She remarried two years later and went East to play music in a band. She works in an office now.

Robert: What happened then with you and Brad?

Mr. M.: Brad lived with my parents for six years until my father got sick. After that, I had Brad in a Catholic boarding school for boys. After I remarried, Brad came to live with us. He has been here ever since, with the exception of a year with his mother.

Robert: Why did he go there?

Mr. M.: Because he wasn't getting along with us, and he wanted to live with her. Then, three years ago, she called me up and said Brad had to leave because he was breaking up their home.

Robert noticed that Mrs. Mercury did not participate much in the discussion. She sat quietly, seldom commenting. Robert turned to her and smiled, hoping to get her involved in the conversation.

Robert: How do you feel about Brad, Mrs. Mercury?

Mrs. M.: I cannot feel toward him as a real mother would. I have our own children to take care of, and they have to come first.

Robert: How does Brad get along with the other children?

Mrs. M.: Brad seems to like them, and they all seem to get along together.

Robert: So they spend time together and seem to get along?

Mrs. M.: But I don't want him babysitting with the children.

Robert: Oh, how come?

Mrs. M.: Because he might molest my daughter.

Robert: Has that ever happened?

Mrs. M.: No, but it could.

Neither Mr. nor Mrs. Mercury could offer any evidence that suggested Brad might sexually abuse or molest his younger stepsister, but Mrs. Mercury continued her suspicions about Brad's intentions.

During this interview, Robert developed a great deal of information that led him to several conclusions. Brad's father and stepmother seemed to provide well for Brad's material needs, but there was an absence of much attention to his emotional needs. Recently, Mr. Mercury had become increasingly distressed at his son's behavior and, consequently, became more rejecting of Brad. At the times when understanding and support were needed, Mr. Mercury became more vindictive and punitive and, thus, aggravated rather than alleviated the problem. On the surface, Brad related well to his father and respected him, but there seemed to be no real warmth and understanding between the two and few mutual interests and activities. Mr. Mercury was rather controlling in his actions toward Brad. In spite of these negatives, Mr. Mercury seemed interested in Brad and wanted to be actively involved in planning for him.

In contrast, Mrs. Mercury seemed not to show much genuine, positive feeling toward Brad. Her only stated concern, aside from being worried about Brad sexually abusing her daughter, was that Brad's behavior affected her husband. As Robert learned later, Brad's feelings about his stepmother were virtually nonexistent, and the two of them seemed to mutually ignore each other. Neither seemed to have made any effort to relate to each other, other than to coexist in the same household.

Through other interviews with Brad, Robert learned that he was aware that he had problems but that he was "all mixed up" about many things. He couldn't really offer a cogent explanation of why he had resorted to stealing cars, other than it made him feel like he was mobile and could go wherever he wanted. Robert learned that when Brad was home he was frequently made to spend entire evenings in his own small bedroom as punishment for some misdeed. Although his parents saw this as appropriate discipline, Brad tended to react to this punishment with rebellion.

Assessment

Robert thought Brad had been hurt deeply on many occasions and seemed to have built a wall around himself to prevent further emotional injury. Perhaps his history of car theft was related to attempts to get attention, reaching out to adults based on his rejection by his important family members. One way or another, Robert wondered if Brad's family members were capable of changing their interactive patterns with Brad. Brad seemed happier when he was at the detention center, interacting with his peers and with caring adults.

Robert decided to refer Brad and his family to the Lennen County Child Guidance Center in the nearby community of Holly Hill for a more thorough evaluation. This would also assist Robert in making a recommendation to the juvenile court about what disposition would be in Brad's best interests. He hoped that the center evaluation would add information to the assessment, assist with planning, and make suggestions for appropriate interventions. He also hoped that someone from the center would recommend that Brad and his family be seen at the center for family counseling, but he was somewhat pessimistic about this possibility.

At the center, Brad was seen by a psychologist and a psychiatrist, and Brad's father was seen by a psychiatric social worker. The center report summarized some of their findings as follows.

> Brad's delinquency may be a reaction to the rejection and emotional deprivation that have contributed to his feelings of depression, anxiety, and guilt. The center staff thought Brad revealed a rather rigid conscience that made him dissatisfied with deviance. The nature of the problem between Brad and his parents has engendered feelings of being unwanted and disappointed. The center feels that it is highly unlikely that the parents would be able to change their attitudes sufficiently to support a program of individual or family therapy. Brad displays some strengths, including adequate intelligence, a desire for more rewarding relationships, and dissatisfaction with deviant behavior. These are factors that could best be utilized in a rehabilitation program away from home.

Robert's impressions of Brad and his family led him to conclusions consistent with those of the center. Brad had substantial strengths and potential but was unhappy with himself in a nonsupportive family situation replete with parental rigidity and rejection. Brad had some strengths, as reflected by his good adjustment and positive conduct in detention. For example, he was permitted to leave the facility with selected groups of boys who were taken to recreational events. Further, he demonstrated how trustworthy he could be when some maintenance repairs were being done to the building and he was given permission to help the staff with certain errands. He could easily have run away in this situation but never did so.

In one way, Brad seemed typical of juveniles who take cars for the forbidden drive or ride. He was just 15 years old and, hence, unable to partake in the appeal of driving a car for another year. Interestingly, Brad did not verbalize the kinds of things juvenile probation officers so often hear. He did not blame his peers or provide other common rationalizations for his misconduct. Nor did he make promises, pleading that if he could just have one more chance he would not get in further trouble. Robert noted that the center did not use the kinds of labels for Brad that are frequently attached to offenders, both juvenile and adult, and this seemed to Robert another sign of strength for Brad.

Planning

Generally, Robert made every effort to keep families intact and to leave delinquent youngsters with their families.

In Brad's case, however, significant factors precluded his return. His biological mother was a great distance away geographically and showed little interest in him. Brad had attempted to live with her earlier, and it had not worked well. The center was unwilling to work with the father and stepmother on an ongoing basis, seeing them as unable to make the kind and degree of changes that would be required for Brad to function satisfactorily at home. His parents appeared not to be motivated to receive help at another agency (for example, Family Services or Catholic Social Services) that could utilize "family preservation" and family-based, in-home approaches or other helping methods. At the same time, Brad's delinquent behavior and conflict at home and school were continuing, if not worsening. He still had almost a year to go before he would be old enough to drive legally. This was likely to be a difficult year for him, since he was feeling so unhappy, depressed, anxious, angry, and guilty.

Brad and his father participated cooperatively with Robert in planning for an acceptable solution. Robert discussed with each of them the possibility of placing Brad in a residential facility or school. Although Brad did not like being in detention, his dissatisfaction was not extreme, and he seemed about as content there as he had been at home. Brad listed three places he would like to live: a residential facility or school, a foster home, and his own home. He realized that he was unhappy at home and really did not wish to be there. Further, he realized that if he returned home to an unchanged situation, he might again become involved in delinquent behavior, and he did not want that to happen.

Intervention

Robert considered several alternatives for Brad: (1) the state training school for delinquents, (2) return to his parental home on probation, (3) placement in a small residential school, and (4) a foster family placement. He contacted a small, private boys' school in the state and discussed the case with the school's director. A social history was sent to the school. At the request of the director of the school, Robert and Mr. Mercury took Brad there for an interview.

After visiting the school, Robert said to Brad, "Well, what do you think of it?" Brad replied quickly with some enthusiasm, "I like it; it would be good for me." Mr. Mercury said, "I think if he went here he could catch up with his schoolwork and get on track." "Yes, this could be a good place for you to get on top of things and settle down," responded Robert. All three were convinced it was the thing to do.

Robert scheduled a final hearing in the juvenile court before the judge. A social history was prepared for the judge with a recommendation that Brad be placed in the school and that his father be ordered to pay a fixed sum per day for his son's care. This had been discussed previously with Mr. Mercury, and he had reluctantly agreed to participate in financing Brad's placement. Finally, Robert incorporated into his recommendation the suggestion that the hearing be made as constructive and positive as possible in tone and atmosphere so that Brad might realize he had actively participated in planning for the placement. Robert hoped Brad would see the placement as an opportunity for him to develop in ways that would be most satisfactory to him.

Brad was brought to the final hearing from the detention facility. Robert, Mr. Mercury, and his attorney were also present. The judge went through the legal aspects of the case, established the facts, including Brad's admission of guilt, and read the worker's summary. The summary was lengthier than most due to the complexity of the case, the center involvement, and the proposed placement. The judge accepted the recommendation and ordered the commitment and payment by Mr. Mercury. A very positive, supportive atmosphere was maintained. Following the hearing, arrangements were made for Mr. Mercury to transport Brad to the school on the following day.

Evaluation

Since this was not to be an ongoing case for Robert, he began writing a closing summary in Brad's case record. Had Brad been continued on probation, Robert would have continued in a case management role. Although Robert had a strong preference for community-based alternatives over placement in an institution, in this case he felt he had recommended the right alternative. It seemed to be necessary and appropriate, although not an ideal choice. Brad's behaviors and feelings, as well as his family's attitudes toward him, provided rather limited options. Both Brad and his father were reconciled to this outcome, participated in its arrangement, and approached it in a relatively positive fashion. Although there are never any guarantees of "cure" in such cases, this seemed a hopeful step and a good plan for Brad's future. Residential care, with a stable, structured, and supportive environment could be therapeutic and constructive for a youngster like Brad. It could be a more neutral setting for him emotionally, and less harsh and repressive than his parents' home.

Robert realized that he had to deal with his own general reluctance to recommend institutionalization. Institutions could be destructive for adolescents. But it could also be dangerous to leave a youngster in a family situation that propels him or her into self-destructive behavior in the community. To have avoided considering an institutional placement might have, in the long run, made things worse for Brad. Robert also realized that he had to guard against overidentifying with Brad, since Brad was an appealing youth who had been hurt by the most important adults in his life and who had many of his emotional needs unmet.

Termination and Follow-Up

The case was closed after the final hearing. One further development was noteworthy. About a year later, Brad appeared at Robert's office unexpectedly. He had recently been released from the school and had returned to live with his father's family. It appeared to Robert that Brad had physically developed and matured a great deal. Brad seemed more settled, happier, and more at peace with himself and his situation than the last time Robert had seen him. He was again attending Rock River High School and spoke of interest in college, just as he had done in earlier discussions. Robert assured Brad that if he ever wanted to talk, they could.

It was not unheard of for a former client involved in the juvenile court and probation department to reappear this way, but it didn't happen often. Perhaps it was a reflection on the quality of the relationship Robert had been able to establish with Brad.

Readings

Garnier, H. E., & Stein, J. A. (2002). An 18-year model of family and peer effects on adolescent drug use and delinquency. *Journal of Youth & Adolescence, 31*(1), 45–57.

Matherne, M. M., & Thomas, A. (2001). Family environment as a predictor of adolescent delinquency. *Adolescence, 36*(144), 655–665.

Rebellon, C. J. (2002). Reconsidering the broken homes/delinquency relationship and exploring its mediating mechanism(s). *Criminology, 40*(1), 103–136.

Discussion Questions

1. *What purpose might Brad's acting out behavior have served?*

2. *What would the prognosis have been had Brad remained with his father and stepmother rather than being sent to the residential treatment facility?*

3. *Why does this case suggest the importance of using the person-in-environment model for assessing the individual?*

4. *How might an adolescent like Brad benefit from a residential treatment center?*

5. *What reactions might you anticipate from a youngster like Brad who had experienced rejection from all the significant adults in his life?*

6. *Robert prepared a "social history" for the juvenile court prior to Brad's hearing. What is a social history, and what would be the purpose of preparing one for the judge?*

7. *Do you think a foster family placement would have been a better alternative for Brad than placing him in a residential treatment center? Why or why not?*

8. *What advantages did a residential treatment center have over other alternatives?*

9. *The social worker was concerned about the possibility of overidentifying with Brad. What does this mean and why was it a possible problem?*

15

A Visit to Dwight's Hollow

Jody Gottlieb and Linda Gottlieb

West Virginia is the only state located entirely in what is considered to be the Appalachian region. Though rich in natural resources, many of those resources have, historically, been controlled by out-of-state interests. The beauty of its mountains stands in stark contrast to the poverty and isolation in parts of the state.

West Virginia lost both manufacturing and coal mining jobs in the early 1980s. With the jobs went many of its young people, leaving West Virginia with the highest percentage of elderly in the nation. Almost 40 percent of West Virginia's children live in poverty, and the state ranks last in the number of adults with high school and college education. Although the state has since placed a priority on economic development, pockets of poverty remain. Southern West Virginia, known for poor roads, lack of water and sewer systems, and a coal-dependent economy, has found growth difficult. In some southern counties, the unemployment rate is much higher than the state average.

The family and community in this case study capture some of the strengths, problems, and characteristics common to families living in central Appalachia.

Lola Jeffries

Lola Jeffries had high hopes for the success of her pilot program. She had been awarded a grant to direct Let's Join Efforts for Our Future (LJEF), an outreach program designed to actively involve parents in their children's education.

Lola had lived in Blair County most of her life. She had worked as a social worker for the Department of Health & Human Resources (DHHR) for almost 15 years. Lola was active in the community. As a parent as well as a social worker, she was concerned about the high dropout rates in her community's schools. Many of her children's friends seemed to give up too readily on their education, and their parents seemed too easily resigned to that.

Lola was also worried about the impact recent welfare reform efforts would have on her community. Although traditionally a very independent people, a long history of exploitation had left many Appalachians feeling helpless, with no chance of controlling their future. With few job opportunities and a reluctance to move from the area, many of her neighbors relied on some form of public assistance. The need for change was pressing.

Some positive changes were already taking place. A new four-lane highway through southern West Virginia

was recently completed, and local organizations were beginning to spring up, seeking funding to work on various issues and problems. Lola thought the climate was right for a team approach to helping families in the region. She had spent the past few months contacting representatives from certain sectors of the community—public services, education, and private enterprise—and had started to develop a network of support for LJEF.

The program's mission was to keep students in school, based on the theory that family involvement is the key to a child's success in school. LJEF would provide support and advocacy services for parents in the school system. It would provide transportation to PTA meetings and conferences; offer adult "tutoring" to help parents keep up with their children's curriculum; explain academic and transitional programs; act as a liaison between parents and community systems; assist with college applications; invite parents to school for "Career Day" meetings; and engage in other activities.

Lola's organization was based on a theory she had about why some Blair County families didn't place a lot of emphasis on education. Having grown up in the region and done research on its people, she concluded that academic achievement was somewhat of a threat to a rural community whose hope for survival was its youth. Success often meant that children would leave the area to pursue opportunity. Thus, people from the region viewed schools as preparing their young people to leave. Further compounding this problem was the fact that cultural stereotypes had led Appalachians to believe they were not as smart or as successful as the rest of society if they wanted to remain in their home community.

Lola wanted LJEF to counteract those stereotypes and restore confidence. She wanted it to be a program where Appalachians would use their talents and resources to make a difference in their own communities. She hoped that the program would start to reverse the process of cultural stereotypes and help parents keep their children in school.

The Chapman family was the first official referral to LJEF. James (J. D.) Chapman was 15 years old and had been a good student until middle school. His grades had started to drop last year, and this semester he had been truant on a few occasions. The school guidance counselor had spoken to the family previously, noting that both J. D.'s sister and brother had dropped out of high school. In their last conversation, the counselor had mentioned Lola's work and asked the family's permission to speak to Lola about J. D.'s situation. The counselor was given permission to speak to Lola about J. D., and the referral had been made. Lola agreed that J. D. was at high risk for dropping out of school and might utilize the services of the LJEF program. She put in a call to the Chapman family and explained the services offered by LJEF. They seemed interested, and Lola made an appointment to come out and visit.

Dwight's Hollow

Lola took the new four-lane highway and headed south. For miles she was surrounded by breathtaking views of tree-covered hills. Occasional signs marked county and state roads. She passed the time thinking about how the beautiful countryside and its natural resources were such a blessing to all who lived there. At the same time, she realized that the terrain presented access difficulties for persons who lived far from larger towns, especially for people who had spent much of their lives nestled in the hollows. The Chapmans lived in Dwight's Hollow, for which there was no highway sign.

Lola's directions had her turn onto Big Creek Road, one-quarter mile off Blair County Road. The pavement soon became gravel and rocks as the road curved around, up and down the hill. Large, modern homes were interspersed with small frame houses, trailers, and some dilapidated shacks. She passed a small, cement block church and looked for the next dirt road on the left.

A row of mailboxes marked the entrance to Dwight's Hollow. Lola had to make a sharp turn onto the narrow road. As she wound around the bends, trees blocked the view of what was ahead. Had another car approached, there would have been little room to pull over. As she proceeded, Lola wondered what kind of a reception she would get from the Chapman family. Her experience told her that despite the fact that some families were suspicious of strangers, persons who lived in the Appalachian region were known for their hospitality and friendliness. She also knew that as a parent from the same school system, the Chapmans might feel a sense of connection with her. She hoped this would provide a place to begin engaging the family in her outreach efforts.

A gravel driveway led up a short hill to the Chapmans' home, a modest-sized brick rancher with an unfinished addition on the back. A teenaged boy came out to greet Lola. Since the driveway was filled with a pickup truck and a gutted automobile, he motioned for her to park in the yard beside a motorcycle. "How do you like my dirt bike?" he asked as she got out of the car. "I just got it running."

"You must be J. D.," Lola answered.

"I bet you're Trish's mother. I know her from school." They stepped into the house. J. D. led the way through the front rooms and into a large paneled den. Several adults and a young child were there, and all introduced themselves to Lola. J. D.'s parents, sister, and young niece were present. Mrs. Chapman offered Lola coffee and asked her to sit down. The room that had looked unfinished on the outside was abundantly furnished. The sectional sofa, chair, and ottoman were comfortable, though worn. A tall gun cabinet stood in one corner; a woodburning fireplace in another. A sliding glass door led back outside. Lola admired an unusual basket on the table. Mrs. Chapman said that she had woven it from pine needles and showed Lola how it was constructed. Lola took this opportunity to casually chat with Mrs. Chapman and the other family members. She realized that the Chapmans needed time to understand who she was as a person before they would want to discuss their family situation. During the conversation, Mrs. Chapman noted that she had heard about Lola's daughter Trish from conversations with J. D., and she asked where Lola had grown up. Lola shared that she grew up not far from there and had come back to work after she had finished her social work degree.

After a time, Lola began to explain in more detail what she had told Mrs. Chapman on the phone about LJEF and the referral. She hoped that they could come up with a plan to help J. D. in school. Both parents agreed. "We hoped all of our children would finish school. J. D., especially, used to be a good student. But it seems that once they get to a certain age, they just don't want to go anymore," Mrs. Chapman ("Call me Pat.") said.

"J. D. thinks he can get by as a mechanic," Mr. Chapman (Harlan) added. "He doesn't think he needs to learn English or geography for that. But I told him not to make the same mistake I did by putting all his eggs in one basket." Harlan and the other family members talked about their situation for a while, and Lola listened.

Some Chapman Family History

Harlan had quit school at the age of 16 to work in the coal mines like his father and grandfather before him. It was a high-paying job with no degree required. Underground mining was a dangerous job at the time. Harlan's uncle was killed in an accident, and Harlan watched his father die of Black Lung disease. Still, when his mine closed in 1984, Harlan had hoped to find another mining job. Demand for coal remained high, but changing technology eliminated a lot of the underground labor needed to produce it. Competition was stiff, so many of Harlan's coworkers relied on Workers' Compensation claims for their new livelihood.

Pat explained that her father was a career politician—the sheriff at the time in Blair County. Harlan assumed he could work for the county if he couldn't get on with a mine. However, before that could be worked out, his father-in-law suffered a fatal heart attack. Harlan worked at odd jobs for a while, some construction work and truck driving, until a bad back made those activities impossible. He was now 47 years old and was receiving disability income.

Pat, 46 years old, lived in Dwight's Hollow all of her life. Her father, besides running for office, was a preacher at the church Lola had passed on Big Creek. His sudden death was a shock to Pat's entire family. Pat had fond memories of campaigning for him, and she still attended his church. Both Pat's mother and sister still lived nearby and were important in Pat's life. They provided the support so often found among the kinship networks of the region.

Pat met Harlan through mutual friends during her senior year at high school. They fell in love. Harlan was already working and making good money. She dropped out of school to get married. Pat had never worked outside the home. She had learned the art of basket making from her grandmother and occasionally sold some of her baskets at county arts and craft fairs. She also did some babysitting for family and neighbors.

When Harlan worked in the mines, he made enough money to build a house and amass a lot of debt. The Chapmans started adding onto their house and were financing a boat, a camper, two cars, and a truck when he lost his job. They sold the boat and a couple of vehicles but eventually had to file for bankruptcy. "It's been rough," Pat said. "We had to go on welfare for a while before Harlan's disability was approved. But we've still got each other, and the Lord has always watched over us."

It was especially rough on the family when their oldest son, Jack, had to leave the state to find work. Jack was married at 17 and worked as a construction worker. He and his wife moved to North Carolina where they both could find jobs. They earned enough to support their family but were not happy. Jack was now 27 and had recently returned to Blair County so his wife could care for her mother who had become ill. The Chapmans were glad to have Jack back but worried about his ability to make a living in the area.

Harlan commented that he understood how his son felt. "A lot of people have asked me why I didn't leave myself. 'This is home,' I tell them, 'and I don't know of another place like it.' People who leave here always want to come back. It's like that old story about the fellow being shown around heaven by St. Peter. In the middle of all the beautiful clouds, the fellow notices a fenced-in area, filled with people looking out wistfully. 'Those are the West Virginians,' says St. Pete. 'If we don't lock them up, they try to sneak home on weekends.'"

Lori, the Chapmans' 24-year-old daughter, had also moved back home, in this case literally. She and her daughter (Jessica, age 3) moved back with Harlan and Pat a few months ago. She was receiving benefits from the state and was working as a file clerk at the Blair County DHHR office as part of a state-sponsored program in which a recipient works in return for receiving state benefits. She

passed her High School Equivalency test and had plans to go back to school. Lori applied for a Pell Grant and hoped to attend a medical technology program next semester at the community college. She and Jessica would have to stay with her parents until she finished school and found a job. Pat, at least, would be paid as a daycare provider for Jessica.

Lori had plenty of questions of her own, and Lola said she would be happy to talk to her. However, first she wanted to discuss J. D.

Presenting Problem: J. D.'s Truancy

With the Chapmans' permission, Lola talked to some of J. D.'s current and former teachers. She learned that his grades were good through most of elementary school but dropped a little in middle school. Routine school testing showed a weakness in language areas, but he had scored high enough in other areas to test average overall. He had not been tested for any learning disabilities.

The only behavior problems J. D. had previously exhibited in school were in the form of good-natured pranks. He had an outgoing personality and a penchant for practical jokes (Harlan chuckled at that observation). J. D. was an eager participant in class discussions, often volunteering answers and opinions, though not always following through with assigned homework. He took advantage of every opportunity to use the school's computers and had participated in the school band, playing trombone.

J. D.'s grades dropped considerably upon entering high school this year. His absences were becoming more frequent, and when he did attend school his participation declined. His English/Language Arts teacher, Mr. Waldrop, suspected that poor reading habits were causing J. D. to fall behind in all of his subjects and that he was probably frustrated and embarrassed.

J. D. commented, "Me and Mr. Waldrop just don't get along. I'm not learning anything at school anyway. Besides, I hardly ever get to use the computers when I need to get online, and that was about the only part of school I liked. That and band." J. D. was not able to participate in band this year because of his grades.

Harlan added, "J. D. is like me. He likes to be outdoors, hunting or fishing or riding his bike. He doesn't have much patience for sitting down and studying. But I don't know where he got his knack for mechanics. He's a natural at taking things apart and putting them back together."

J. D. proudly added, "Everyone in the hollow asks me to fix their cars." He noted that he had developed an interest in cars and bikes by helping a neighbor rebuild an old automobile. J. D. began using the Internet at school to learn about particular makes of cars and to locate hard-to-find parts. He had found some parts for his dirt bike online and had talked the seller into a trade for some old tools.

"J. D. could talk anyone into anything," Pat added. "He talked me into letting him have that bike, as dangerous as I think those things are. He's going to be a politician like his grandfather."

Despite all the speculation about J. D.'s future, he really hadn't decided to be a mechanic or a politician. In fact, he was tired of people talking about his career before he was ready to choose one. He added, "I'll want a good-paying job—that's all I know."

Lola asked J. D. to tell her more about school. Mr. Waldrop's class was not the only one in which he was having trouble. J. D. admitted that school had become difficult for him. All of his subjects required more homework and studying than in the past. He felt Mr. Waldrop, in particular, expected a lot, and he didn't like having to read aloud in front of the class. He couldn't read as fast as the other students could. J. D. didn't think it was possible to make up what he had already missed this year. In addition, this school was much bigger than his previous one, and he felt a little lost.

J. D. acknowledged that the new school did have some advantages. The computer and science labs had up-to-date technology. J. D. enjoyed his time in both. There were also some interesting electives to take, if he could ever get caught up in his basic subjects.

Assessing the Situation

J. D. was intelligent and inquisitive. He had taught himself mechanics by reading and research, so he had demonstrated that he was capable of good study skills. J. D. also demonstrated his analytical abilities through his use of computer technology at school. His behavior in his classes suggested that he possessed some strengths in interpersonal skills, including the use of humor.

J. D. seemed to be a little overwhelmed. He knew it would take a lot of effort to keep up with the required schoolwork, and he indicated that he was afraid he wasn't capable of it. He also felt uncomfortable talking to his teachers about his concerns about schoolwork. He seemed to recognize that he needed to work on his reading skills but was not clear how to get help for this.

The Chapman family all seemed genuinely concerned about J. D. The family seemed close and mutually supportive. However, the family system had recently changed with the return of the two children. Harlan and Pat had the added concern of providing for Lori and her daughter Jessica. In addition, they worried about Jack's ability to support his family due to the lack of employment opportunities. Lola thought that, despite the family's strengths, so much was going on that it was difficult to give J. D.'s situation the attention that was needed. It

seemed to her that the family also seemed a little overwhelmed.

Goals and Tasks

Lola talked with the Chapmans about how she might help ease their situation. Harlan and Pat both wondered if Lola could talk to people at the school about how to address J. D.'s needs. They expressed some frustration over not being able to make good connections with the teachers there, partially because they had felt uncomfortable in expressing their concerns about J. D.'s recent drop in school performance. With assistance from Harlan and Pat, Lola helped to identify some goals and activities that could be worked on by everyone.

Mr. Waldrop, J. D.'s English/Language Arts teacher, seemed like a good person to contact. Lola explained that if she could help them connect with Mr. Waldrop, he might have some resources for and suggestions about how J. D. could work on his reading skills. Harlan and Pat agreed to accompany Lola to meet with Mr. Waldrop in hopes of discussing how they could all make things better.

The visit to school was productive. Mr. Waldrop said that at the beginning of the year he may have started out on the wrong foot with J. D. when he labeled him as the "class clown." He offered to help J. D. get back on track in his class by allowing J. D. to complete a research project for extra credit, and he offered to help him with the project.

In return, the Chapmans volunteered to help J. D. with his reading if Mr. Waldrop could make suggestions about how they could proceed with this help. The conversation was productive, and Mr. Waldrop provided some good examples of how the Chapmans could help with J. D.'s reading skills. Pat mentioned that J. D. felt uncomfortable reading in front of the class, and Mr. Waldrop agreed to keep that activity to a minimum for J. D., at least for the time being.

Lola took the opportunity to talk with the school social worker, while she and the Chapmans were visiting Mr. Waldrop. Lola asked if the social worker could suggest that the school provide a tutor for J. D. to help him get caught up with his academic work and to help him improve his study habits. Unfortunately, the school social worker did not have any concrete suggestions about how to connect J. D. with this type of resource.

Luckily, Lola had recently met with Gail Lewis, a retired reading teacher who had agreed to volunteer with LJEF. Upon returning to her office, Lola put in a call to Mrs. Lewis, and she agreed to help J. D. with his reading. Mrs. Lewis lived a few miles away on Little Creek Road and would be able to come to the house to work with the family. She could help J. D. set up a daily study schedule and show the family how to work with him on his reading.

After that, it would be up to them to implement the reading plan and monitor the schedule. The Chapmans readily agreed to this arrangement.

Lola also had some business sponsors for LJEF. Motorcade, a local car dealership, had agreed to donate one of its used computers and would upgrade the modem. J. D. could use the computer, but an Internet connection would be a monthly expense. Pat immediately spoke up, offering to use some of her forthcoming babysitting income to pay the Internet connection charge, contingent on J. D. following his study plan. J. D. told his mother, "I'll pay you back by selling some of your baskets on the Web." He liked the plan.

Lola suggested they write an agreement recapping the immediate plan. Pat would keep in touch with the school, Mr. Waldrop, and the guidance counselor. Pat would call Mrs. Lewis, and Harlan would take J. D. to Motorcade to pick up the computer. J. D. agreed to bring home his assignments each day, and Pat and Harlan would keep track of how much time and help he needed to complete them. They signed the agreement.

Lori and Welfare Reform

Lori hoped J. D. would succeed and graduate from high school, as she wished she had done. She noted, "It's degrading being on welfare. I plan to tell Jessica that she'd better finish high school and go to college."

Lori was looking forward to community college but was worried about being able to attend class, study, be a mother, and work 20 hours a week at the same time. She explained that college didn't count as a work activity needed for eligibility for government assistance. If she didn't find a job near the school, she would lose not only the check, but also her transportation allowance needed to get there. She confided in Lola, "I don't think that's fair. I'm lucky that I have my parents to babysit, but how am I supposed to spend any time with Jessica? I know you used to work for the DHHR, Lola, so maybe you know something about it?"

Lola acknowledged that it was, indeed, the policy. She offered to call the college for Lori about a Work-Study job. As for Jessica going to college, Lola pointed out that children tend to do best in school if read to at an early age. Lori could make that part of Jessica's bedtime routine, thus assuring them of some quality time together every day. Also, Jessica might benefit from attending the Head Start program while Lori was at school. Lola would ask Head Start to send an application.

Follow-up

The family's relationship with LJEF was a productive one. The Chapmans met with J. D.'s teachers several times, getting tips on how to keep J. D. focused on his studies at home. Eventually, the Chapmans met with the school social worker and were able to negotiate for a tutor for J. D. in social studies, math, and science. The social worker also took some time to explain the vocational programs available to J. D. if he decided to pursue his interest in mechanics.

Lola made a follow-up visit to the Chapmans before the end of the school year. J. D.'s school attendance had improved, as had most of his grades. His grade in Mr. Waldrop's class, in particular, had improved significantly. J. D. was playing in the band again, and the Chapmans were planning to attend the band's performance at the Spring festival.

Mrs. Lewis had mentioned having J. D. tested for Attention Deficit Disorder, but Pat and Harlan were not yet convinced they should do that. J. D. was, however, adhering to a daily study plan. Mrs. Lewis had suggested he read whatever interested him at first, and she had brought an issue of *Popular Mechanics* with her. She then helped set up a schedule, allotting time for each subject based on difficulty level. Pat would question J. D. about each session. If he followed his schedule, he could have the rest of the evening free.

J. D. was making good use of the computer and had introduced the other family members to it. He had designed a Web page to sell his mother's baskets. Harlan was in charge of packaging, and the Chapmans had a small cottage industry in the works.

Lori had started community college and a Work Study job. She contacted Head Start for Jessica, only to learn that its bus would not come into the hollow. At Lola's suggestion, she talked to other parents in the hollow and planned a car pool to transport the children to and from the bus stop on Big Creek. Jessica would begin Head Start in the fall.

Encouraged by her success, Lori decided to take some action about the state's "college-not-counted-as-work-activity-for-welfare-benefits" policy. She had contacted members of the state legislature and was now in the process of organizing others in the same position to start a letterwriting campaign.

Things seemed to be looking up for the family, and they wanted to thank Lola for all of her help. Pat offered Lola a beautiful basket filled with her homemade jam and invited her to come visit any time.

Readings

Gandara, P., Gutierrez, D., & O'Hara, S. (2001). Planning for the future in rural and urban high schools. *Journal of Education for Students Placed at Risk,* 6(1/2), 73–94.

Wells, B. (2002). Women's voices: Explaining poverty and plenty in a rural community. *Rural Sociology,* 67(2), 234–255.

Zook, L. J. (2002). The Smiths: A rural family. *The New Social Worker,* 9(2), 6–7.

Discussion Questions

1. What traits of Appalachian culture were brought out in this case? What are some cultural stereotypes of Appalachia, and how could they contribute to the problems in the area?

2. What assumptions did you make about the racial and cultural background of the Chapman family?

3. What were some of the strengths in the community? What were the strengths in the family? How did LJEF build on those strengths?

4. Why was an outreach program preferable to an agency-based one?

5. How did Lola's community ties help in her work with the program and the family? What potential problems could arise from those ties?

6. *What are some effects of long-term unemployment?*

7. *What welfare reform issues affected the family? Why did Lola agree to help Lori?*

8. *Should Lola have accepted the basket with the homemade jam?*

9. *In this case, the worker decided to try to change a state policy governing the welfare system, even though her involvement with the family was over. Why is this an appropriate role for a generalist social worker?*

16

No Mad Dog Looks: Group Work and Mediating Differences

Cynthia Duncan

Sandy Townsend worked with high-risk students in several rural school districts. As part of her field practicum, she was assigned referrals from school personnel and was expected to assess and help with a wide range of problems. Most of her work was with individual teens and their families.

Sandy received a referral from a junior high school principal in a district that enrolled about 40 percent Latino and 60 percent non-Latino students. Apparently, there were several Latino teens who had been fighting in school and in the neighborhood. The police had been involved twice, and it was rumored that the students were becoming more aggressive toward each other, making threats, and planning an organized confrontation. The principal provided Sandy with a list of names of the girls involved but little other information. The final words of the principal were, "See if you can do something before they all get kicked out of school for the rest of the year."

Engagement: Preliminary Information

Sandy began by individually interviewing three junior high students. She asked them to describe how they saw the conflict, what they wanted, and who else was involved. Based on the information she received from these interviews, she contacted and interviewed three other teens who attended the local high school. She was able to develop the following information.

1. All the students indicated they wanted to figure out a way to stay out of trouble and stay in school. The students involved were divided into two groups of about the same size.
2. All expressed the sentiment, "If she/they would just stop, we wouldn't have a problem." Each group felt the other was at fault.
3. Most of the actual fighting had occurred between two girls, Angelica and Veronica, who were identified as leaders of their respective groups. Both Angelica and Veronica had first cousins, Esmerelda and Blanca, who were part of their groups and who felt obligated to defend their viewpoints. The presence of strong family ties helped to reinforce the solidarity of each group. All the girls Sandy interviewed made comments about "us and them," suggesting strong feelings of loyalty to their groups.

4. There was one other noticeable difference between the two groups. Angelica's group members had grown up in the community, and Veronica's had more recently moved into this rural neighborhood from a large urban area. According to one of the girls, Veronica and her friends had belonged to a gang before moving to this community.
5. Although members of both groups expressed some interest in getting along with each other, no efforts to problem-solve had taken place, either through their own efforts or through school counselors.

The Planning Process: Establishing a Group

Sandy wondered whether offering the students an opportunity to discuss their differences in a group would help diffuse this potentially dangerous situation. Her initial assessment of the possible membership of a problem-solving group suggested that the students involved in the conflict were amenable to some form of intervention on her part, but she was unsure how to proceed with such a plan. Sandy decided to proceed with the planning stage of this group effort in a systematic way, and she took paper and pencil and made some planning notes.

Establishing the Group's Purpose

Sandy began by reviewing the potential purpose for a group that could help settle some of the differences among the students. She recalled her charge from the junior high school principal and noted that she had been asked to help these students begin to act more responsibly toward each other and keep them from getting into a conflict that would result in their being suspended from school. Sandy decided that if she could bring all the disputing students together, she might have a chance to help them mediate their differences and open up more positive lines of communication. This beginning purpose seemed to be reasonable, and she hoped the members of the two groups would agree.

Assessing Potential Sponsorship

Since the original referral had come through a principal at the junior high school, Sandy thought she would be able to use the school facilities to hold a group meeting.

She noted, however, that most of the school counselors' and social workers' work was done with individual students. She would have to make contacts with some school officials to interpret the purpose of the group and explain how working with the students in a group would be more beneficial than working with them individually. In this sense, Sandy realized that she would be pioneering group work services and should take care to inform school officials and seek their support.

Assessing Potential Membership

Although some of the students expressed interest in meeting together, there were several potential differences among members that could affect the plan for the group. Some students were from junior high, and others were in high school, which would necessitate finding a mutually convenient time and place for getting them together. Furthermore, she was concerned about the amount of time the group members would miss from classes because the optimal meeting time seemed to be when members were in school. All of the girls were bilingual, and Sandy spoke only English. She was concerned that she might not understand the subtlety of their communications and might lose control if the students spoke Spanish or used colloquial expressions she didn't understand.

Recruiting Members

Because Angelica's and Veronica's supporters were already identified, efforts to recruit each of the members into Sandy's mediating group would focus on working with the two group leaders. Sandy would make a special effort, however, to contact each student individually and secure her agreement to attend. After each conversation, she would write the potential member a short note, confirming their conversation and thanking her for agreeing to attend the group.

Orienting Members

During her conversations with individual members, she would orient each to the purpose of the group. She would state the purpose in tentative terms, suggesting that the members would have the opportunity to discuss the purpose and vote on it at their first meeting. She anticipated that members would have questions about how the group would be run. Sandy would try to clarify group procedures and promised to do her best to help each member stop fighting and begin to talk to each other. She also felt it was her job to help members communicate with each other, and she would try to get them to vote on some basic rules of participation at their first meeting. Most of Sandy's conversations with potential members were quite positive. Sandy felt that each member was "appropriate for the group," because all had some desire to make things better and had demonstrated a willingness to compromise.

Composing the Group

Because the composition of the mediating group would be determined by being a member in either Angelica's or Veronica's group, Sandy realized she had little control over actual group composition. She recognized that all potential members held some common characteristics, including Latino heritage, language characteristics, age and life stage, and a beginning agreement on wanting to make things better between all involved. Each of the girls also had several values in common, including loyalty to her family ties and relatives and pride in her Latino heritage.

The girls also had diverse characteristics that could possibly affect the group, including differences in geographic background and life experience (urban and rural) and some differences based on age and grade attended. It seemed to Sandy that these differences could be minimized if the members could concentrate on their common values and strengths.

The structure of the proposed group would be interesting, because bringing both groups together would mean that the new group would have two strong leaders, each with her own following. Sandy wondered how she could encourage both Angelica and Veronica to share leadership of the new group and avoid conflict based on extragroup loyalty. In the early stage of the group, the structure would clearly be determined by previous group loyalties.

Angelica's Group	*Veronica's Group*
Angelica (junior high)	Veronica (high school)
Esmerelda (junior high)	Blanca (high school)
Sonia (junior high)	Rosa (junior high)
Sylvia (high school)	Yesenia (junior high)

The new group would be small, and with only eight members, Sandy felt comfortable leading it. She felt it would be best if the membership were fixed, so she decided on a closed membership group in which membership would be determined from the beginning and no new members would be added.

Contracting for Group Procedures

Sandy wanted to begin the group with as few rules as possible. Still, she felt it would be best to have potential members agree to a few rules governing their conduct in the group. She would ask the girls to agree to:

• Attend all group sessions as scheduled.
• Arrive on time and be prepared to discuss the business of the group.

- Listen carefully to what each member says. Wait until the other member has finished before speaking. No interruptions.
- Refrain from violence or threats of violence toward other members during group meetings.
- Keep what is said in the group confidential. Refrain from discussing what is said in the group with other people.

Sandy also composed several rules that would govern her own behavior. She would tell each member that she would:

- Make sure the group started and ended on time.
- Help members feel protected and not allow members to threaten each other.
- Provide a quiet, private place where the group could meet. Provide some refreshments for members.
- Evaluate each group session with the members.
- Treat what was said in the group as confidential, although she would be telling the principal how the group was doing without mentioning names or exactly what was said by whom.
- Remain neutral in her dealings with group members.

Preparing the Environment

Sandy would need to find a private, comfortable room that would ensure privacy during meetings. She felt the room should be smaller than a classroom but large enough that each member would "have her own space."

Sandy decided she would speak to counselors at both schools and explain the mediation process. They could be instrumental in helping to reinforce the girls' attendance. She would also talk to the principal who made the original referral about obtaining some money for refreshments.

One other issue concerned Sandy. She recognized that she might not be in the best position to understand cultural issues that were at work in this situation. She had read several articles on working with Latino groups in *The Journal of Social Work with Groups* but had little experience doing group work. Sandy decided to contact Maria Gil, a fellow student who was a bilingual Latino worker at the local mental health center. Sandy would explain the situation to Maria and ask if she could be present at the mediation session to cofacilitate the group and help provide her with a cultural perspective. She would meet with Maria before starting the group so that they could discuss their approach, and she would contact the group members.

Intervention: The First Group Meeting

Schedules were arranged so that all participants arrived at the same time. The staff conference room was used for the mediation session. The conference room was furnished with a large rectangular oak conference table and comfortable chairs. As everyone entered the room, Angelica sat on one side, and Esmerelda, Sonia, and Sylvia joined her. Veronica sat across the table, and Blanca, Rosa, and Yesenia sat with her. After greeting the girls as they entered, Sandy and Maria sat together at one end of the table. Sandy began the meeting by reviewing the purpose for the group and the beginning ground rules.

Sandy: I want to welcome each of you to this mediation session today. Before we start, I want to introduce you to Maria. Maria is a social worker who works in our community. She has volunteered to be here today to help with the group. Maria wanted to be here today because she is concerned about the fighting.

Maria: I don't know all of you, so would you please tell me your names? Would you start? [she asked, pointing to Sylvia, who was sitting farthest away from Maria.] (Each girl introduced herself.)

Sandy: I want to remind everyone that I will be talking with the school counselors and the principal after we meet today to tell them, in general, how this meeting goes. I will report whether you have been able to reach an agreement among yourselves about the situation. I will not be sharing exactly who said what. Is that OK with all of you? (The group members responded with a collective yes.)

The first thing I would like to do is to state the purpose for the group. As I discussed with all of you, we are here to help solve the differences you have had and to open up communication among all of you. You can discuss and modify the purpose, but for now it will help direct our conversations together. That is the purpose for this group meeting.

Veronica: How do we know that Angelica and her group won't want to do all of the talking?

Angelica: We can make rules for all of us.

Sandy: When I met with each of you to explain mediation, we talked about the ground rules. I've written them down and tacked them on the wall behind me. Let's take a look at them.

Maria pointed out the rules that had been agreed on and reviewed each one by repeating it and making sure each of the girls was paying attention. The rules were:

- Maria and Sandy will remain neutral.
- What we say in here stays in here.
- No personal attacks and no fighting will be allowed.
- One person speaks at a time.
- Everyone will have a chance to be heard.
- Being here means we are willing to work things out.

Sandy felt the tension in the room and observed that the girls were quiet but glaring at each other. She wondered whether this was really going to work. One by one,

Sandy asked each girl to agree to the ground rules. Each girl said "yes." Sandy began to explore the problems between the two groups.

Sandy: We'll start by asking one of you to tell us how you see the problem; then we'll ask someone else to restate it to make sure we all understand. Who would like to start?

Angelica: Veronica wants to fight me all the time. She calls me names; she calls all of us names. She says stuff about us behind our backs. She won't say stuff to my face; she's just chicken I guess.

Sandy: Angelica, remember the ground rules. Calling someone a chicken is a personal attack. Your comments about Veronica wanting to fight are your perception of the problem. Is there anything else you want to say?

Angelica: OK, sorry. But if someone says stuff and wants to fight me, I'll fight. They just need to mind their own business.

Sandy: Veronica, could you restate what Angelica said, how she sees the problem?

Veronica: She calls us names too.

Sandy: Veronica, remember the ground rules; you'll get your chance to tell your side of the story. Right now, I'd like you to restate what Angelica said.

Veronica: OK, sorry. Angelica says we call her names and want to fight her, and she doesn't want to fight but she will.

Sandy: Is that about what you said, Angelica?

Angelica: Yeah, they just need to mind their own business.

Sandy: Veronica, would you tell us how you see the problem?

Veronica: OK, well, it's like this. We're new here, and we don't know anybody. And some kids told us we better watch out for Angelica and Esmerelda because they like to fight. And pretty soon we hear they're calling us names, and they want to fight because they think Blanca is messing with her boyfriend. And she wasn't even near her boyfriend. So, hey, we don't want to fight, but they're telling all these lies about us and wanting to fight, so we'll fight.

Sandy: Angelica, could you restate what Veronica said, how she sees the problem?

Angelica: Veronica, we heard about that party where Blanca was hanging all over Jose.

Veronica: Who told you? They lied; we weren't there!

Sandy: Angelica, Veronica, stop! Remember the ground rules. Right now, I've asked Angelica to restate what Veronica said about how she sees the problem, OK?

Angelica: OK.

Veronica: OK.

Angelica: Well, Veronica thinks we like to fight everybody and that we've been calling them names and saying lies about them.

Sandy: Veronica, is that about it?

Veronica: Yeah, and we don't want to fight, but we will.

Sandy thought the rules seemed to be working for the girls, providing them with some protection from potentially explosive responses. The girls seemed to be thinking more about their responses instead of just trying to "answer back." Sandy figured that she would continue the process of problem definition until each of the girls had a chance to contribute.

Sandy: So far, Angelica has said that she thinks the problem has to do with name calling and people talking behind her back. She says she doesn't want to fight, but she will. Veronica says the problem has to do with name calling and people saying things that aren't true. And she doesn't want to fight, but she will. Is that about right so far?

Angelica: That's about it; you're a good listener.

Veronica: I think that's right.

Maria: Who else would like to tell how they see the problem?

Esmerelda: Well, these girls are new. And we heard they were gang members, and they really think they're tough. We heard they were calling us names and that Blanca was messing with Jose.

Blanca: We don't want any trouble, and we don't mess with anybody's boyfriends. We heard they were telling lies about us. Then Esmerelda called me and made all these threats, so that's when the fighting started.

Sonia: We heard they were saying we couldn't go near the Seventh Street Park or they'd get us. I think everybody has been talking trash and things got out of hand, and everybody has been listening to everybody else.

Veronica: The park is near where we live; we like it there.

Rosa: I think we're all saying the same thing, all the name calling, and threats, and everybody talks.

Sandy thought everyone was looking more relaxed. They all seemed to be genuinely surprised about what was being shared. Sandy wondered if this was the first time they had actually talked to each other.

Sandy: Have any of you actually talked to each other face to face before today?

Angelica: No. Can we just talk to each other now?

Sandy: Well, yes, we can. But if the ground rules aren't followed, I'll stop the discussion.

Rosa: I think Carlos has had a lot to do with this. I think he's trying to get us to fight.

Esmerelda: Yeah, he and Mike said they'd like to see how those girl gang members fight.

Blanca: Who told you I was messing with Jose?

Angelica: Sophie and Linda.

Blanca: I don't think they were even there.

Angelica: I heard you were looking for us last Friday night. Carlos and Mike said you were driving by our house throwing your signs.

Blanca: We know about our signs; you don't.

Veronica: Sandra said Carlos told us you were looking for us and you wanted to fight.

Rosa: That last fight started because of those mad dog looks you threw us in the hallway.

Sonia: Well, when that gets started, we're gonna fight.

Blanca: My mom said if I get in one more fight, we're moving to Alaska!

At that point, everyone in the room laughed. Sandy and Maria noticed that the tension in the group was subsiding. At least the group members had one thing in common: a sense of humor. Sandy was not quite sure what the girls meant by "throwing signs," but she had her suspicions.

Sandy: Let's continue our discussion.

Veronica: It's true we were in a gang, but we're not now. And we're trying to have a better life here. We don't want to fight, but we will if we have to.

Angelica: I didn't want to fight you, but everything I heard you were saying about me made me so mad I didn't care.

Sandy: I want to summarize what's been said. This is the first time you all have sat face to face and talked. A lot of people have been saying things that you have said or done, but you are saying that these things are not true. While all of you are willing to fight to settle things, the fighting has caused problems for you at school and for some of you at home. Is this about right? (The group agrees.)

The next step in mediation is for us to brainstorm ideas that could become part of an agreement for getting along and not fighting. We won't decide if a particular idea will work or not; we'll just come up with as many ideas as we can. Maria will write your ideas on the board. You can list serious as well as silly ideas that might work. We want to generate as many ideas as we can, and don't comment on the ideas until we are finished listing all of them. Want to give it a try?

The girls generated about 15 ideas. Maria wrote each on the blackboard, and the girls discussed them one by one. After the discussion, the group voted on the ideas they wanted to include in the agreement. Maria wrote the final ideas on a clean piece of paper, and each girl signed it. The contract read:

WE AGREE: No dirty looks. No mad dog looks.
Don't believe what everybody says.
Talk directly to each other; confront the person who talks.
If you don't talk about me, I won't talk about you.
No sign throwing.
No territories.
No threats from cars.
Forget the past and start over.

Veronica: What if there's a problem with this; what if someone breaks the agreement?

Sandy: Should we meet again and see how the agreement is working out?

Girls: Yes. (in unison)

Maria: Good, I'll make copies for each of you before we leave today. I guess we can try to meet again in about two weeks.

As the meeting ended, Sandy and Maria observed that the girls were polite but still regarded each other with some suspicion. Maria remarked on one particular cultural issue that emerged and interpreted it to Sandy. She explained that eye contact among adolescent Latino females can have different meanings. In particular, the girls had mentioned "mad dog looks," which can be used to express a verbal obscenity or challenge. Direct and sustained eye contact can clearly be disrespectful. This behavior and its accompanying meaning could be done in the school hall or in a classroom, and a teacher or staff member might not know what was going on, especially if it led to a fight.

Although the new girls expressed a sincere desire to leave the way of the gang behind, it was being re-created in the community. There was a small park in town, and some new graffiti was seen there. A rumor began to circulate that Veronica and her friends had started to claim it as their territory. They seemed quite willing to let go of their turf when the agreement was reached.

It seemed important at the next session to give the girls an additional opportunity to get to know each other if they were interested. Sandy contacted Linda, the junior high school librarian, who was skilled at working with students on an interpersonal level. Linda agreed to come to the next group meeting and do a structured exercise designed to "break the ice" and help the girls get to know each other better. Sandy, Maria, and Linda would all attend the next meeting of the group.

Intervention: The Second Group Meeting

In two weeks, the girls met again to review the agreement. There had been one minor problem. Angelica and Veronica had a personal problem with each other, but they talked with Linda and had worked it out. There were no reported violations of the agreement, and according to the principal of the junior high school, the girls seemed to be staying away from each other.

Sandy began the second meeting by summarizing how things seemed to be going. She also reinforced the girls' cooperation with each other in honoring the agreement.

Sandy: Since the agreement is working well, Maria and Linda and I would like to suggest that we spend some time together today getting to know each other a little better. We will ask you to get into groups of three and to do that by picking the people you know the least. We have a list of four questions for you to answer. Each group can go outside and find a comfortable spot. You can talk there and will need to return in 20 minutes. What do you think? (The group agrees.)

Veronica: Can we go off the school grounds?

Sandy: We need to stay on the school grounds in the front of the building. Anything else?

Blanca: Do we just talk, or do we have to ask each other these questions?

Sandy: You might find that if you talk with each other, you can learn the answers to the questions. Be good listeners!

Sandy was glad questions had been asked and thought once again that it was good to provide structure for the group members. She also knew that her authority might have been questioned by Veronica and Blanca, but this was a normal process for this stage of the group. Questioning the leader could indicate that members were being more independent and taking more responsibility for the group.

When the girls returned, they seemed animated, and some were even laughing. Sandy asked the group members to share what they had learned. Maria reviewed the questions the girls were supposed to discuss. She wrote them on the board; they were:

• Where were you born?
• Where were your parents born?
• What would you like us to know about you?
• What do you want for your future?

Angelica: Veronica lives in a house with 13 people and one bathroom. Her mom and her uncle are trying to find jobs.

Rosa: Angelica lives with her stepdad and her half sister. He never lets her go anywhere. She doesn't know what she wants to do with her life.

Esmerelda: Rosa lives with her second stepdad; she doesn't know where her mom is or who her dad was. She wants to finish high school and get a good job.

Blanca: Esmerelda lives with her aunt and uncle. They were born in Mexico, and she was born here. She wants to finish school and get married!

Sonia: Blanca lives with her aunt and Veronica. She gets mad a lot because someone is always in her stuff. She thinks she wants to graduate, but she also wants to marry somebody rich.

Yesenia: Sylvia is lucky; she lives with her sister and her sister's boyfriend. She's trying to find a job, and she wants to graduate and go to college. Her mom is in Mexico, and she doesn't know about her dad.

Sylvia: Yesenia lives with her mom and her sisters and brothers. Her dad was killed in an accident two years ago. She wants to finish high school and get a good job.

Blanca: Sonia lives with her mom and her uncle and her sister. She wants to move to a big city after high school.

Maria: I feel really sad as I listen to all of you talk. There is so much loss here. I also feel proud of you. Most of

you want to finish high school and have a better life. I get the impression that you are all strong enough to work on your feelings of loss and anger and that you can get along at school. There are people in your school and in your community who can help.

Sandy: I am in your schools two days a week; I'd be glad to talk with you individually. Also, your school counselors can talk with you. Maria works at the counseling office on Second Street.

Maria: For the next few weeks, I'll come to school during lunch time if anyone wants to talk. If you'd like to talk with me outside of school, we could set up a time to meet.

Sandy: There are two weeks left of school. Does this group need to meet again?

Veronica: Let's meet right before school is out, and let's bring food.

Angelica: I'll bring chips and salsa.

Maria: I'll bring some too.

Sandy: OK, two weeks from today, bring food.

Intervention: The Third Group Meeting

The girls entered the room with sacks and purses full of food, and they began to unpack. Sandy noticed that the members worked together to coordinate things and put out the food. She wondered if the group had moved into the performing stage, when members reach their highest potential for cooperation and work. Although it would be possible to make this session a working one, Sandy decided to review the progress the group had made and ask how they thought things would go in the future.

Sandy: Since this is our final meeting, should we review the agreement?

Veronica: No, everything is OK, let's eat. What did everybody bring?

Angelica: Sandy, can we just talk today? We won't interrupt.

Blanca: Maria, what did you bring? You should see Veronica eat, and she just had lunch!

Sandy: Yes, I think today we can just talk. I'd like to know if you think your agreement will work during the summer and what your plans are for the summer.

Angelica: I'm going to summer school. Yuk.

Maria: I brought some chips, salsa, and some candy; who wants to try some?

Veronica: I'm going to work; I just got a job at the bakery. I think I'm going to join that Mexican dancing group too.

Maria: That's good. Will you make a lot of money this summer?

Veronica: Yes, I think so.

Sandy: Have there been any problems with the agreement?

Angelica: No, just that once, and we went to Linda and Veronica and I talked. The main thing is to confront others who talk. Every time now I say to someone, did

Veronica really say that? Let's go see her and ask her about it. And they always say they don't want to, so I know she didn't say it.

Veronica: Yeah, I say, well, let's go see if Angelica says that now, and they won't go with me.

Sonia: We also told some people about our agreement. Now I think they know we won't fight like before.

Sylvia: Look at you girls eat! This whole place smells like salsa.

Sandy: Do you think you will all be able to get along in the same school next year?

Sonia: I don't think we'll be great friends or anything, but I don't think we'll fight.

Veronica: We won't see each other much, and if we hear stuff, we'll know what to do first.

Maria: You worked this out great! When we first met, your goal was to find a way to stop the fighting and to stay in school. There haven't been any fights, and you have all stayed in school. Each of you has had a part in this success.

When the time was up, the food was gone.

Readings

Barrera Jr., M., Biglan, A., Ary, D., & Li, F. (2001). Replication of a problem behavior model with American Indian, Hispanic, and Caucasian youth. *Journal of Early Adolescence, 21*(2), 133–158.

Franklin, C. G., & Soto, I. (2002). Keeping Hispanic youths in school. *Children and Schools, 24*(3), 139–143.

Malgady, R. G., & Zayas, L. H. (2001). Cultural and linguistic considerations in psychodiagnosis with Hispanics: The need for an empirically informed process model. *Social Work, 4*(1), 39–50.

Discussion Questions

1. Why was it important for Sandy to keep the school principal and others informed about her plans?

2. What are the possible advantages of having a worker from the same culture as the group members? Are there any possible disadvantages?

3. Why was structure so important in working with the group? What might have occurred if there had been less structure?

4. When members first got together in the group, what benefits were achieved by making each girl summarize what the previous speaker said? What skills was the worker trying to teach?

5. In the brainstorming session, Sandy did not let members critique ideas until everyone had finished. What were some of the reasons for this prohibition?

6. *The worker decided to use a group approach to try to resolve the problems identified in this case. Do you think working with the girls individually could have achieved the same results? Why or why not?*

7. *Why was it important to have the group members discuss and vote on the purpose of the meeting?*

8. *The worker in this case commented that she did not have control of the group membership. What are the advantages of having the ability to select group members?*

9. *What were the advantages of closing the group and not allowing any new members to enter?*

17

Deanna's Dilemma

Jannah J. Hurn Mather
Robert F. Rivas

Deanna had worked at the Empathy Drug Rehabilitation Center for about six months when she encountered her first dilemma. She was asked by her supervisor, Jean, to start a group for adolescents recently discharged from local residential drug abuse facilities. As a BSW-level social worker, Deanna had extensive experience with children and adolescents but only on an individual basis. Jean's request that she start a group would extend the frontiers of her practice, and Deanna was not sure she was ready to explore new worlds.

As she discussed the idea of the group with her supervisor, she said, "Jean, look, I'm not sure I can handle a group. I don't know how to compose or lead one. I've never done this before." Jean responded, "Deanna, there is a first time for everything, and I would really like you to try this. I will be willing to help by discussing the group with you and making suggestions." With some anxiety, Deanna launched into planning for the group.

The Planning Stage: Designing the Group

Deanna began planning by working out the purpose for the group with her supervisor. Jean explained that local adolescents recently discharged from residential drug rehabilitation programs needed additional support to abstain from further drug use. These youngsters generally had problems with self-esteem and peer pressure, resulting in drug use. Each member might benefit from forming relationships with others who shared similar concerns. Perhaps a positive peer culture could be established where members could extend understanding and support to each other. Deanna formulated a short statement of purpose and read it to Jean: "The purpose of this group is to extend mutual support and understanding to each other while we help each other abstain from drug use."

Jean noted, "That sounds great for a start. Remember that the group should have some say in what its purpose should be. The group has to have a feeling of ownership about its purpose, and to establish this you need to discuss the group's purpose during the early stages of the group."

Deanna noted, "Jean, you sound like the group itself is one of my clients."

Jean's face lit up as she enthusiastically reinforced this idea, "You must have been reading my mind; the group is actually one of your clients! In addition to the individuals in the group, you devote attention to the group as a whole,

helping the group grow and taking care of any problems that might interfere with its development. Group work is complicated because you need to keep one eye on the individual within the group and the other on the group as a whole. Of all the rules about groups, this is the prime directive." Deanna hoped all her thoughts would be so insightful as she wondered what to do about further planning.

Jean explained that there were several issues to consider when planning for a group. Assessing potential membership was a good place to start. In this case, members would be referred to the group by other organizations, so it was particularly important to establish relationships with those referral sources and explain the purpose for the group. In addition, Deanna would have to discuss and explain the proposed group to her own organization, taking care to gain organizational support for her new project. She might also need to discuss the group with members from the community to gain acceptance and community sanction for the group.

Jean also discussed how members would be recruited. By using existing referral sources, such as other rehabilitation centers, there should be an ample supply of potential members. Advertising the group by announcements on local radio and television stations was also discussed as a possibility.

Deanna realized she would need to decide what rules, if any, to follow when composing the group. She reasoned that members should have some common characteristics and needs for being in the group but should be sufficiently different and unique that they could learn new behaviors from each other. A balance of men and women would be desirable, especially so that members could explore how gender affects drug recovery. A mixed-gender group would also help create a more realistic atmosphere for members facing other issues associated with adolescence and young adulthood.

Several other planning issues faced Deanna. She decided she would like the group to be a closed one, beginning and ending with the same members rather than adding members as the group progressed. She also decided to make the group a time-limited one in which it would meet for only ten sessions. Having a closed, time-limited group would possibly help the group be more cohesive. Since the members would be young people, she felt that short meetings of about an hour and a half would be best. She planned to have refreshments during the meetings, possibly during a break in the middle of each meeting.

For Deanna to learn from her first group experience, she designed a brief evaluation plan to get feedback about how the group progressed throughout its development. She also designed a short consumer survey to be administered at the end of the last group session. She hoped the data she collected would be useful for her future group efforts.

Several teens were identified as potential members for the group.

Billie, age 14, was hospitalized for alcohol and drug abuse and discharged about three weeks ago. She had a two-year history of alcohol intoxication on an almost daily basis. Although currently not using alcohol, she admitted having difficulty reintegrating into her peer group.

Al, age 17, had a three-year history of marijuana use. During that time, he "got high" approximately three to four times a week. Although he has been "clean for three months," his parents made his continued residence at home contingent upon attending a support group for teens.

Ron, age 16, had been "getting high" since he was 10. He had been in several treatment programs in another state. He recently went to live with an aunt but was later admitted to an intensive community-based outpatient program. He stated it has been easier to stay off drugs because he did not know anybody using them.

Terry, age 16, was recently discharged from an inpatient mental health center where she received care for about six weeks. She was admitted there following an overdose of alcohol and "bennies." She now attends family therapy twice each week.

Jeff, age 16, was recently released from a detention center for car theft. He was high on crack when he was arrested. He noted that it was hard to avoid getting high in his neighborhood with all the "deals" going on.

In addition to reading the case files on each of these potential members, Deanna contacted and interviewed each of them to explain the purpose of the group, assess their motivation, and familiarize them with group procedures. Deanna also used this time to decide on their appropriateness for the group and to contract with each of them individually. Overall, she thought these members would have potential for working together, and they seemed interested in attending.

As the last part of the planning process, Deanna arranged for the room to be used for group meetings. She chose a small room with comfortable chairs, taking care to assure privacy for group members. Making financial arrangements was not quite so easy. She made a small budget request for supplies and refreshments but was told there was no budget line that would cover such a request.

Deanna found it strange that such a large agency would not have budgetary arrangements to cover her request and decided to pursue this policy issue with her supervisor.

At her next meeting with Jean, Deanna presented her work on planning for the group. Jean agreed that all seemed to be prepared for the beginning of the group, and they decided to start as soon as a meeting time could be arranged with all the members.

Deanna suggested that she keep summary recordings of each meeting, particularly focusing on group dynamics, so that she and Jean could discuss the progress of the group. Jean agreed and told her that recording some of the issues of the group would help both Deanna and Jean in their supervisory sessions. Excerpts from Deanna's summary recordings are presented next.

The Beginning Stage: Introductions and Struggles

First Session

I opened the first group session by having everyone introduce themselves. We did a short exercise called "the name game," which helped members remember each other's names. Another exercise, called "treasure hunt," helped members find out a few interesting facts about each other, and I sensed that the members became less anxious after this exercise. I made an opening statement of the purpose of the group, but this didn't seem to create much discussion. Members were cautious about sharing much about themselves at this point. I tried to tell them what my job would be as leader, and we discussed some of the beginning rules for the group. Some of the rules agreed on were: (1) everyone will be a good listener, (2) no one should talk until the other person was finished, and (3) we should all be supportive of each other and not criticize each other's behavior.

During this first session, Al had a question about confidentiality. I responded that what was discussed in the group was to remain confidential. However, I pointed out that there might be compelling circumstances that could affect whether I could maintain the confidentiality of what members said. The group seemed to accept this caveat without much discussion. We continued on with the meeting, briefly discussing how members felt about the purpose of the group, how they could work out some individual goals, and how they could help each other work on their goals. With the exercises, introductions, and discussions, the first meeting seemed to go quickly. I sensed that the members were forming as a group.

Second Session

With the success of the first meeting, I was relatively confident that the second would go well. Wrong! I'm still not sure how things got so out of hand. I should have sensed they were feeling anxious about something; they were so quiet when we started the session. I tried to think of what might be bothering them but to no avail. I realized I wasn't much of a mind reader, so I just asked them what was bothering them. The group became somewhat anxious over this question, and Billie asked me about the issue of confidentiality. It was all downhill from there! The group erupted into an argument, with several group members accusing each other of being "snitches." I tried to refocus the discussion on what I had said about confidentiality in the first session, but members seemed more interested in questioning each other's intentions about keeping information in the group confidential. I have to admit that I was feeling pretty anxious, but I allowed the group members to continue their heated discussion. I did get them to form their own rule about sharing information about the group with persons who were not members. They seemed to be reluctant to share personal information with each other, choosing instead to accuse each other of violating confidentiality by saying that "some people" were discussing the first meeting with people outside the group. I think the members are supersensitive to issues of privacy, and I will have to pay attention to this. I did get them to focus on their feelings about wanting privacy, and this seemed to calm the members down some.

The group members seemed to carry on their discussions without me. I'm not sure I should have let them, but they seemed to do well. At the end of the session, I asked them to "process the group," and they had some interesting insights about why the session was so stormy. I couldn't help feeling that little was accomplished in this session, but the members did get to know each other better.

The Working Stage: Defining and Working on Goals

Third Session

I hoped to get members to work on identifying some individual goals for themselves. Although this didn't exactly occur, we were able to identify some common themes faced by members. One of the major issues confronting all the members was concern about returning to an inpatient setting. Members felt they were always in jeopardy of being readmitted to a residential program, and they expressed real fear about making a mistake that would result in a readmission.

We were able to identify some ways they could talk to their parents about this fear, and Ron role-played telling his mother about his fear of returning to residential treatment. Billie did a nice job of playing his mother, and I think the group learned about themselves from participating in the role-play. Members of the group continued to discuss their "fears" regarding returning to an inpatient setting. I tried to redirect the group discussion to deciding

on additional rules for the group. I asked them to restate the group's purpose, but only Jeff remembered (thank goodness). He said members should be giving support and understanding to each other and helping each other stay off drugs. Most members questioned whether the group was actually doing this. They seemed to look to me as if to say, "Why don't you do something to keep us to our agreement?" And they became silent during the rest of the group meeting.

Following the session, I felt pretty responsible for some of the disorganization in the group. I wondered if I should have been a more autocratic leader or should have continued to let the group go where it wanted to go. I do think the group left today with a sense of its purpose, although I don't think members felt the group was very effective.

Fourth Session

Once again, the members raised the issue of confidentiality. I thought we had agreed on what this meant. But the group members seemed to be in the mood for a fight, and they chose this issue as a weapon. Several members started accusing each other of breaking the rule of confidentiality. Chaos broke out in the group, and all I could do was sit there and think, "Beam me up, Scotty!" I could really use some help here; I'm not sure what is going on with this group. I guess I will have to do a more in-depth assessment of group dynamics. In addition, I'll have to do another assessment of the individual personalities in the group.

Fifth Session

I started out today's session with three questions. The members seemed to be very interested in all of them, and we had a lively discussion. The three questions were:

1. What is our policy on confidentiality, and why do we have it?
2. What are the limits of confidentiality in the group, and what "compelling reasons" would anyone have for reporting what went on in the group to other people?
3. How could I, as a leader, have better handled the confidentiality issue?

We talked about each of these questions, mostly in generalities. I couldn't seem to get the members to self-disclose their feelings about confidentiality, but I sensed that they were struggling with what rules were important to them as a group.

Finally, Jeff disclosed that he was uncomfortable about what I would share with his parents. He asked whether I would tell them anything if he disclosed in the group that he was having problems keeping clean. I guess all the members were wondering the same thing, since there was a major silence in the group after Jeff asked me his question. I did the best I could to tell Jeff and the other members about what I considered the limits of confidentiality and my responsibility as a social worker. Briefly stated, I said I would feel compelled to discuss their situation with someone if I felt their actions, especially drug use, would pose a threat to their own or someone else's safety. Other than that, what was said in the group would remain in the group. This seemed to be agreeable to the members. Their body language seemed to indicate that they were somewhat relieved to finally understand this.

Sixth Session

I opened the session by acknowledging the members' concerns about rules. I directed the discussion by asking each member of the group to discuss his or her feelings about the rules of the group. I structured this exchange by writing all these comments on a flip chart and identifying the differences between their concerns over rules and their feeling of anger at being placed in residential treatment. I remember one exchange we had that seemed particularly meaningful.

Deanna: There are many things we fear in our lives, and we talked about some of those fears last week. However, I think it is important that we begin to discuss any fears you have in terms of the rules of the group. Who would like to start?

Jeff: Why do we have to have rules?

Ron: Yeah, why? Can't we do our own thing in here?

Al: Because we have to be patrolled and controlled. So we have to have rules. Right?

Billie: I think it's important to have some rules, or some of us won't always get to talk.

Ron: Well, I still don't want what I say in the group to be repeated to other people outside the group.

Deanna: So maybe the feeling of being controlled by rules comes from a fear of being put back into a residential treatment center. Maybe this has something to do with being fearful of trusting one another. What about for you, Billie?

Billie: I just want to stay out of trouble. Rules don't bother me, and I'm not worried about what's said because I don't plan to be getting in any trouble. Maybe that's what's really wrong. People are planning to do something, and they're worried about others finding out.

Terry: Even if I did do something, I wouldn't tell. I'm too nervous about it.

Deanna: So perhaps another fear has to do with whether members can stay straight, and if not, will someone put you back in the hospital or treatment center.

Jeff: The hospital is crazy. There's no way I'm going back there.

Deanna: That's why we are meeting as a group, helping each other to stay out of the hospital or residential treatment center. Maybe we need to give and get support in

the struggle to be clean. Let's discuss how each of you might use the group to do that.

The members discussed their struggles about remaining drug-free. Ron noted that he felt like everyone was watching him and waiting for him to break the rules his parents had given him. Several of the members seemed to agree with this, and a lively discussion took place about how they could "prove themselves" to their parents, relatives, and teachers. There were some good discussions by individual members today. Each member formulated two goals: to find new ways to stay drug-free and to talk to their parents and teachers about their progress. Overall, members seemed to support each other, and it was nice to see the group agree on something for a change. Most of the members thought this was a good session. We agreed that we should continue discussing this theme for the next few sessions and work on individual goals. I felt we had finally reached an understanding of our purpose and that members, not just me, "owned it."

Seventh Session

The group members began to focus on how they might use the group time to support their issues. Discussion of this issue took up most of the group session, and the rules of the group were again discussed. Each member reported on how he or she was doing and how they had tried to talk with their parents and teachers about their concerns. I felt good about the fact that all of the members seemed to take their individual goals and tasks seriously.

Most of them reported some positive reactions from their parents, and this seemed to diminish their fears about being readmitted to a hospital or residential treatment center. Most of the members said they felt they had some power over their own lives when they got positive responses from their parents. This was not the case for Jeff, who said his parents thought he was "high" when he started talking to them. Other members made some good suggestions to Jeff about how to convince his parents he was sincere, and Ron and Billie even offered to talk to his parents about Jeff's efforts in the group. Jeff agreed to give it another try and to call Ron and Billie if he couldn't convince his parents of his sincerity.

It felt good to see individual members reaching out to each other. The group mood seemed to be one of "mutual aid," and it seemed that members were taking more responsibility for the group. I didn't have to direct the conversation today as much as usual. I actually felt more like a member than a leader. I wonder if this is OK?

Eighth Session

This was another good meeting. Members again discussed their efforts to stay drug-free. Terry reported that she was asked to speak about teens and drug use for a school assembly program. She was a bit reluctant to do so and asked the other group members for advice. Members made several suggestions, and they helped convince Terry that she had the ability to contribute to this important program. Members also helped Terry organize her thoughts about the proposed presentation.

I thought the whole group actually learned a lot from this activity, and I kept busy helping members generalize the issues they brought up to their own lives. It seems like the group is making some good progress on individual as well as group goals.

The Ending Stage: Ending and Evaluating

Ninth Session

With only two sessions left, I thought it would be a good time to bring up the ending of the group. Since we had contracted for only ten sessions and since the end was near, I hoped we could use our time productively if we kept sight of our scheduled ending. Wrong again!

When I opened the group by bringing up ending and terminating, the group again lapsed into silence. I thought to myself, "Am I in some alternate universe here, or is the group just ignoring me?" The group then proceeded to pick up on how Terry's presentation went. After learning that Terry had been wildly successful, the group went on to discuss how hard it was for them to stay drug-free.

Although I thought this was a great discussion, it seemed to me that members were ignoring my initial comments about ending the group. In fact, they busied themselves making plans for future presentations at their own schools, asking Terry for suggestions and encouragement. I had to intervene just before our time was up because the group seemed to be denying that the group was scheduled to end after only one more session. Ron said he was not ready to leave the group and was afraid that if the group ended he would probably go back to using drugs. Jeff echoed this sentiment, reminding me that there were lots of kids at his school who sold drugs, and he was again being approached by some of them.

Although it compromised my original plan, I explored these feelings with Ron and Jeff, as well as with other group members. I again pointed out the plan for ending after the tenth session and asked if members weren't ignoring my opening statement. This resulted in some good discussions about members' fears about "going it alone." Several members asked if we could extend the life of the group so that they could continue to support each other in a formal way. I agreed that during the next session we would conduct a formal evaluation of the group to see what progress we had made and plan from there. I asked each member to write a few paragraphs about the strengths and weaknesses of the group experience and to bring these in for our next session.

Tenth Session

All the members had done their "homework," and we had a good discussion of the strengths and weaknesses of the overall group experience. I also had a chance to administer my "homemade" evaluation questionnaire (thank goodness for my social work research instructor). Members generally felt the group was a very positive experience and asked me to approach my supervisor about continuing the group for an indefinite period of time. I was a little reluctant to promise that this could be done since our contract called for this session to be our last. I agreed to talk to my supervisor and get back to them.

Supervision: Deanna and Jean

Deanna and her supervisor met regularly to review her summary recordings of each meeting. Deanna used these sessions to learn about the group processes and dynamics and to get ideas from Jean about how to practice her leadership skills. Jean was quite supportive of her efforts, pointing out how she had struggled along the way to understand the normal stages of development for this type of group and how she had allowed the group to determine its own direction as it moved through the forming, storming, norming, and performing stages.

Deanna pointed out that her evaluation efforts produced data suggesting the group was accomplishing its purpose and meeting the individual goals of the members. She shared that she felt the group was finally becoming a cohesive unit and that in a number of instances members were able to provide mutual aid to each other.

Finally, Deanna brought up the issue of continuing the group. Although Jean was skeptical at first, it was decided that it might be possible to extend the group if members were committed to working together on new individual and group goals. Deanna added that she felt this was the case and asked permission to make the group contract an open-ended one. Jean responded, "Make it so!"

Readings

Etheridge, R. M., Smith, J. C., Rounds-Bryant, J. L., & Hubbard, R. L. (2001). Drug abuse treatment and comprehensive services for adolescents. *Journal of Adolescent Research, 16*(6), 563–590.

Molidor, C. E., Nissen, L. B., & Watkins, T. R. (2002). The development of theory and treatment with substance abusing female juvenile offenders. *Child & Adolescent Social Work Journal, 19*(3), 209–226.

Muck, R., Zempolich, K. A., Titus, J. C., Fishman, M., Godley, M. D., & Schwebel, R. (2001). An overview of the effectiveness of adolescent substance abuse treatment models. *Youth & Society, 33*(2), 143–169.

Discussion Questions

1. *How did the purpose of the group evolve throughout the stages of the group intervention?*

2. *What might some additional individual goals be for each member?*

3. *What planning issues did the worker face? What other planning issues might have been considered?*

4. *What specific rules would you propose for this type of group? How do rules or norms develop over the stages of group development?*

5. *What issue seemed to be of primary concern to the group as a whole? How did the worker deal with this issue? How would you have dealt with this issue?*

6. *How did this case illustrate the normal stages of group development? What group and individual behaviors are typical of each stage?*

7. *How would you develop an evaluation design and instruments to monitor the progress of individuals in the group and evaluate the success of the group as a whole?*

8. *What are some of the issues of adolescence and adulthood the group members might face that could be better dealt with in a coeducational group?*

9. *What are the advantages and disadvantages of having a "closed" group rather than an "open group"?*

18

Ari and Simone: Notes from the Group

James X. Bembry

Betsy S. Vourlekis

Ari and Simone became co-leaders for a group of 15 at-risk sixth-grade students enrolled in a community service program through their junior high school. The community service program was sponsored by the Woodville City School System but administered by the Bethel County Family Service Agency, the employing organization for Ari and Simone.

The community service program identified potential students in the beginning of sixth grade, asking for referrals from the guidance department and the administrators of the Woodville School System. The purpose of the program was to foster students' self-esteem as well as their personal and social responsibility through doing voluntary work with the elderly. Student volunteers play important roles with the elderly, visiting them weekly at the Red Rock Nursing Home in Woodville and providing conversation and activities to people who are limited in their abilities to have outside contacts. The program runs throughout the school year, and students are encouraged to stay in the program through the eighth grade.

Together with their 15 students, Ari and Simone plan as a group. They discuss expectations for each visit and plan activities for each week, some involving one-to-one interactions between the student and the nursing home resident and others involving the students and residents together in a large group. Ari and Simone accompany the students to and from the nursing home and monitor the group and individual interactions, providing on-the-spot help during the students' time in the nursing home. A key element of the program is the "reflection session," which takes place every third week. For the reflective session, students remain at school, meet as a group, and discuss the experiences they are having together.

Ari and Simone's group work actually involved three levels of intervention.

1. Conducting the reflection sessions every three weeks and helping group members reach their individual goals.
2. Helping the group engage in task planning for the students' visits and aiding the development of the group as a whole.
3. Mediating the interaction between students and residents and facilitating the interaction of the group with the larger social environment of the nursing home.

In essence, Ari and Simone have three client systems for which they are responsible: the individual, the group as a whole, and the group's environment. In the following pages, we will follow the work of Ari and Simone by reviewing their summary recordings of some of the group sessions.

Engagement

During this stage of the group's development, Ari and Simone are challenged to open up the boundary of interaction between themselves and the other group members. At the same time, they remain aware of the students' needs to eventually engage positively with the nursing home residents. Their structured approach to engagement is accomplished over the first two meetings of the group.

First Meeting

At the beginning of the first group session, we entered the classroom where the students were gathered by their teachers. Although we had individually interviewed each of the students, it seemed we didn't really know them when we walked into the room. They were so quiet, and they seemed to look at us with some degree of suspicion. We introduced ourselves again and reviewed the overall purpose of the program. There were no questions, and there seemed to be little reaction from any of the group members. We were pretty worried by that time, wondering if a nonverbal group would be waiting for us at each of our sessions together.

Things seemed to liven up when we dumped the contents of our paper bags on the table in the front of the room. We brought masking tape, rope, Vaseline, glasses, cotton, and a few other things. We asked for volunteers to try an exercise, and to our surprise, several members volunteered. We explained that we wanted to simulate how people they would be working with might experience their disabilities, and this seemed to pique the members' interest. They allowed us to bind them, somewhat, to their chairs. Tape was placed over the mouths of some to simulate an inability to talk. Others had thick wads of cotton placed over their ears to simulate hearing impairment. For others, we gave eye glasses smeared with Vaseline to simulate failing sight. We watched for signs of uneasiness or discomfort and would not have forced participation by any group member who had directly or indirectly expressed an unwillingness to participate.

After all the members were assigned their "disabilities," we asked them to walk around and talk to each other. This produced some interesting reactions, and we were later able to focus our discussion on the meaning of disabilities and their fears associated with visiting a nursing home. Members noted that people with disabilities might experience a loss of freedom, especially living in a restricted setting. We ended the session by asking which students would like to make the lives of the nursing home residents a little happier by visiting them on a weekly basis. All seemed to be interested.

In planning this strategy, Ari and Simone considered the age of the participants and decided on an action-oriented experiential approach rather than formal discussion. They reasoned that an experiential approach would be effective in getting the group's attention (starting where the client is) and would make it easier for the members to recognize and talk about their feelings and concerns. The laughter, animated discussion, and unanimous agreement to participate confirmed that this tactic worked.

The second session continues the engagement process. Although the first session was successful, and obviously a lot of fun for everyone involved, Ari and Simone were acutely aware that the students were about to embark on a serious endeavor requiring them to interact in a new social environment. With this in mind, they decided that the second session would focus on the rights, rules, and responsibilities of participating in the program. They also attempted to structure this session in a way that would be appealing to sixth-grade youngsters, emphasizing concrete evidence of their program participation and special identity as group members. Over the course of the second session, students were given nametags, a journal they would be allowed to personalize with their own decorations, a T-shirt, and a contract.

Second Meeting

We began the session by passing out nametags and T-shirts with our program logo. We also handed out blank journals to members, noting that we would be asking them to keep track of their thoughts and feelings during their experiences in the program. We spent some time allowing members to decorate the covers of their journals, and this seemed to warm up the group.

After this activity, we asked the members to have a discussion on the rights and responsibilities involved in being enrolled in the program. We considered this to be the first substantial discussion of our "group contract" for the members. We also outlined what we thought our job responsibilities would be with the group. After discussing this for a while, we asked for feedback. There wasn't much in the way of objections, so we had a brief discussion of the

nursing home and its rules and regulations, following up with more discussion of our "contract."

Once again, we tried to open up some avenues of communication. It seemed to us that the members learned best from the concrete emphasis on the mutual expectations we provided. We also tried to introduce the reality of what they would be facing when they entered the nursing home for the first time. It seems like the group came together for a while, especially when we handed out the T-shirts and let them decorate their journals.

After answering a few more questions, we emphasized that all the members would be expected to live up to the contract and that they would be responsible for evaluating the group experience twice each semester. We ended the session by asking members to make entries in their journals. Since we were to begin our visits to the nursing home the next week, we asked members to write about their expectations of their first visit.

Third Meeting

The big day finally arrived, and students seemed ready to make their first visit to the residents of the Red Rock Nursing Home. The group members were very rambunctious on the bus ride to the nursing home, and we constantly had to ask them to remain in their seats. When we arrived at Red Rock, their behavior changed dramatically. Members were greeted by staff and given a tour of the facility. They were encouraged to ask questions and, finally, were introduced to some of the residents. The students toured the facility in an orderly manner and asked many appropriate questions of the staff. They were obviously nervous when they were introduced to the residents. Many students lingered in the background, seemingly afraid to come forward and introduce themselves. Eventually, group members warmed up to the residents and spent about a half hour talking and exchanging information. Afterward, some members asked if they could take the residents back to their rooms. A larger group of students wanted to visit the nursing home gift shop before leaving.

On the ride back to school, we attempted to talk about the visit. However, the members once again engaged in a good deal of inappropriate behavior, making any discussion of the visit impossible.

Assessment

Over the next several sessions, Ari and Simone engaged in the formal assessment of individual behaviors and group processes. They drew on their observations of and experiences with the members, attempting to assess individual member needs and the overall needs of the group as a whole. Their assessment also took into account the environments in which the group operates, both at school and at the nursing home.

The conclusions drawn from their initial assessment guided them in planning and carrying out intervention strategies on several levels, including determining the theme for the group's first group reflection session. In addition, their assessment of the age and attention span of the members suggested that interventions should be structured around activities rather than around formal, lengthy discussions. Assessment of the group as a whole was more difficult, since the group operated in two distinct environments (school and nursing home) and since the group seemed to be in its beginning, forming stage.

Intervention: The Reflection Session and Visits

As part of the program design, a reflection session takes place about once each month. The purposes of the reflection sessions are twofold. The first purpose is to reinforce the positive experiences of members in the program and to process problems in individual and group functioning. To accomplish this, reinforcement sessions are used to teach students to identify and express their feelings in a supportive fashion. The second purpose is to build social skills (that is, critical thinking, communication, problem-solving, self-esteem, and so forth). Using the experiences at the service site, individual and group accomplishments are stressed, and social skill development is noted and reinforced.

Fourth Meeting

This meeting was to be our first real reflection session. We decided to keep to our original idea of designing the group sessions around activities and other action-oriented interventions. We prepared some role-play situations we thought would simulate possible situations the members might encounter at the nursing home. We hoped members would consider these situations and practice appropriate responses. Wrong! The session did not go as well as we had hoped. Members had a difficult time taking the role-play situations seriously, and they engaged in a lot of disruptive behavior. It got so bad, and the members got so out of control, that we decided to end the session a little early.

We debated afterward, wondering if we should cancel the next visit to the nursing home until the group got itself together. We had a bit of a disagreement about what to do. We consulted the literature on groups and started to recognize that, in addition to having members with individual behavior problems, the group was also moving out of its "honeymoon" period and beginning to deal with issues of dominance, power, and control. We discovered that this "storming" period is typical of most groups, particularly groups for adolescents.

We decided that it was important for the members not to feel that they had failed so early in the program. This seemed particularly crucial since the members had a history of failing, at least in the school setting. We decided that before they boarded the bus for the next nursing home visit, we would remind the members of the group contract and hope for the best.

Fifth Meeting

We reminded the members about the group contract and the responsibilities they had accepted when they entered the group. The bus ride was again noisy, but as the members entered the nursing home their behavior became more acceptable.

Recognizing that both the students and the residents needed help and structure to ease their awkwardness and discomfort, we prepared two activities for this visit. The first involved mixing the residents and group members on teams to play balloon volleyball. Before the activity, we reminded the students to be gentle with the more fragile clients and to make sure everyone was involved in the game. The group members did such a great job that before long they attracted an audience of staff members and visitors who cheered for their favorite teams.

In the next activity, the students played a "name game," where each person introduced himself or herself and invented a nickname that rhymed with each individual's name. The activity was very successful, and everyone had a good time.

The bus ride home was again boisterous, but we noticed that the discussions were focused on what took place at the nursing home and not on the usual name calling and roughhousing.

Sixth Meeting

We prepared an activity for this session that required each student to pair off with a resident. It took some prodding to get some of the students to pair off individually, but eventually each of the students found an elderly partner and participated in the activity. Overall, it was a good day at the nursing home.

Unfortunately, the bus ride back to school turned into a fiasco. David and Stephen, who had been vying for leadership of the group, had a fight, and we had to break it up. This seemed to create a form of group contagion, and as we separated the combatants Graham and Neil also exchanged heated words. Other members started acting out, at least verbally. It was a bit like putting out a series of small fires—as one was taken care of, another popped up. There was little opportunity to process this event once we returned to school. The principal had learned of the physical altercation on the bus, and she informed us that she would "handle it."

Reassessment: Using Supervision

Ari and Simone met with their supervisor, Janice, to get some guidance on how to assess the group's functioning.

They explained that the group had been on a roller coaster ride, sometimes functioning at a high level at the nursing home and at other times plunging into disorganization at school and on the bus. They noted some consistent patterns of how members communicated and interacted with each other. They also discussed issues of social control within the group, assessing roles, power, status, and leadership within the group. On a particularly positive note, they suggested that, despite the recent bus episode, the group seemed cohesive and seemed to have developed a strong group culture of helping others. Ari and Simone noted some consistent patterns in the way the students related to one another.

On the negative side of their assessment, they described the group's communication pattern as each person attempting to talk louder than the next, with members displaying disrespect for each other and engaging in constant name calling. They felt this pattern led to the altercation after the last session.

Ironically, the members' behavior was quite different in the nursing home. Ari explained that the environment of the nursing home seemed to have a calming effect on the group. The members were respectful, gentle, and sensitive to the cues given to them by the elderly residents. Janice sensed their frustration and attempted to help them understand that for this group's short time together, it was quite an accomplishment for the members to have performed so well at the nursing home. She reminded them of an article she had asked them to read when they were planning the group. According to the author, "unpredictability is the rule" when working with a group of adolescents. Janice helped Ari and Simone review the developmental stages adolescents undergo and reminded them that for these members, swings in group behavior are closer to normal than abnormal. However, Janice was quick to point out that the group's behavior with each other outside the nursing home was inappropriate.

Ari and Simone agreed that the root of the problem the members had with one another seemed to be their inability to communicate appropriately. Based on this assessment, Janice suggested that the next reflection session might focus on beginning to solve this problem.

Intervention: Advocating for the Group

Several days before the reflection session was to take place, Mrs. Miller, the principal of Woodstock school, telephoned Simone to inform her that because of their fighting she had decided to expel David and Stephen from the group. Simone asked Mrs. Miller if she had informed the boys of this decision, and the principal indicated that Simone was the first person she had notified. Simone requested that she not take any action until she and Ari could discuss this with her, and Mrs. Miller agreed.

Ari and Simone met with Mrs. Miller to discuss the situation and advocate for the group. They were upset that Mrs. Miller would make a unilateral decision about the group, and they felt the group should be involved in any decision to remove members. During the meeting, they were careful to express understanding of the principal's ultimate authority, and they attended to her needs to maintain order. After some negotiation, they convinced her that it was important to the development of the group that, whenever possible, group members participate in decisions affecting them. Mrs. Miller agreed to allow Stephen and David to remain in the group for the time being.

Intervention: Reflective Role Reversal

Ari and Simone thought about how to set the right tone for the upcoming reflection session. Without overemphasizing the negative behavior, they wanted to get the group's attention and suggest that their bus behavior was inappropriate. They felt it was important for the members to recognize the destructive group process that had developed and begin to do some problem-solving. They also wanted the group to recognize that they had done an excellent job at the nursing home. They decided to maintain an activity orientation to their intervention sessions.

Seventh Meeting

As an intervention strategy, we created a role-play in which we would act out the members' behavior, both on the bus and in the nursing home. As the students entered the room for the session, they found us standing in the middle of the room with a sign that read "school bus." Ari painted it a nice yellow and black, so there would be no mistake about the environment we wanted to simulate. Once the students were seated, we began calling each other names and otherwise mimicking the behavior we had seen from members when they were on the bus. The members were momentarily confused but soon started laughing and taking sides in the staged disagreement. Just as abruptly, we stopped arguing and picked up another sign reading "nursing home." We began to talk softly and act out the students' positive behavior at the nursing home. After a few minutes, we stopped and let our actions speak louder than words.

After a short silence (which seemed to last forever), we began a discussion of what the members had seen in our acting efforts. Members noted the differences exhibited in the two scenarios, and several admitted that their behavior toward one another was inappropriate. We emphasized that their behavior in the nursing home was evidence that they were capable of acting differently. We helped the group begin problem-solving, and they identified respect as an important factor in how they wanted to be treated by each other. They decided that treating each other with respect should be incorporated into the rules for the group, and we asked each member to write this in their group contract. We also asked them to write about our role-plays in their journals.

Although we have a feeling that this was a powerful session for the members, we recognize it will not end all the inappropriate behavior displayed in the group. Nevertheless, we are satisfied that we are making progress and that the group is developing a more positive culture of mutual aid.

Ari and Simone continued to meet with the group throughout the school year, sometimes at school for reflection sessions and other times at the nursing home. They observed the group becoming more cohesive and cooperative over time. The group progressed from its "storming" stage through the stages of "norming" and "performing." Several of the members seemed to learn new ways of communicating, both with each other and with older adults. Ari and Simone received several reports from teachers, who generally remarked that the group members seemed to have matured as a result of their experiences in the nursing home.

Termination and Evaluation

At a reflection session toward the end of the school year, a group member remarked that when the group returned to the nursing home in September some of the residents might not be there. Simone asked what she meant, and the member replied, "You know, they might move or something, or maybe they might go back home." Ari and Simone had anticipated that the group might have concerns about leaving the nursing home. They had planned to use the next-to-last reflection session to discuss this. Also, although it was not addressed directly, they believed some group members feared that residents to whom they had become attached might die before they saw them again.

Simone decided to raise these issues for discussion. The students expressed a wide range of feelings related to ending for summer vacation. Ari and Simone encouraged them to express their fear of residents dying, since this was a possibility. The group requested that Ari and Simone maintain contact with the nursing home and notify group members if any of the residents did pass away. Ari and Simone agreed that they would be responsible for sending notices to group members.

Ari and Simone used the last reflection session to summarize what had taken place over the year and to celebrate their experiences together. At this last meeting, students were presented with certificates of achievement and small gifts made by the residents of the nursing home.

They asked students to write a journal entry about what they had learned from the group, and students volunteered to read their journal entries. Ari and Simone also sent a short questionnaire with a series of open-ended questions to each of the members' teachers. In this survey, they asked for feedback about changes in behavior and any feedback they had heard about the community service project. Generally, teachers were most positive. Even Mrs. Miller, the principal, seemed quite positive about the group, noting that David, Stephen, Graham, and Neil seemed to have potential for getting along together again. Perhaps the best evaluation of the program came from one of the members, who commented that she couldn't wait for summer to be over so she could "come back to Woodville."

Readings

Kinnevy, S. C., & Healey, B. P. (1999). Bicycle-WORKS: Task-centered group work with high-risk youth. *Social Work with Groups, 22*(1), 33–49.

Lomonaco, S., Scheidlinger, S., & Aronson, S. (2000). Five decades of children's group treatment—an overview. *Journal of Child and Adolescent Group Therapy, 10*(2), 77–96.

Rhodes, J. E., Bogat, G. A., Roffman, J., Edelman, P., & Galasso, L. (2002). Youth mentoring in perspective: Introduction to the Special Issue. *American Journal of Community Psychology, 30*(2), 149–154.

Discussion Questions

1. Ari and Simone chose an activity designed to simulate living with a disability. What purposes did this activity serve?

2. How did Ari and Simone intervene to build the culture of the group?

3. How did Ari and Simone help the students recognize their strengths?

4. The two workers were required to mediate between the school and the group to prevent expulsion of two group members. What skills were important in this process?

5. What purpose was served by the group members interacting with the nursing home residents?

6. *Why did the workers give the group members nametags and T-shirts with the program logo on them?*

7. *Based on the workers' experiences in this case, what might you expect to occur during the "storming" period of a group's development?*

8. *What is the purpose of having a group contract?*

9. *Had the workers allowed the principal to kick two members out of the group, what do you think the reaction of the other members might have been? Give your reasons.*

III

Macro Practice: Communities and Organizations

Generalist practitioners work in larger systems such as neighborhoods or communities, institutions, organizations, and society as a whole. Social workers often intervene by working with individuals and small task groups to promote changes that have small, moderate, or far-reaching effects. Whether seeking small changes in organizational policy or larger changes to promote social and economic justice, the generalist needs to know how these systems operate as well as how individuals behave in each system. The cases presented in this section demonstrate some of these dynamics.

The first case in this section, *Project Homeless*, was written by Gloria Alexander. It is the account of a community task force designed to study and work with the community problem of homelessness. This community change effort focuses on research and assessment of need, work with task groups, and community planning for services. It stresses the importance of diversity of representation in social action strategies. JoAnn Ray contributes a wonderful example of how research skills can be important when effecting change at a macro level in *Transitional Homes for Young Street Mothers*. In this case, the worker carries out exploratory and needs assessment research to inform her change efforts. Her research helps the community respond to the needs of this population at risk and demonstrates case-to-cause advocacy and program planning.

Grafton H. Hull, Jr., provides an excellent example of how workers can effect small but important changes in organizational policy in his case, *The Appointment Letters*. The scene is set for a clash of values between the chief executive of the organization, who wants to save money at the expense of client privacy, confidentiality, and self-determination, and the workers who hold their clients' interests above those of the organization. Readers will learn how ethical issues can be difficult to manage in an organizational climate that has other priorities. In *The Evergreen Boys Ranch: A Story about Jack and Diane*, Robert E. Rivas documents the efforts of two BSW social workers who use group work and advocacy skills to effect major changes in a dysfunctional agency. Again, major ethical issues present themselves in this case, and there are no easy solutions. The case stresses planning and intervention at a large system level, issues of diversity, and the vulnerability of workers who seek to find social justice for clients who are victims of unethical organizational policies and practices. Dennis Eikenberry revisits this theme in *The Willow River Developmental Disabilities Center*, but in a different way. The case documents how a worker sought to achieve social justice for consumers of service in a center for the disabled by using the legal system, group grievance, and state regulatory agencies to assure appropriateness of services for the population.

In *Managing Margaret's Care*, Kimberly Strom-Gottfried provides a unique case that involves a single woman struggling with managed health care. It underscores the challenges facing everyone who deals with the new emphasis on managed care systems, while providing some insights useful for social workers dealing in this arena. In *From Case to Cause: My Name Is Jess Overton*, Donna McIntosh traces the story of a woman who moves from being a survivor of domestic violence to a legislative advocate. It is an excellent example of how effective social work practice can include empowering consumers of service to enter the policy practice arena.

Terry L. Singer provides a global perspective to oppression and refugee resettlement in his case *Community Work with Refugees*. Here we follow a social worker who employs multilevel systems skills in working for social justice. Carla Sofka also provides insight into multilevel system work with a community response team dealing with a personal and community tragedy. Her case, *When Life Changes in an Instant*, reminds us of how persons at all system levels can both experience and respond to trauma and life-altering events that occur in our communities.

Each of the cases contained here not only has implications for generalist intervention but also has applicability to policy practice and other large system efforts important to social workers. They suggest that the role of the social worker is unique among the helping professions, maintaining both a case and a cause focus.

19

Project Homeless

Gloria Alexander

Presenting Problem

Homelessness existed in Mapletown, a rural town in northern New England. But unlike urban areas where homeless people were visible, the homeless in Mapletown were invisible. They moved in with relatives and friends for short-term stays until they could find more permanent living arrangements. Their situation was further complicated by a fear of disrupting their "hosts'" rental arrangements with landlords, who would not be happy about additional tenants in their rental units and houses. This situation resulted in homeless families "hiding out" for fear of landlord reprisals. Under these conditions, homeless families experienced a high degree of stress, financial strain, and disorganization.

These and other dynamics were discovered by students in a social work program at Wilton College, a private, liberal arts college located in Mapletown. Students studied the nature and extent of homelessness as part of a course titled "Project Homeless." The course involved a research component, which included data collection and assessment, and a practicum opportunity to raise community consciousness about homelessness and to advocate for development of services to homeless families.

In response to students' interest in having a positive impact on this difficult social problem, Dr. Amanda Worthington, the course instructor, and Ms. Claire Delune, a social worker from United Services, helped students establish a community coalition to address the need for services in the county. Several community agencies were interested in the homeless population, and many were already delivering some services to homeless families, albeit in a temporary and fragmented fashion. A community coalition would be an ideal way to bring these and other interested parties together to share information and perhaps to share resources.

The Planning Stage

Amanda and Claire began the planning process for developing a coalition on homelessness by acquainting students with some key people in the community who might be interested in the problem of homelessness. After identifying possible coalition members, students discussed the possible beginning purpose of such a group. It was pointed out that the actual purpose of such a task force would eventually emerge as a product of the group itself. However, to give the group an initial direction, a beginning

purpose was assigned. The students considered these initial goals for the coalition:

- to increase community awareness and acceptance of the problem of homelessness,
- to consider the need for emergency shelter space for homeless people,
- to explore the long-term need for transitional and low-priced housing arrangements for homeless families, and
- to facilitate coordination of existing services for homeless people.

Many other planning issues were discussed, including the size of the potential group and its composition, meeting place and time, and physical facilities needed. In addition, the students explored grants and sources of financial support to provide emergency and transitional housing. The need for operating funds was also discussed, and fund-raising possibilities were brainstormed. Finally, students discussed who or what particular agency should take the leadership role or help "staff" the group.

Engagement: Planning and Beginning the Group

Claire was asked to be the initial facilitator of the coalition. She staffed the group by providing her agency's resources to contact other interested people in the community who might attend an information-sharing meeting. Her agency also volunteered the use of its community meeting room for the group meetings. Since the mission of the United Services agency was to address current community problems, the agency felt the proposed group would be most appropriate for its sponsorship.

Engagement and Planning Issues

The First Meeting
Claire opened the first meeting by asking the participants to introduce themselves and tell the name of their organization. Several people represented organizations in the community, some came as concerned citizens, and Dr. Worthington and several students introduced themselves and shared information. The following people were sent as official representatives of their agencies:

Clement Wilcox, Manager, Mapletown Housing Authority
Jane Grant, Director, Department of Social Welfare

Brenda Long, Director, American Red Cross

Angus Kennedy, Director, Public Relations, Mapletown Hospital

John Allen, Staff, Community Development Program

Joy Williams, Director, Health Department

Alice MacDonald, Pastor, Mapletown Methodist Church

Roger Thompson, Regional Coordinator for Human Services in the Public and Private Sectors

Vivian Brown, Director, Center for Victims of Family Violence

The meeting began with the attendees discussing the purpose of the group and the problem of homelessness in the community. Claire began the meeting.

Claire: I'd like to thank you all for coming here today. It is wonderful to see so much interest in homelessness in our town. This meeting is a result of a research project done by social work students at Wilton College under the leadership of Dr. Amanda Worthington. You will find copies of the research project on the table. If you have any questions, please address them to Dr. Worthington and the students.

Clement: I will read this report after the meeting and contact Dr. Worthington if I have any questions. (Other participants took copies of the report and reviewed them.)

Claire: That sounds like a good idea; it will save us time to get organized. Now we should begin to discuss the purpose of this meeting.

Angus: I would like to know how many homeless people there are in Mapletown?

Claire: This is an important question. According to the research done by the students, 789 people were identified as not having a permanent home.

Roger: If this is the case, why are there so few people living on the street?

Amanda: The research shows that the majority of homeless people in Mapletown are from our area and are not able to find affordable housing. This forces them to have short-term stays with family and friends.

Joy: This is often the situation for single teenage mothers and their children who come for help at the Health Department.

John: We have seen an increase in the number of families who come to our agency for help with housing.

Angus: What are some of the reasons a greater number of families are seeking help with housing?

John: From my experience, two of the major reasons are lack of affordable housing and high unemployment.

Brenda: I would like us to consider the possibility of a transitional housing arrangement for homeless people.

John: Our agency has transitional housing for residents in nearby Brantly.

Claire: It might be helpful if you would share information about the transitional housing, perhaps at a future meeting.

John: I'd be happy to do that.

Jane: I believe we also need to consider provision of an emergency shelter. When transients come to our agency, we often send them to a motel to stay overnight because we do not have an emergency shelter.

Alice: I believe we need to increase community awareness about the extent of homelessness in Mapletown and promote coordination of services for homeless people.

Claire: Let me try to summarize for a moment. We have identified several issues that could be part of our purpose as a coalition. They are: increase community awareness, explore emergency shelter and transitional housing, and coordinate existing services for homeless people. Does that about summarize it? (The group agrees.)

Participants had an opportunity to get acquainted and learn that a sizable number of people in Mapletown were without a permanent home. Members also learned there was a need for affordable housing and discussed ways it could be provided through emergency and transitional housing. Participants also had an opportunity to express their interest in forming a coalition, developing a purpose, planning for future meetings, and continuing the students' research by forming a research subcommittee.

Claire felt it was important to involve group members in the planning and work of the group as early as possible. This would help their feeling of group ownership and develop their commitment to its goals. For example, John Allen, the worker from the Community Development Program, was asked to share information on existing transitional housing at a future meeting. Others were asked to serve on a subcommittee. In addition, research information was made available to all members, allowing them to be more informed about the problem of homelessness and serving to disseminate and promote utilization of the students' research findings. These beginning actions began the process of building group cohesion.

Data Collection: The Subcommittee Meeting

The research subcommittee of the coalition consisted of Angus Kennedy (hospital), Alice MacDonald (minister), Dr. Worthington (college), and two social work students, Andrew James and Nancy Bright. The two students had participated in the original research done by their class, and this assisted the subcommittee in reviewing the research findings.

The purpose of the research subcommittee was to more fully assess the problem of homelessness in Mapletown. Students began by reviewing the professional literature on homelessness, including information from the National Coalition on Homelessness, studies on homelessness in Ohio and New York State, and several local newspaper articles. Two people who ran a day program for the homeless in a neighboring community were asked to speak to the subcommittee, providing helpful information and personal insights.

In conjunction with their social work research professor, the students designed a research strategy to more accurately estimate the number of homeless in Mapletown. They designed a questionnaire to collect various categories of data about people who were homeless in Mapletown. Their primary strategy for data collection involved interviews with people from community social service agencies to obtain information about the numbers and types of people receiving assistance who were considered homeless.

The students had planned to interview homeless people on the street but found none. One of the students, a resident of Mapletown, suggested that the police and the city council "warned out and passed on" most homeless people because it was bad for the local tourist economy. However, they were told that there were places near the church, under a bridge, and behind the Department of Social Services where homeless people camped out at night. Students were able to informally talk to several homeless individuals and one family who lived in their car.

The interview process went very well, with students receiving cooperation from all the agencies contacted. They were able to collect information on the number of homeless people served by each agency, the factors that led to their situation, and the kinds of resources provided. They found that there were multiple reasons for homelessness in Mapletown, including lack of affordable housing, transience, catastrophe, domestic violence, unemployment, mental illness, and emotional or behavioral problems. The community agencies provided several types of services to these people, including information and referral, safekeeping of valuables, meals, housing referrals, educational services, job training, alcohol and drug counseling, medical services, family support services, information on cash assistance, emergency cash, clothing, advocacy, temporary shelters (motel), peer counseling, legal advice, low-cost cash loans, and landlord lists.

Students estimated that there were about 750 homeless people in Mapletown. About 80 percent of these were residents of Maple County; the others were from other counties or from neighboring states. Females were disproportionately represented among the ranks of the homeless, possibly because of the increased incidence of domestic violence in Mapletown. (Students were able to verify this by interviewing the chief of police.) About 50 percent of the people listed as homeless were children.

The coalition research subcommittee wondered whether there could have been duplicated reports of homelessness by the service providers. To obtain an unduplicated count, the subcommittee asked the three organizations that served the largest number of homeless people (the Health Department, the Department of Social Welfare, and the Community Development Program) to review their records for the past three months and collect demographic and other information on their cases. For reasons of confidentiality, these data were given to the regional coordinator of Human Services, who compiled an unduplicated list of homeless people served by these organizations in the three-month period. He reported the results in aggregate form, and the data supported the students' original estimate of homeless people in the community.

The research findings were compiled in a research report written by Professor Worthington. The research subcommittee would submit their findings at the next meeting of the coalition. Meanwhile, Professor Worthington made plans for how to disseminate the research report to maximize its impact on the community. On the local level, a presentation would be made to the Community Resource Group, made up of representatives of community organizations. Newspaper coverage was arranged by a student through a friend who was a reporter. Findings also were shared on the state level at a housing workshop in the Annual Forum on the Federal Budget and Social Planning led by the state's U.S. senator and her staff. In addition, a report of the findings would appear in newsletters of community organizations in the state. A copy would also be sent to the U.S. secretary of Housing and Urban Development.

Assessment and Goal Planning

The Second Meeting

Claire began the meeting by asking the subcommittee on research to report their findings to the coalition. Later she helped the group explore its purpose and goals. The following excerpt illustrates some of the issues raised.

Claire: Now that you have heard the report of the subcommittee on research, do you have any questions or comments?

Angus: It seems to me that the problem of an emergency shelter needs to be dealt with first.

Jane: I agree. As I mentioned in the previous meeting, when transients come to the Department of Social Services for emergency shelter, we have to place them in a motel room, which can be very expensive.

Brenda: I believe we should also keep in mind the need for transitional housing. A large number of people need a more stable living situation, especially people who are victims of domestic violence.

Joy: This is also true for people who have been released from the state mental health facility.

Alice: From the research findings, it appears that a number of resources are available for homeless people but there is no coordinated information and referral source. I believe we should work on coordination of services for homeless people.

Roger: I agree with Alice about the need for coordinated services. I also feel that there is a need to increase community awareness about the problem of homelessness. Most of our community political leaders don't have any idea about this.

Claire: It sounds to me as if the key areas we listed in our purpose have been reaffirmed by these findings. I suggest that we divide into committees to work on these needs.

Amanda: I would like to involve the students in developing an overall plan for development of emergency and transitional housing to the coalition.

Claire: That sounds like a good idea.

Brenda: I would like to serve on a committee to explore housing sites.

Jane: I would too.

John: I would like to work on a grant development committee. I think we should consider funding sources before we decide what we want to work on.

Claire: Fund-raising is very important; we do need to consider how we could raise some money to keep the work of the coalition going. It sounds like we also need to explore grants that might be available for aid to homeless people, particularly for emergencies and for transitional housing. Community awareness seems to be an issue here too.

Vivian: Joe's Pub has volunteered to have a Celebrity Bartenders Night to raise money for the homeless.

Roger: That sounds like a good idea. However, I believe the drinks should be nonalcoholic. Homelessness is often linked to alcohol in people's minds, and this could reinforce that idea.

Claire: How many of you feel that the drinks should be nonalcoholic? I see from the hands raised that we are all in agreement. Before you leave today, I would appreciate it if you would sign up for one of the committees.

Amanda: I think all the ideas presented today are worthy of our attention. I'm concerned that we don't seem to have a consensus on which idea has priority.

Claire: Amanda is right. We need to decide on the first-priority goal or at least keep in mind what goals are guiding our work here. This way we can avoid a fragmented approach.

Joy: I agree. We already have fragmented services for the homeless. We don't want to be going off in different directions; we want to coordinate our efforts.

Claire: Let me suggest that we first agree on goal priorities. If you remember our initial purpose for being here and, more specifically, our beginning goals, we can decide on a beginning direction for the coalition. Our goals were: community awareness, considering emergency and transitional housing, and service coordination. Is there an order inherent in these goals? Where do we begin?

In this last interaction, the group struggled with setting priorities and determining how to work on its varied goals. In essence, the group began its second stage of development, characterized by a period of "storming" among members. Varied opinions were expressed, and it was difficult to coordinate the priorities of members. Claire redirected the group to again consider its priorities.

Also in this meeting, further discussions took place on homelessness and its causes. Eventually, the group set community awareness as its first priority and agreed to maintain communication among group members, with Claire serving as liaison and staff person. The coalition met two more times to plan the fund-raiser and continue its discussion on how to raise community awareness of homelessness.

Intervention

The Fifth Meeting

After the Celebrity Bartenders Night was held, the coalition met to hear the results and consider further work. Raising community awareness continued to be the group's first goal.

Claire: I would like to open the meeting with a report of the Celebrity Bartenders Night at Joe's Pub. We raised $1000, which is to be used to provide services for local homeless people. The evening was a great success, with a large number of people attending. Entertainment was provided by local musical groups and the antics of the celebrity bartenders.

Angus: I saw a good article about the event in the *Mapletown News*. It featured pictures of two Mapletown town council members serving drinks. Keeping our politicians informed and involved will help raise community awareness a lot.

Claire: I agree. We raised a sizable amount of money, and we have had some good coverage of our efforts in the press. We might want to consider other ways to raise community awareness.

Clement: It was a great evening. I suggest we try to make a public presentation on what we have learned about homelessness in Mapletown. We could advertise it in the paper and try to get more of our town council members to attend. (The group agrees.)

John: I think that would be a good idea. It might be important to keep ourselves before the public eye. This will continue to raise consciousness about the problem. It's about time the community dealt with this! I also think we need to move on establishing an emergency shelter, soon.

In this meeting, the group heard about the successful fund-raiser and discussed the resulting community awareness this event fostered. The coalition heard sub-committee reports that indicated that most members were hard at work planning and carrying out individual tasks. The group continued to struggle with its direction but kept its primary goal in mind. The events up to now gave members of the coalition a sense of goal accomplishment, which fostered a feeling of mutuality and cohesion. It also marked the beginning of the group's "norming" period, when the work of the group was planned and the means to carry out the group's work was discussed. In addition, the group increased member motivation by successfully carrying out its tasks and reaching its short-term goals.

The Seventh Meeting

At the sixth meeting, the group voted to work on establishing an emergency shelter. The group members all agreed that their agencies would work together to establish the shelter and that this should be a collaborative effort. This goal became the next priority. At the seventh meeting, the following dialogue occurred.

Claire: The social work students have completed their plan for emergency and transitional housing for homeless people in Mapletown. Nancy Bright will present their recommendations.

Nancy: The major goal of our plan is housing for the homeless in Mapletown. The first subgoal is emergency shelters, and the second is transitional housing. The coalition would operate under the auspices of the Community Development Program for the short term and consider becoming a separate incorporated body in the future. We have made a detailed analysis of the goals and activities associated with providing housing, and we think this is a project that can be accomplished. (See Figure 3.)

John: I guess I should let you all know that the Community Development Program has allocated money for an emergency shelter. We want to open it as soon as possible.

Nancy: While I think this is great, I would like to see the coalition have some input into how the shelter would be run.

John: What do you mean by that?

Nancy: Well, we have all worked hard on this whole issue of homelessness; we all have good ideas to contribute. For example, some of us would like to help design policies and procedures for the shelter. What would its intake policy be? Who would the shelter serve and not serve? I'm sure others have thoughts about the shelter.

Angus: I agree. I believe the coalition needs to have input into the policies and rules before the shelter is opened.

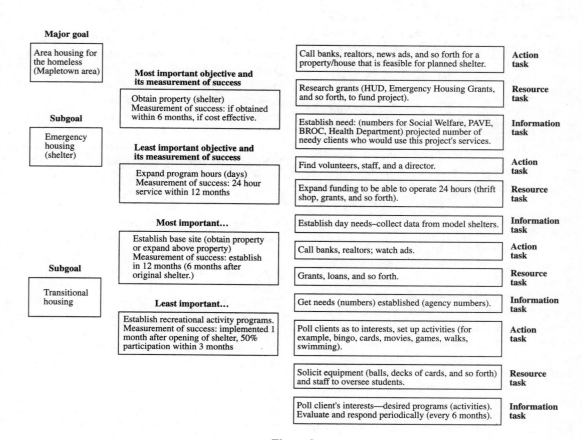

Figure 3

John: We have found a house that can be used as a shelter, but we need to decide right away or it will not be available.

Alice: I think we need more time for planning before a house is rented.

John: I am afraid that the property will be rented if we wait.

Claire: Let's think about possible policies and rules for the shelter and bring them to the next meeting. Then we can decide about a shelter site.

At this meeting, the students presented a model for planning the establishment of emergency and transitional housing. John Allen wanted to obtain and open a shelter site without considering policies, rules, and other planning considerations. Members of the coalition did not agree with him. Claire Delune supported the idea of planning and suggested policies and rules be discussed at the next meeting. Conflict was emerging in the group, and a good deal of tension was brewing between John and other coalition members.

The Eighth Meeting

Claire: This meeting is supposed to concentrate on recommending policies and procedures for the proposed shelter. Any thoughts on this issue? I would like to hear your suggestions.

John: The home I wanted to rent for a shelter is not available now due to our delay in making a decision. I found another house appropriate for a shelter and rented and furnished it. I did not want to lose this house.

Angus: I thought we were going to discuss policies and rules before securing the shelter.

Brenda: I have to tell you that I'm upset because you and your agency went ahead with the rental without involving the coalition.

John: I felt I couldn't wait for input from the coalition. However, we could use suggestions for shelter rules.

Claire: I think we need to have a subcommittee from the coalition visit the shelter and get an idea of what might be needed for policies.

The Ninth Meeting

Nancy Bright, Joy Williams, and Alice MacDonald agreed to serve on the subcommittee to recommend policies, and they visited the shelter site. They met and made a list of recommendations they intended to bring to the full coalition. However, at this meeting the conflict between John Allen and other coalition members became more intense because John and his agency seemed to be working independently on the shelter project and not cooperating with the coalition. At its next meeting, two weeks later, the coalition found the situation had changed further.

Claire: I would like John to bring us up to date on the progress of the shelter.

John: We opened the shelter yesterday and have several homeless people living there.

Nancy: Our subcommittee met to work on the shelter rules and policies, but no one from the Community Development Program called to ask about them. Now the shelter is open without the necessary policies in place.

Joy: I am very upset that you and your agency went ahead without our input on policies.

John: We had several homeless people who needed a place to stay, and we felt we had to open the shelter for them.

Claire: We need to discuss the role of the coalition in developing a shelter and find out if John and his agency are going to work on their own. Let's put this on the agenda for the next meeting.

The coalition members were very angry at John because his organization opened the shelter without consulting them or without having adequate policies and rules in place. Conflicts increased between John Allen and other coalition members, and several meetings were devoted to discussing this issue. John Allen did not attend these meetings, although he was encouraged to come. Problems occurred at the shelter because of the lack of rules.

Later Developments

Susan Green, another Community Development worker, came to one of the meetings instead of John Allen. She reported that the agency had to close the shelter because of lack of funding and hoped to open another shelter when they secured additional funds. Members of the coalition again expressed their desire to have input into the process of planning for the shelter.

Several months later, the Community Development Program opened another emergency shelter. They had more structured policies and rules. Case management was provided for the homeless residents to link them with community resources and to assist them in finding employment. However, problems arose between male and female residents, and a mother and her child had to move because of the inappropriate behavior of some of the residents. After five months, this shelter was closed because of lack of funding.

Soon after the close of the second shelter, John Allen left the Community Development Program, and a new director, Jean Wright, was hired. Claire met with Jean Wright to discuss the problems the coalition had encountered with the Community Development Program. Jean was very concerned about what had happened and expressed her desire to cooperate with the coalition in developing a shelter and transitional housing. She chose to represent the Community Development Program on the coalition, and she attended regularly.

To promote cooperation among the coalition members and to raise community awareness of the nature of homelessness, the coalition members decided to sponsor a conference on homelessness. Representatives from state and local organizations shared information on their work with the homeless, and a number of community residents as well as a few state politicians attended. Members of the coalition were pleased at the results of the conference, recognizing that this was an indicator that the group had moved into its "performing" stage and was accomplishing its goals.

Evaluation: Looking Back and Looking Ahead

The coalition members wanted to evaluate their work to help them plan for their future. Claire and Andrea developed an interview questionnaire that could be used to find out how the community viewed the work of the coalition and if the purpose and goals of the coalition were important to community residents. Each coalition member selected several key people in the community to interview, including the town manager, the manager of the Housing Authority, the director of Social Services, a member of the clergy, and other citizens. The consensus of the people interviewed was that the coalition needed to continue to work on its purpose and goals and to focus on transitional housing.

The coalition members discussed whether they should become incorporated or become part of an existing agency servicing homeless people. Jean Wright suggested that the coalition become an advisory committee of the Community Development Program to work on the development of transitional housing. The coalition members met with Jean Wright and Community Development Program board members to discuss this possibility. Because of the positive change in the Community Development Program's leadership, the coalition was asked to become an advisory committee to the agency's board of directors. This was a recommendation originally made by the social work students of Wilton College, and they were especially pleased at this outcome.

The coalition was able to achieve its purpose in several ways. Community awareness was increased by the conference on homelessness and the bartenders night at the local pub. In addition, coalition members spoke about their work to various community groups and civic organizations. Local politicians were also involved in the coalition's activities, fostering political acceptance of the coalition's purposes and projects. A new emergency shelter was established, and although several refinements were needed, it served the needs of several homeless people.

The coalition assisted in planning for transitional housing, and members assisted in writing grant applications. Although this was a long-term and formidable task, good progress was made. Members of the coalition worked with elected representatives at the state level to sponsor state legislation for funding transitional housing.

Case managers carried out coordination of services for homeless people at the shelter. Their input was especially important to planning for transitional housing. Case managers provided important statistical and anecdotal data to state legislators by testifying before a legislative committee. This further supported the need for transitional housing legislation.

The students involved in the project learned a number of things about homelessness in Mapletown and about the community social service system. These included:

1. The nature and extent of homelessness in Mapletown.
2. The hard work and extended length of time it can take for a community to become aware of a social problem and for the organizations in the community to work together to resolve it.
3. The necessary steps involved in establishing emergency and transitional housing: planning, selecting an appropriate site, applying for funding grants, preparing a shelter for occupancy, establishing policies and regulations, staffing, placing residents, case management, and other shelter operations.
4. The importance of power and political issues, for a small group, the community, and on the state level when carrying out a macro-level intervention.
5. The group dynamics of a task group and the group work skills needed by the leadership to confront conflicts and help the group accomplish its purpose and goals.

Readings

Biggerstaff, M. A., Morris, P. M., & Nichols-Casebolt, A. (2002). Living on the edge: Examination of people attending food pantries and soup kitchens. *Social Work, 47*(3), 267–277.

Mizrahi, T. (2001). The status of community organizing in 2001: Community practice context, complexities, contradictions, and contributions. *Research on Social Work Practice, 11*(2), 176–190.

Oakley, D. (2002). Housing homeless people: Local mobilization of federal resources to fight nimbyism. *Journal of Urban Affairs, 24*(1), 97–117.

Discussion Questions

1. *As you think about your own hometown, consider where homeless people stay in your community. If you knew of a homeless family, where would you suggest they go for assistance with shelter?*

2. *What are some of the factors that may lead a person to become homeless?*

3. *What services besides shelter do the homeless require? What other needs do the homeless have?*

4. *Present one reason supporting and one reason in opposition to John's decision to open a shelter for the homeless without involving the other members of the coalition.*

5. *What is the purpose of periodically summarizing the group discussion?*

6. *What might explain the finding that most of the homeless population in this community consisted of women and children?*

7. *What power issues arose in the coalition? Could they have been prevented?*

8. *Identify two different needs assessment methods used by the coalition to determine the actual number of homeless in the community.*

9. *One of the follow-ups in the case involved planning for "transitional housing" for the homeless. What does this mean? What other groups might benefit from this type of service?*

20

Transitional Homes
for Young Street Mothers

JoAnn Ray

Background

Pat was excited about her practicum placement with New-Path, the city's program serving homeless youth. She was especially interested in the problems of youth, and this agency served really troubled kids. NewPath had an excellent reputation in the community, and Pat had heard that she could expect excellent field instruction and supervision.

Pat's first duties were to learn about the kids and their needs by doing intakes. It would give her a chance to really understand the kids and some of their situations. She was also interested in gaining experience conducting a self-help group and perhaps helping develop a new program. Pat's field instructor, Mary, had also suggested that Pat consider completing a small research project. Pat had done well in research, but the idea seemed a little scary. She hoped she could get some help if she had the opportunity to actually carry out a research project of her own. At the end of her first supervisory meeting with Mary, Pat exclaimed, "I'm so excited! I'll be getting some really valuable and challenging experiences here."

Pat learned that the boys and girls at NewPath had multiple needs. These children most often came from conflict-ridden, violent, abusive families. Their schooling was often interrupted. They frequently abused drugs and alcohol and were often involved in illegal activities. Many had lived in a series of unsuccessful foster homes, and life was difficult for them. Mary explained, "These are troubled youngsters. We try our best to meet their basic needs, such as food, shelter, clothing, and school. We need to do this in ways in which the kids can accept the help we offer."

Engagement

It was the pregnant and parenting young mothers who concerned Pat so deeply. Pat had recently completed an intake with Sandy, who was 15 years old, pregnant, and living wherever she could find a place. She was presently staying in the emergency shelter provided by NewPath. Foster care had not been successful, and Sandy could not return to her own abusive home. Pat agreed to help Sandy get welfare benefits, a place to stay, and medical care. Sandy had many other needs as well, such as schooling, warm clothing, baby things, recreation, and transportation. The list seemed long. Pat wondered whether she could really help Sandy enough.

What concerned Pat even more was that there seemed to be so many young girls like Sandy. This was the third pregnant or mothering street kid she had talked with this week. In one of her supervisory sessions with Mary, Pat brought up her concern.

Pat: We really should be able to do something more for Sandy and the other young mothers too.

Mary: I agree. The young mothers have special needs. We do what we can, and so do some of the other agencies. But their needs are not addressed in a comprehensive manner in the community.

Pat: What can we do?

Mary: You might want to study some of the problems experienced by these young mothers and help us develop a special program for them.

Collecting and Analyzing the Data

Pat was delighted and decided to accept Mary's suggestion that she learn more about the young mothers. Wondering how to get started, she remembered that the first thing to do when planning for a new program is to "define the problem."

Pat: First, I guess we need to review what we know about the young moms. There must be something in the literature about young street mothers.

Mary: That's a good place to start. Any ideas?

Pat: The evaluation report you gave me to read would be useful. Perhaps we could analyze the existing data in the agency files; there must be good records on these kids.

Mary: Pat, it sounds like you have some good leads to pursue. Go ahead and start investigating your ideas. If you need help or more ideas, let me know.

At the next session with Mary, Pat related what she had learned from her investigative work. Her follow-up study indicated that half of the girls who were considered street kids were either pregnant or had a child within two years of their "street status." The Program Evaluation Report on NewPath, which had been completed by Pat's research teacher Sally Smith, compared the needs and problems of boys and girls served by the agency. Girls had higher rates of sexual and physical abuse. They were more apt to be depressed and more likely to have attempted suicide. Pat really began to appreciate the circumstances of these youngsters, and inside, she felt a deep concern for them.

Pat asked her research teacher if it were possible to analyze the intake data of the agency, perhaps to get a reading on the needs of this population. Sally helped Pat generate a printout. The plight of teen mothers looked grim. Girls who were pregnant or mothering at the time of intake indicated higher rates of abuse, suicide attempts, depression, family conflict, and drug use than did non-mothering girls.

In addition to carrying out this secondary analysis, Pat talked with two of the young mothers who were "hanging out" at NewPath. The girls had come for dinner, and Pat, remembering them from the intakes, had asked them whether they would talk with her about their needs. The young mothers were eager to talk. They spoke freely about their needs and noted similar concerns, including needs for housing, medical care, financial help, day care, education, and counseling. Two comments from the young mothers stood out in Pat's mind.

Sandy: I have welfare benefits. But it is not so easy to get along with my caseworker, and it's really hard to find someone who will rent to me. People don't want to rent to kids.

Carrie: There never is enough money, especially for baby things. I don't know who to ask for help.

Pat reflected on her conversation with Sandy and Carrie. These young moms had so many needs and seemed so alone in the world. Both the young moms and their babies were at risk for multiple problems, and they weren't getting services they needed. She brought this up to Mary in another session.

Pat: Why aren't the young moms getting the services they need?

Mary: A number of agencies serve these young mothers, but there is little coordination between agencies. Often the girls slip through the cracks.

Pat: Uh huh, how come?

Mary: And some of the agencies have policies that restrict them from serving adolescents.

Pat: And these kids have had lots of bad experiences with agencies too.

Mary: These street kids do not respond to the usual social work methods. They have learned not to trust through their life experiences, and a social worker must earn trust first by providing concrete help.

Pat: Like providing meals and clothes.

Mary: Right. As I said before, we have to find ways to reach out that these youngsters will accept. Otherwise, we become just another unresponsive agency.

Pat wondered how other social workers viewed the problems and needs of young mothers. She decided to ask them by designing an exploratory study. Pat asked Mary to help her develop an interview schedule and decide which agency representatives should be interviewed. They decided to interview workers who worked regularly with young mothers and some agency representatives whom they thought should also be providing services.

The list of questions was not long, but the interview would be semistructured, with room for follow-up and clarifying questions. Overall, Pat wanted lots of details. Her interview schedule included:

1. Do you provide services to out-of-home teen mothers? If not, what are the reasons for not providing services?
2. What services do you and your agency provide?
3. What do you see as the needs of the young street mothers?
4. What difficulties do you or your agency experience in providing services to these young mothers? What are the major challenges you face in working with this population?

In the next few weeks, Pat interviewed several workers. There seemed to be agreement that young street mothers were very needy and difficult to reach. They reported that the girls often appeared angry or sullen. They did not keep appointments very often and were almost impossible to locate because of their frequent moves. One worker for a drug and alcohol program stated that her agency could not accept minors. A subsidized rental program had a similar policy. Overall, Pat found out that most agencies did very little for this population, especially since the young mothers appeared to be resistant to their help.

Based on her interviews, Pat concluded that the young mothers and their children were at risk for continued homelessness, drug and alcohol use, abuse by their families, and other social problems. These young women had unique problems that were not being comprehensively addressed by any one agency in the city. She also concluded that there should be a program that provides young mothers with a more comprehensive range of services.

Planning and Intervening

Pat decided to accept her field instructor's invitation and develop a plan for a program for young mothers. She discussed this with Mary at her next meeting.

Pat: How do you think I should proceed?

Mary: You might consider forming a task force composed of people interested in services for young mothers.

Pat: Yeah, I like the idea of a task force. The more input I can get from interested people, the better the program design will be.

Mary: A task force will also share the ownership with the agencies who serve these young mothers.

Pat: Who should be on the task force?

Mary: Which of the agency representatives you interviewed appeared to be most helpful or concerned?

Pat: I'll have to review my notes, but I think I can identify a few who would be committed to the purpose of the group.

Mary: Actually, the idea of group purpose is about the most important consideration you need to make. You probably need to formulate a brief but clear statement of the purpose for the group before you start to consider composing it.

Pat: It sounds like you think I need to be more thoughtful about planning for the group before I rush in without thinking.

Mary: No need to be worried; most workers don't do enough planning for the groups they lead. You have a chance here to learn how to do it right. Let me make some suggestions.

Pat: Sounds good. What constitutes a good planning process?

Mary: As I said, it begins with a clear statement of the purpose for the group. If you are not clear about that, the members will be confused. Next, consider the potential membership, but don't forget sponsorship. This means that the group should have some official sponsor, such as NewPath. You will also need to recruit and orient members and give some consideration to how you will compose the group. Finally, don't forget to prepare the meeting environment, you know, room, refreshments, and other things.

Pat: Sounds pretty complicated!

Mary: Doesn't have to be. It all comes together, and planning pays off.

Mary and Pat selected four social workers from agencies that were providing services to the young mothers to be on the task force. Pat also asked Sandy, who was willing to give the viewpoint of the young mothers, to serve on the task force. The Task Force for Out-of-Home Teen Mothers consisted of:

Jennie, a social worker with Children and Family Services,
Mike, a social worker with the public schools,
Cindy, a social worker with the Health Department,
Lisa, a social worker with Family Counseling Services,
Sandy, a client from NewPath, and
Mary and Pat, social workers from NewPath.

The task force met for the first time and discussed the purpose for the group. After some preliminary discussions, they reviewed the findings from Pat's research.

Lisa: The statistics sure give a bleak picture of the young mother.

Jennie: But we don't know enough about how these young mothers are surviving on a day-to-day basis.

Cindy: That's true. We don't know what agencies are helping them, or who else is providing them with help.

Lisa: Or even what their unmet needs are.

Mike: I think we need more information before we can design a program to meet their needs.

Pat: Do you think we need to talk with more of the young moms?

Jennie: I think we need to know about how they survive on a day-to-day basis.

Sandy: I've talked with Penni and Vickie—you know, two of the young moms like me—and they said they would like to talk.

Pat: That sounds promising. What else do we need to know?

Cindy: I would like to know about the health problems experienced by the moms and their children.

Mike: Whether they plan to go to school.

Jennie: Who helps them, and how? babysitting? emotional support?

Lisa: What are their relationships with their parents and with the fathers of their kids?

Pat was a little disappointed that she had to go back to do more research. She wanted to get on with the planning. Pat met with her research teacher, Sally, to discuss the design of a new research study. Sally really sounded excited that Pat's study would be responsive to the expressed needs of the task force members, and she reminded Pat that program planning took time. She also mentioned that carrying out additional research based on the suggestions of task force members would add to the cohesion of the task force. In the long run, the research project would get the members of the task force more involved in program planning, and this was important.

Sally: What would you like to learn from your research?

Pat: I've listed the questions mentioned by the members of the task force. Here is my revised list of questions.

Sally: Those are very good questions and can probably best be obtained through qualitative research.

Pat: I think so.

Sally: Do you want to use any quantitative data, perhaps from standardized instruments, too?

Pat: I suppose it might be useful to get some measure of what services they are using, maybe from a list.

Sally: We could also use the Community Services Checklist I developed for this community. How about some objective measure of these young women's levels of depression, or how they feel about being a mother, or the types of stress they encounter?

Pat: Are there—what did you call them—standardized measures of these variables I could use?

Sally: I'll help you locate some.

Pat's questionnaire turned out to be much longer than she had anticipated. It had some really interesting questions designed to obtain qualitative data. These included the following.

1. Who helps you with all you need to be a good mother?
2. Who helps you financially? with emotional support? babysitting? advice?
3. What is a typical day like for you and your child(ren)?

4. How has your alcohol and drug use changed since you became pregnant?
5. How has your relationship with your own mother and father changed since the birth of your baby?
6. What is your relationship with the baby's father? How has your relationship with the baby's father changed?
7. What are your plans for further schooling?
8. What are your hopes and dreams for your baby?

Pat included the Zung Self-Rating Depression Scale, selected items from the Kanner Daily Hassles Inventory, and the Community Services Checklist. Sandy was willing to be interviewed for the pretest, and Pat made minor changes to the questionnaire based on what she learned during the pretest interview.

Pat and another student, Theresa, interviewed 25 young mothers. The mothers spoke very freely about their situations and needs, and a great amount of information was developed. Sally helped Pat compile and organize the data and understand the computer printouts that resulted. Pat summarized the qualitative and quantitative data in a report. As she was completing the report, she wondered how to handle a detailed account given by one of the young mothers on how she was trying to survive without welfare benefits.

Sally: Your examples of what the young mothers think and feel really adds richness to your study, Pat.
Pat: I think Penni's situation is especially interesting.
Sally: Is she the young mom who is not on welfare?
Pat: Uh-huh. But I'm afraid that in a city this small, she might be identified based on what she has said. I don't think I can guarantee her anonymity if I quote her statements.
Sally: Yes, the report will be made available to the community.
Pat: Maybe I'd better delete that vignette on how Penni is making it without welfare benefits.
Sally: I agree. We need to respect our clients' confidentiality and privacy. In addition, we guaranteed anonymity

to your respondents, and to violate this would be a serious breach of research ethics. It would also destroy the rapport we all have worked so hard to establish. I'm really glad you picked up on this issue.

The research findings indicated that the young women were very proud and devoted mothers. Most had some parental support, especially from their mothers, and most had friends they could depend on. Only about half of the young women had a relationship with the child's father, and in many cases this was filled with conflict. They were living on welfare, at a poverty level, and lacked money to cover daily needs. Many experienced health problems, as did their children. Most were receiving social services, most often welfare, public health, and emergency services. They experienced a high level of stress, often related to economic, social, health, and personal concerns. Many were depressed, some seriously. They were experiencing the stresses of trying to raise a child at such a young age with limited income and support. All had common goals for their children, including a life better than their own. Most wanted to complete school or a training program so they could become independent.

The task force thought Pat's research was extremely helpful in identifying the needs and wants of the young mothers. They spent a good deal of time reviewing the findings and discussing what they could do about them.

Pat: What kinds of services do the needs of these mothers suggest?
Sandy: I seem to be very much like the other young moms. I need housing especially and help with my child, more money, and training. I want to think about my future and the future of my baby. But I'm also caught up in daily survival issues.
Mike: Let's diagram the needs of the young teen mother.

The group developed a map of the factors affecting the typical street kid mother. (See Figure 4.)

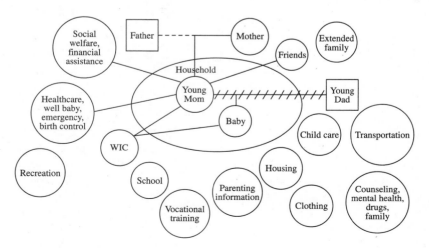

Figure 4

Intervening and Ending

The task force settled quickly on the need for designing a comprehensive program for the young mothers. They would plan to provide a transition living situation supervised by a social worker. The transition home would provide six young mothers with a place to live while they improved their own independent living skills. There would be classes on parenting, communication skills, job readiness, and self-esteem building. Day care would be offered. Pat and Mary wrote a grant for federal funding for the project. The data from Pat's research and the data from the intakes at NewPath were useful in establishing the need for the program.

Federal funding was obtained after a rewrite of the grant request. The funding source was especially impressed with the research needs assessment that supported the proposal. Nancy, a local newspaper reporter, heard about Pat's research and the grant that Mary and Pat had written. The newspaper article suggested that interested citizens could help with the project through donations. Mary and Pat made several presentations, and two church groups decided to help furnish the NewPath Transitional Home. Pat completed her practicum, and, once the proposal was funded, she accepted the position of social worker for the transition home.

Readings

Bogard, C., & McConnell, J. J. (1999). Homeless mothers and depression: Misdirected policy. *Journal of Health & Social Behavior, 40*(1), 46–63.

Goldberg, J. E. (1999). A short term approach to intervention with homeless mothers: A role for clinicians in homeless shelters. *Families in Society, 80*(2), 161–169.

Kissman, K. (1999). Respite from stress and other service needs of homeless families. *Community Mental Health Journal, 35*(3), 241–250.

Discussion Questions

1. *What other ethical concerns besides maintaining confidentiality must be considered when conducting research?*

2. *How else besides individual interviews might Pat have collected data on the young mothers?*

3. *How could Pat's research data be used to make changes in policies that restrict services because of age?*

4. *What social work roles, besides researcher, did Pat play in the vignette?*

5. *Based on your knowledge of human behavior, what kinds of needs would you expect most pregnant homeless teens and homeless teens with babies to have?*

6. *If you were designing a program to serve this population, what kinds of services would you provide? Would your services be available free, at low cost, or paid for fully by the users? Explain your answer.*

7. *The supervisor in this case observed that many workers begin groups without adequate planning. Can you think of reasons workers often start groups without planning carefully for what they are going to do?*

8. *Why was sponsorship of the task force an important consideration?*

9. *The research conducted by the student used both quantitative and qualitative data. Describe why both types were important.*

21

The Appointment Letters

Grafton H. Hull, Jr.

Presenting Problem

Geof Hernandez sensed that the mood in the general staff meeting of the Marquette County Department of Human Services was getting tense. Clashes between workers and the director were becoming more common—so common, in fact, that the director had canceled general staff meetings for a couple of months. Once again, the issue was money, this time overlaid by a conflict between values. There did not seem to be a middle ground between the two sides, and acrimonious questions and retorts were becoming all too frequent.

This particular problem erupted when the director, in an attempt to cut costs, decided to end the practice of workers sending appointment letters to clients. These letters were used with clients who lacked a phone or could not be reached by phone, and they allowed workers to notify clients that they would be visiting in a week or two. The letters read as follows:

> Marquette County Department of Human Services
> 1415 East Main Street
> East North Overshoe, WY 34512
> (414) 673-9800
> Date
> Name of Client
> Address of Client
> City, State, ZIP Code
> Dear Client's Name:
> I have scheduled a visit to your home for *Day, Date, and Time*. If this arrangement is not convenient, please call me at (414) 673-9800 so that we can schedule an alternative time. I look forward to talking with you.
> Sincerely,
> John Hansen
> Social Worker II

Clerical staff members had complained to the director that it took too much time to type these letters and that the cost was unnecessary. The office manager had calculated the cost of each letter and convinced the director that the agency could save both clerical time and money by ending the practice. When the director announced the policy, some of the staff objected and questioned how they were supposed to let clients know they would be coming for a home visit. His response was that there was no need to announce these visits in advance; workers could just visit when they needed to.

Bob Bumpers, a fiery unit supervisor, attacked the director immediately. "You're ignoring clients' rights. This hardly shows respect for their worth and dignity. No one

could expect to get an appointment with you without scheduling the visit ahead of time," he said. "Why should clients be treated with any less respect?" Other workers joined the chorus of objections, but to no avail. Arguments about clients' rights and worth and the dignity of clients were lost on the agency director. A former probation officer, the director did not share the same social work values held by his staff. His concerns were efficiency, cutting costs, and avoiding criticism from members of the county board, values that to him were much more salient. In fact, he was often amazed by his workers' advocacy on behalf of clients. The meeting ended with loud grumbling and the usual hustle and bustle to get on with the day's work.

Gathering Data about the Problem

For Geof and Bob, this situation was a clear case of organizational policy acting as an impediment to effective service delivery. In their discussions, they considered various possible interventions. Since the issue was of direct concern to line workers, it was important to consider their opinions in the matter. The following week, Geof had a supervisory session with one of his line workers, Ron Rivers. Ron was exasperated. "I wasted a full hour of my time yesterday because of that stupid appointment letter situation. I made a visit to Mr. Topp's home in La Grange." (Mr. Topp was a single individual living in a small town at the far end of the county.) "It took 25 minutes to drive out to his home, and he wasn't there. If I could have sent the appointment letter, this wouldn't have happened." Ron was justifiably irritated, especially since this could happen repeatedly with his clients, many of whom lacked phones.

When Geof related this story to Bob, Bob nodded his agreement. "I was talking with John Hansen (one of the most experienced social workers in his unit). John is also upset over the appointment letter policy change. He asked me whether the director might consider sending out postcards as an alternative to the letters. I told him the idea had merit and that I'd take it up at the next staff meeting."

Assessing the Problem

Geof and Bob assessed the situation similarly. Both felt deeply that the director's action was wrong. It violated clients' rights to privacy and to equal treatment, and it complicated both workers' and clients' lives. Clients' rights to self-determination were also affected, since they should have a right to participate in setting dates for meeting times.

Geof, a supervisor in another unit, was not as vocal an adversary with the director as was Bob. He preferred to use methods other than confrontation to accomplish his goals. Together, however, they could advocate for clients' rights most effectively. Both were aware of their conflicting ethical responsibilities (loyalty to their agency and colleagues, including the director, and responsibility to their clients). The director would not change his mind based on value arguments alone. Other approaches would be necessary.

Planning for Change

Since the director's primary objection appeared to be financial, they decided that the intervention they pursued must emphasize this. Also, since the director would not want to lose face, the topic must be handled in a nonthreatening manner. Brainstorming the situation, the two supervisors began to formulate their plan. Their plan for resolving the conflict would require tact, quiet argument, and sound facts. Belligerence would be met by the same from the director. Because Bob had been so vehement in his dissent during the previous general staff meeting, he suggested that Geof take the lead in addressing the appointment letter matter in the next administrative staff meeting. "I'll try not to aggravate Mr. Scrooge," said Geof, using their sometimes affectionate nickname for the director. "I'll mention Ron Rivers' experience and focus on how much this cost the county. We know what Ron is paid per hour and how much it cost for mileage out to La-Grange and back. A conservative estimate is $21, which covers $10 per hour in salary plus mileage of about $11. The director said it costs $5 to send out each business letter, or at least that's what he read somewhere. That means the policy cost the department a net of $16 multiplied by the number of times this is likely to happen. I think this might help move the director off dead center. That's when you might want to present John's idea about the postcards. The cost is minimal, and he might just buy it. Whatever we do, let's not get him so upset he cancels the administrative staff meeting. This is the only place we can still present ideas to him."

Bob agreed, "I'll try to stay calmer this time. I know he has his own problems."

Intervention

A week later, the director called the administrative staff together. This group was composed of all unit supervisors, the office manager, and the deputy director. Once the administrative staff meeting was under way, Geof told the story of Ron Rivers and the wasted trip. Geof said he'd calculated the mileage cost the county was obligated to pay to cover Ron's travel to Mr. Topp's home. He had also added in the cost of Ron's time, which had been completely wasted. Finally, he argued that this represented only one worker's situation and that many, many similar experiences could be expected. "I know the cost of Ron's wasted trip far exceeds the savings achieved by not sending the appointment letter. I also know you are always looking for ways to better manage costs in the agency, and this looks like it might end up costing us a great deal more."

Bob then brought up quietly (uncharacteristically for him) John's suggestion about the postcards. "Perhaps the department could prepare preprinted postcards the worker would simply address, write in the proposed time of the visit, and sign. This would save clerical time since no letters would have to be typed, and the cost of postage would be significantly less. Since the postcards would not have to carry any other identifying information, no one happening to see the card would know whom it was from. Thus, clients' privacy would be preserved."

The director pondered this suggestion for a few seconds. "OK, I'm impressed that you two found a way to save money rather than spend it," he said, smiling. He asked the office manager to arrange for printing the cards. Bob and Geof asked the director to announce the new policy at the next general staff meeting, and he agreed.

Evaluation, Termination, and Follow-up

The policy change was announced as promised, and the postcards were tried for several months. Workers were generally happy with the system, although many still preferred the old appointment letters. The director still searched for ways to cut the budget, and Geof and Bob remained committed to serving clients in as humane a fashion as possible. However, the underlying tensions that characterized the mood in the agency were never fully resolved. Because they arose from basic value differences and dissimilar communication styles, they did not lend themselves to easy solutions. In fact, they would become the basis for future problems until the director decided to retire.

Readings

Glasby, J. (2001). Money talks: The role of finance in social work education and practice. *Social Work Education, 20*(4), 493–498.

Goldberg, M. (2000). Conflicting principles in multicultural social work. *Families in Society, 81*(1), 12–22.

Horwath, M. (2000). Identifying and implementing pathways for organizational change—using the framework for the assessment of children in need and their families as a case example. *Child & Family Social Work, 5*(3), 245–255.

Discussion Questions

1. *Bob and Geof chose to intervene in the administrative staff meeting rather than in the general staff meeting. What are some possible reasons for choosing one meeting over the other?*

2. *What provided Bob and Geof with the sanction to undertake this change in their own agency's policy?*

3. *Bob's initial verbal attack on the director violated at least one section of the NASW Code of Ethics. What was the violation?*

4. *Why did Bob and Geof ask the director to make the announcement of the changed policy at the next general staff meeting?*

5. *Assuming that the director of the agency refused to change the policy of appointment letters even after hearing the arguments made by Bob and Geof, what further strategies for change could be considered? How would the NASW Code of Ethics influence these strategies?*

6. *Differences based on values tend to be harder to resolve than differences based on facts. What factors contribute to this situation?*

7. *Although the situation was resolved successfully by raising the subject of the postcards in an administrative staff meeting, there were other alternatives that could have been used to make the director aware of this possible solution. Identify two possible approaches that might have been used.*

8. *The director had canceled staff meetings to avoid conflicts that occurred there. What conflict resolution methods besides avoidance might he have considered?*

22

The Evergreen Boys Ranch: A Story about Jack and Diane

Robert F. Rivas

Jack and Diane had just taken new social work positions at the Evergreen Boys Ranch (EBR), while Jack was doing graduate work on an MSW degree. Evergreen Boys Ranch was a 20-year-old residential institution for boys between the ages of 8 and 16. Located in a desert area 20 miles from a large city in the Southwest, the ranch served boys who were referred by the state's Department of Social Services and by local Departments of Juvenile Probation.

Jack and Diane were assigned to provide social work services to boys who lived in the ten group homes located on the grounds of the 200-acre residential institution. Jack was expected to be one of the ranch's group workers, leading group activities and special interest club activities, while Diane functioned as a school social worker, providing services to older boys attending local community schools. Both Jack and Diane were also expected to provide assistance and consultation to group home staff, consisting of married couples who lived in the group homes located on the ranch.

This was an important employment opportunity for both Jack and Diane because it included an apartment on the ranch for them to live in and provided a small salary for each. Both were very excited about starting to work at EBR, wanting to make a contribution both to the boys and to the ranch. This was their first professional employment since receiving their BSW degrees.

Engagement: First Impressions

During their first days at the ranch, all seemed especially well and orderly. The ranch group homes were well kept, and the boys seemed to like their group home parents. The boys seemed to have very difficult problems, however. Several were caught with alcohol and drugs in their group homes, and some of the older boys appeared to intimidate the younger ones. In addition to the usual period of "testing behavior," Jack and Diane had to deal with two instances of boys running away and being picked up by the State Police.

Jack and Diane sought assistance from the assistant executive director of EBR, the ranch official who had originally interviewed and hired them. (They were anxious to meet the executive director, but he was on an extended fund-raising trip and was not expected back for a few more days.) The assistant director assured them that the boys were just engaging in "testing behavior" and that things would settle down after they had established themselves as the ranch social workers. However, in talking to one of the group home staff, Diane had learned that most of the boys in her group home were considered to be "rejects" from other cottages who posed behavior problems and were transferred out for disciplinary reasons.

Jack's concerns were reinforced by an incident that occurred the next day. While playing basketball with some residents of his cottage, he heard loud yelling and screaming, accompanied by crashing noises, coming from the ranch's recreation room. Feeling a sense of responsibility for checking out the disturbance, Jack approached the recreation room with measured determination, unable to imagine who or what might be involved. Upon entering the recreation room, he observed a middle-aged man throwing the furniture around and screaming, "This is the last time they'll use this place and not clean up after themselves." Using his best nonjudgmental interpersonal skills, Jack replied, "Can I help you?" The man never looked at Jack and simply left, grumbling as he departed.

By this time, Diane and the assistant director had arrived at the scene of the disturbance. Jack could tell by looking at the troubled expression on Diane's face that all was not well. The assistant director also seemed troubled, as he said to Jack, "I see you have met our executive director!" The knowing glances exchanged between Jack and Diane suggested to both that it was going to be a long day. On the way back to their apartment, the assistant director explained that the director had just returned from a long trip and was agitated at the boys for not respecting ranch property. He assured Jack and Diane that their next meeting with the director would be more cordial.

Data Collection

Later that week, Jack and Diane attended their first staff meeting, where they were formally introduced to the executive director and to the other staff members. They observed the director lead a group discussion about disciplinary policy. The session consisted of the director instructing group home staff to design a strong structure of rewards and punishments for the boys in their care. Participants were also reminded that several boys had run away lately, suggesting that discipline needed to be reinforced.

Jack was not as interested in the content of the group discussion as he was in the group dynamics he observed.

The communication patterns seemed to be rather unilateral in that the director did most of the talking. Most of the more recently hired group home staff appeared to be disturbed by what the director was saying. (Diane pointed out their nonverbal communication: crossed arms and legs, guarded facial expressions, furtive eye contact among new staff.) Most of the group home staff who had been at the ranch for several years seemed to reinforce what the director was saying by nodding their heads and by contributing ideas for discipline plans. Diane whispered to Jack, "There seem to be two groups, the new and the old. What's going on here?"

Jack replied, "I don't know, but it is time to find out." The meeting ended, and all returned to their duties.

Later that night, Diane left the apartment to visit some neighbors, John and Pat, who were group home parents and also new to the ranch. Diane was intent on getting their reactions to the staff meeting, and she hoped they could shed some light on the inner workings of EBR. As she was admitted to John and Pat's group home, she found several other group home staff seated in the living area, discussing recent happenings at the ranch. The discussants regarded her with suspicion and became silent as she sat on the floor with them. As she had been known to do before, Diane pressed her luck and came right to the point, inquiring, "So, is it me, or is something weird going on here?"

Diane's openness, assertiveness, and risk-taking behavior prompted others in the room to test the waters of self-disclosure. As a result of the ensuing group discussion, the following information was developed.

1. There appeared to be two distinct factions among the group home staff: the new group home staff employed less than two years and the group home staff employed two years or more (several staff in this category had been employed for more than ten years). There appeared to be little interaction between the two factions.
2. Members of the more experienced staff appeared to be loyal to the executive director and satisfied with the ranch's policies and practices.
3. It was rumored that experienced staff, including members of the administrative staff, believed in and used corporal punishment to make the ranch boys behave. Some of the punishment was purported to include hitting, slapping, and spanking residents. Residents who ran away from the ranch were restricted from all activities.
4. There had been a large turnover of group home staff. Although the exact numbers were unknown, it was estimated that 12 sets of group home staff had left ranch employment in the past two years.
5. New staff were given very little orientation to ranch policies. Staff training was infrequent and consisted of lectures from the executive director.
6. It was estimated that more than 20 residents had run away from the ranch in the past 12 months.

7. Several of the boys seemed to have serious adjustment problems (two had recently attempted suicide), but there were no specialized social or psychological services available to residents.
8. Although ranch policy permitted parents to visit on the first Sunday afternoon of each month, only a few boys received parental visits. Home visits were permitted for Christmas vacation.
9. Although 20 percent of the residents were of Latino background and 15 percent were Native Americans, there were no staff members (other than Jack) who were members of these cultural groups. It appeared that no effort was made to train staff to be culturally sensitive to members of these groups.
10. Conditions in the group homes varied greatly. The more experienced staff had their maintenance requests taken care of immediately, had better furniture and decor, and had their homes painted annually.
11. There appeared to be a problem with the group home food supply system. Several of the less experienced staff reported that the food seemed inferior to that sent to more experienced staff.

As the informal group discussion ended, Diane and the others decided to think about how to develop additional information in a systematic way, with an initial goal of trying to make things better at the ranch. Diane knew, however, that effecting change in a large, complicated system would be difficult.

Assessment: Organizational Problems

It was obvious to both Jack and Diane that things had to change. Foremost in their minds was that the residents of the ranch were currently at risk for abuse and neglect at both an individual and an institutional level. Any efforts to influence institutional policies and practices and to explore the ranch's problems with the administrative staff could place the residents in a more difficult position. Finally, Diane and Jack considered their own situation. They were both new staff members who depended on the ranch for their salaries and security. They also recognized the need to be loyal to their employing agency. They didn't want to be known as troublemakers, but they knew that their social work ethical code of conduct required them to place their clients' interests before their own. Thus, they struggled with the first major ethical dilemma of their careers.

Based on these important considerations, on information they had developed through talking with some of the boys, and on other observations made during their employment, Jack and Diane discussed their overall assessment of the situation at EBR.

1. The policies and practices of Evergreen Boys Ranch appeared to place the ranch residents at risk for unethical

practices by some of the group home parents. The administrative staff of the ranch seemed to tacitly approve of corporal punishment, deprivation of parental visits, lack of appropriate and culturally sensitive services for ranch residents, and inadequate physical and emotional care.

2. The executive director of the ranch appeared to exercise strong control over many of the group home parents. He dictated overall organizational policies and practices that appeared to have detrimental effects on several of the ranch's residents. His personal behavior seemed to border on the unprofessional.
3. Boys who were admitted to the ranch were socialized into the existing structure of the ranch, and this structure did not consider the special needs of boys and families from Native American and Latino cultural backgrounds.
4. The ranch had a very high turnover rate for group home parents, which contributed to a lack of stability in helping relationships between staff and the boys.
5. The ranch had a very high rate of runaways, which suggested that ranch residents were unsatisfied with the services they received and perceived that they were at risk for physical and emotional abuse.

Jack and Diane thought they had enough information to come to this generalized assessment. It was difficult for them to begin to plan for how to make things better. They decided to ask some of the group home staff to come to a strategy meeting at their apartment. During this meeting, they hoped to present the staff with their assessment. Perhaps, they thought, others would share their assessment and would want to join them in trying to improve things at the ranch.

Goal Planning: Organizing for Change

Diane took the lead, organizing another evening meeting of group home staff. Five other couples attended, and two others provided temporary coverage in the group homes while the meeting took place. Evening meetings of staff were a regular event, mostly for the purposes of socializing, ordering a pizza, or relaxing after a busy day. However, this meeting was a somber event that took on a conspiratorial climate, accompanied by feelings of "revolution in the air." Diane led the discussion and took the first part of the meeting to review the facts she and Jack had developed and to share a synopsis of their assessment of the problems at the ranch.

Although the group seemed to reach consensus on the facts and assessment, there were strongly divided opinions about what to do to bring about change. About half of the group wanted to plan for "change from within," which included talking with other group home staff and bringing up their concerns with the administrative staff. Several others

wanted to take their complaints to the local newspaper and ask a reporter to visit the ranch and write an exposé of the ranch's policies and practices. Heated discussion took place well into the night, and there was a good deal of self-imposed pressure on the group to reach consensus on a plan. Finally, the group agreed on the following plan.

Intervention strategy #1. They would send a delegation to the executive director to discuss their concerns. Diane and Jack were chosen to accomplish this task.

Intervention strategy #2. Should strategy #1 not work, it was decided to send a delegation to the Department of Social Services and to the Department of Juvenile Probation to ask these agencies, which placed boys at the ranch, to investigate the ranch's policies and practices.

Intervention strategy #3. It was decided that involving the media would be a last resort, to be used only if nothing else worked.

Diane explained to the group that these strategies followed a pattern favored by professional social workers—namely, using collaboration and negotiation before using conflict. Most of the group agreed that this made sense. However, one group home staff member continued to insist that going to the media would be the only acceptable alternative to him. The meeting ended without convincing him otherwise.

Intervention: Planned and Unplanned

Jack and Diane made an appointment with the executive director for that afternoon and arrived early. While waiting in the reception area, they heard him talking loudly to a boy who had committed an infraction of ranch rules. The director had apparently suspended the boy's parental visit as discipline for the boy's behavior, and the child left the director's office in tears.

The director asked Jack and Diane to be seated in his office while he spoke with the boy's group home staff on the telephone. Jack noticed that the director's office contained an extremely large rectangular table with the director's chair at one end and two chairs at the other. Communicating with the director under this spacial arrangement would be difficult at best, but they decided to accept the arrangement and do their best.

As Jack and Diane started their presentation, they noticed that the executive director was becoming increasingly uncomfortable. He could not maintain eye contact with them and would look off into the distance, appearing to ignore their presentation. In addition, he would continually rearrange items on his office table without appearing to notice that this behavior was distracting and rude. In her most effective nonverbal way, Diane urged Jack to move closer to the director by moving her chair about halfway down the table. Jack caught on, and with this move the director stood up and began pacing the floor, still appearing not to listen to their presentation.

After Jack and Diane had finished, they assured the director that they and the others had only the interest of the residents in mind and that all were willing to work hard to make things better. The director thanked them for their interest and paused while he collected his thoughts. He noted that he had the confidence of the ranch's board of directors and that they supported the current policies and practices of the ranch. He suggested that some of the complaints were unfounded and were the result of discontented employees who were not able to adapt to the style of the ranch. He suggested that those who could not fit in might benefit from additional staff training. Jack noted that many of the group home staff he had spoken with might not agree with the director's assessment but that he would mention this to the rest of the group. Diane asked if it would be possible to form an ad hoc task force to study the group home discipline policy of the ranch and make recommendations for improvements to the executive director and to the board. The director replied that most group home staff were "too busy to be bothered with additional group meetings." Diane thanked the director for his attention to their concerns, and she and Jack left to return to their apartment.

As they were leaving the director's office, Diane and Jack encountered the boy who had been in the director's office prior to their meeting. They noticed that the boy had red marks on his face and was crying. When Jack asked what was going on, the boy replied that the director had slapped him on the face several times because he had failed to do his required chores. Jack and Diane walked the boy to his group home and spoke with the resident staff about the incident. They were told that this was not the first time the director had used corporal punishment in dealing with ranch residents.

Jack and Diane knew that they had encountered a reportable incident of suspected child abuse, which would have to be discussed with their immediate supervisor. They immediately contacted the assistant director but were told that they should not interfere with the authority of the executive director. Both Jack and Diane knew they were ethically and legally bound to report this incident to the Department of Social Services, and they did so when they returned to their apartment. Meanwhile, Jack made appointments for the next day with institutional placement officials from the State Department of Social Services and the Department of Probation.

Jack and two group home staff were able to meet with representatives of these agencies and present the facts as they knew them. They urged that an investigation into the policies and practices of the ranch be initiated, and Jack noted that he had filed a complaint of suspected child abuse with the local Child Protective Services office of the

Department of Social Services. The representatives were sympathetic and assured Jack that they would begin an investigation.

That evening, Jack answered the door of the apartment and was greeted by Don Bowers, a local newspaper reporter. Don was somewhat famous in the local community for his investigative reporting. Jack suspected that Don was at the ranch because he was contacted by one of the group home staff who had decided not to follow the intervention plan protocol agreed on by the group. Diane suggested that they not talk to Don until they had a chance to discuss what had transpired recently with their group of interested staff. Don said he received a call from a staff member who reported all that was happening at the ranch. He suggested that he was going to write an article about the ranch in this week's paper, with or without their help. Jack politely declined to give an interview and insisted, along with Diane, that they stick with the original intervention protocol. As agreed upon, going to the media would be a last resort.

Later, several group home staff met with Jack and Diane to discuss recent events. Notably absent was the one staff member who had insisted on presenting the situation directly to the media. It was clear that he had obviated the consensus opinion and taken matters into his own hands. The group discussed what to do next, and it was agreed that they would wait for the promised investigation by the state agencies.

Evaluation: The Rest of the Story

Although Jack, Diane, and the group had tried to approach the change effort in a logical and systematic way, their actions initiated a process of events that profoundly affected the status of the ranch and its residents. The state agencies appeared on the ranch and began an immediate investigation of policies and practices, concluding that much needed to be changed. At the same time, the local Child Protective Services Agency arrived (with the local county sheriff) and interviewed the executive director, as well as some of the residents and employees of the ranch. Don Bowers, the investigative reporter, was present during some of these activities and filed a story that appeared on the front page of the major newspaper in the area. Local television stations carried feature stories of the ranch happenings, including live broadcasts from the ranch.

The net effect of these events was most disturbing to the ranch residents, who did not fully understand why all this was happening. Jack and Diane spent a good deal of time with groups of boys who needed support and reassurance. Many boys acted out their fears about what might happen to them as a result of the investigations and media coverage. Ranch staff tried to assist the boys to understand the processes that had been set in motion and tried to help the boys through the climate of crisis.

The board of directors held an emergency meeting and heard staff and resident testimony about ranch policies and practices. Jack made a presentation of his and Diane's concerns as professional social workers, suggesting that the ranch should be reorganized, that policies and practices should be reviewed, and that the executive director should be suspended from involvement with the ranch until the board reviewed his performance. The board also heard testimony from several influential community leaders who urged that the executive director be retained, that employees involved in the change effort be terminated, and that the board give the executive director its vote of confidence.

As the board considered its position in a closed executive session, Jack and Diane reflected on how their good intentions and their "planned change effort" had developed into a series of crises and unplanned consequences. Ranch residents had been placed in personal and psychological jeopardy as a result of their actions, and despite their efforts to provide supportive counseling, Jack and Diane felt responsible.

After its meeting, the board held a press conference with most of the local media representatives in attendance. The board had voted to suspend the executive director, reorganize the administrative structure of the ranch, and initiate a staff–board committee to review and revise ranch policies and practices. A decision was also made to reduce the number of residents served by the ranch, and the board authorized the staff to review the status of each resident and make recommendations about who could be placed at home or at another suitable placement.

Eventually, the board appointed an interim executive director who would be responsible for reorganizing the ranch's administrative structure. Diane was offered the position of interim assistant director, which she accepted, and she helped in studying and redeveloping ranch policies and practices. Jack continued to function as the social worker for the ranch, assisting in the return of some ranch residents to their families and helping connect others with their families for regular visits. He also assisted some of the residents in accessing needed psychological and social services.

The Evergreen Boys Ranch gradually became a more stable, viable resource for children in the state, owing, in part, to the efforts of Jack and Diane and other interested staff members. About a year later, Jack and Diane left the ranch and accepted employment in another state. For Jack and Diane, life went on.

Readings

Gambrill, E. (2001). Social work: An authority-based profession. *Research on Social Work Practice, 11*(2), 166–175.

Oliver, M. N. I., Yutrzenka, B. A., & Redinius, P. L. (2002). Residential paraprofessionals' perceptions of and responses to work-related ethical dilemmas. *Mental Retardation, 40*(3), 235–243.

Witkin, S. L. (2000). Ethics-R-Us. *Social Work, 45*(3), 197–201.

Discussion Questions

1. *Of the two ethical dilemmas confronting the social workers, which carried the greatest risk to them personally? Why?*

2. *If the board of directors had not suspended the executive director, what other options remained open to Jack and Diane?*

3. *What reasons can you think of for Jack's refusal to talk to the reporter? Do you agree with his decision? Why?*

4. *The assistant ranch director told Jack and Diane that the kids in their care would settle down in a bit, despite the fact that they were "rejects" from other cottages. What ethical concerns do you have with the assistant director's statements?*

5. *Do you agree with the strategy to first approach the executive director with the group's concerns? Describe your reasons.*

6. One member of the group did not agree with the rest of the group regarding the best method to use in proceeding. If you were the group leader, what might you have done to help assure that this person did not sabotage the group's efforts?

7. When you cannot predict the outcome of your planned change effort with any degree of certainty, should you decide not to try to implement your plan? Why or why not?

8. If you were asked to gather data to help determine whether the ranch had fulfilled its mission, what kinds of information might you seek? What information would you need first?

9. In this case, the social workers are acting as advocates for all residents of the boys ranch. Typically, advocates act only when those they are representing are in agreement with the worker's assuming this role. Explain why this situation is different from a typical advocacy case.

23

The Willow River Developmental Disabilities Center

Dennis D. Eikenberry

The Willow River State Developmental Disabilities Center was home to 500 people with varying needs and abilities. All of its residents carried a primary diagnosis that included such categories as developmental disability, general mental retardation, cerebral palsy, autism, birth injury, or epilepsy. In addition, they had other medical and behavioral involvements that provided various challenges to staff responsible for their care.

Located in a rural, pastoral setting, the center was far from the hustle and bustle of modern urban life. The site for the center was selected by the legislature around the turn of the century, when the prevailing intent was to remove disabled people from society, protect them, and give them a chance to "live with their own kind." Current national and state policies provided a major departure from this approach, dictating that attempts be made to integrate or reintegrate people with disabilities into the mainstream of society. The intent of this policy was to help the disabled experience life as normally and independently as possible while providing them with the supports necessary for that to happen. Residential services, vocational training, and case management needs were the responsibilities of the center.

A variety of habilitation programs were part of the total treatment services provided by the center. Most programs took place in the centrally located "Education Center." Here, people from all residential areas gathered each day to receive work-related training. There were, however, about 100 residents who were no longer eligible for educational services because they were over 18 years of age. It was this group of 100 people who eventually became the client system in a large-scale class action grievance filed on their behalf by a social worker at the center.

Data Collection and Assessment

Juan Rivera became disturbed at what he perceived to be a lack of adequate "active treatment" for residents of the center. Juan was a seasoned veteran of the mental health movement, having been involved in moving the mentally ill from large institutions to community residences and providing them with necessary supports from neighborhood comprehensive mental health programs. While Juan was responsible for case management services

for some of the residents, he became concerned about how the center treated all members of the "over 18 group" in the center's Education Center.

Juan was one of several professionals who participated in an organizational task force responsible for designing and implementing agency programs. As educational program planning proceeded, often over Juan's objections, it seemed to be driven by the needs of the institution rather than by the needs of the people designated as consumers of the program services. In one particular educational program, those residents who were in the "over 18" category were placed in groups because there was space available, rather than because of their identified educational needs or plans.

In composing all groups, people were assigned to a particular group because they were friends or got along with other members. Professional staff were likewise assigned to work with groups in a less than systematic fashion. Rather than consider their educational talents or qualifications, workers were assigned to groups based on no apparent criteria. These practices led to many unhappy groups with much disruptive behavior on the part of the residents. Workers spent an inordinate amount of time dealing with negative behavioral episodes of residents, including running away (eloping) and attempting to harm themselves or others. In essence, workers mostly provided custodial care rather than organized and active treatment. It was clearly a system problem.

Juan assessed the problem as involving two complicated issues. First, assignment of residents to educational groups was random, depending on where space was available. Goals for each member were not specified, and group goals did not necessarily match members' needs. And there was no individualization of service, program, or treatment. Second, the planning process designed to facilitate the program features appeared flawed, favoring the needs of the institution over those of the service consumers.

Planning: Collaboration, Negotiation, and Conflict

Despite Juan's several efforts to register his concerns with his supervisor and the center's administrative staff, there seemed to be no recognition that the system wasn't working. The power structure of the institution was clearly acting, in Juan's opinion, in a way that violated the rights of the organization's service consumers. While not the only voice advocating for individually designed services, Juan's opinion was clearly not considered important by anyone on the planning group. Each time a concern of this nature was raised, it would be quickly discounted, often because it would take too much time and effort.

Wondering what avenues of change might be followed, Juan researched some important background information. He found that residents of centers for the developmentally disabled have rights guaranteed by federal law and state statutes. These various laws are interpreted and result in administrative policy and rules. In addition, parts of the law provided procedures for registering complaints on behalf of consumers, including violations of residents' rights under federal and state law.

The Department of Health, Bureau of Quality Compliance and Care defined grievance procedures and appointed staff to investigate complaints. Information about clients' rights was routinely made available to all residents who lived in the state facilities, to their parents or court-appointed guardians, and to all other professionals who worked at state facilities. Although staff from each facility were designated to be on-site investigators of complaints and grievances, the Department of Health conducted independent investigations of grievances related to clients' rights. Four stages or steps are available in a grievance procedure.

1. The investigator from the institution reviews all the facts and holds an informal discussion with all parties involved. If the matter is not resolved to the complainant's satisfaction, a report of the findings is provided to the institution's administrator.
2. The institution's administrator reviews the report of the findings and issues a formal written decision to the complainant.
3. The complainant may appeal the administrator's decision and forward the complaint to the Client Advocacy Program (CAP) within the State Department of Health and Social Services. A CAP grievance examiner conducts an investigation and issues a written decision to the complainant and other interested parties.
4. Either the institution's administrator or the complainant may appeal the decision of the CAP grievance examiner to the administrator of the Department of Health and Social Services, who will review the grievance, conduct an additional investigation, and provide a written decision within prescribed time limits.

Juan realized that his concerns involved a large number of consumers and that they were not all able to understand that their rights to "active treatment" might have been violated. He also realized that as a social worker he had the ethical responsibility to advocate on his clients' behalf,

place their interests before those of his employing organization, and seek to change organizations such as the center to be more responsive to its consumers' needs. With these principles in mind, he decided to file a group grievance on behalf of those residents who did not seem to be receiving the most planful care available to them.

Intervention: The Group Grievance

Independently, Juan prepared a formal statement documenting what he felt were systematic violations of consumers' rights to active treatment. According to agency policy, the grievance was received and assigned to an institutional staff member to investigate.

The agency investigator, in completing the first step in the investigation, "was unable to find a plan, operational manual, or descriptive model on file that included anything resembling a planned, thought-out road map for the educational program" Juan had cited. The investigator recommended that the institution establish "a curriculum for this program containing a statement of aims and specific objectives and indicating some selection and organization of content, including a plan for evaluating outcomes for participants."

Juan felt that these findings supported the need for change within this educational program. He also recognized that additional sanction from an administrative level would be needed to implement the recommendations that came from the investigation. To facilitate this, he requested that the recommendations be reviewed by the executive officer of the institution, thereby initiating the second step in the grievance process.

This action resulted in the administrator charging the manager of the educational program "with the responsibility of having on-hand an up-to-date description of the program, including minimally, a statement of philosophy, list of objectives, and an outline of the program components and model." In addition, the program manager was "to establish individual treatment plans for all participants in the educational program, establish and review individual lesson plans or work plans to determine what problems of program implementation and problem solving were needed, and meet with all staff to evaluate program effectiveness."

Although it seemed that he had won a victory for consumer rights, Juan's feeling was short-lived. The program manager did respond with a bare outline of program goals and very general goals for program participants, but actual implementation of these features was not forthcoming. In fact, on several observation visits to the educational program, it seemed to be "business as usual," with participants receiving no individualized services and staff unable to articulate specific goals or desired outcomes for individual participants. It became clear to Juan that a policy was only as good as the people who were responsible for implementing it. He decided that further action was needed.

Wishing to accomplish more, Juan requested that the grievance be considered according to the third step in the process. The Client Advocacy Program investigator, who was an attorney, would conduct a thorough investigation and make further recommendations. Upon assignment to the case, the new examiner met with Juan and reviewed the grievance. Juan was able to articulate several issues for which the consumers he represented sought relief.

1. The program should have a statement of purpose, stated goals, measurable outcomes, and a plan for evaluating those outcomes.
2. A formal curriculum should be established, with sequencing requirements that would allow participants to move through the curriculum at their own pace.
3. The program should concentrate on definable skills and should be directed to simulate typical experiences of the work world.
4. Participants should be assigned to groups based on clear criteria and on common levels of ability and need. There should be a required ratio of one staff for every four participants.
5. Assignment of staff to groups should be based on the educational needs of the participants. There should be a continuity of staff assignments to groups, and staff should have specialized training from the institution on meeting the disabled population's needs.

The grievance examiner's investigation was accomplished in four months. It involved many interviews with staff, observations of several work groups, and review of pertinent, documented program information. Juan met frequently with the investigator, and he sensed, for the first time, that the grievance was being taken seriously. With the expertise of the new investigator, and with Juan acting as a consultant and mediator, there appeared to be hope for large system change.

The final report was issued by the CAP investigator and reviewed by the administrative staff of the institution. The following are excerpts from that report.

1. In the context of a structured adult education or vocational program, the lack of a complete and accurate program description creates a high risk that resident rights violations will occur. Structured adult education or vocational programs must provide sufficient opportunities to meet residents' needs, as well as document how those needs are met through evaluative research methods.
2. Staff monitoring, evaluation, and responsive team work are needed to guarantee the level of participant individualization required by law. Programs must also have the clear capability to be developmentally progressive for the individual.

3. Lack of a program description detailing the program rationale, goals and objectives, plan for meeting those objectives, and method for evaluating program effectiveness makes effective review of a program unnecessarily difficult. In the law, the inability or failure to provide documentary evidence almost invariably mitigates against the party whose inability or failure has deprived consumers of these rights to "active treatment."
4. Legal compliance of the entire educational program is at issue here. The core concept within the federal law is that of active treatment. Active treatment requires a high degree of individualization. This individualization is achieved through the Individual Program Plan (IPP) process carried out by an interdisciplinary team. The IPP and team processes are designed to ensure that the selection and organization of the program, distribution of staff, and other resources all flow from the collective individual needs of the clients. Rather than distribute clients among available program resources, the primacy of the client's assessed individual needs must guide program decisions.
5. The conclusions of the grievance process reinforce residents' rights to a system of decision making and quality assurance provided under federal law. Subversion of these processes violates these rights. Federal law requires implementation of the Active Treatment Plan (ATP) by all staff who work with residents. Programming should be organized to correspond to the rhythm of activities that characterizes the normal work day residents will encounter in the community.

The recommendations of the grievance examiner corresponded to the recommendations made in steps 1 and 2 of the grievance process. This level of review, however, not only added detail about what had to be included in the educational program but also gave "force of law" to the rationale for implementing these program features.

It was recommended that the institutional administrator ensure that all involved staff understand the program's organization and operation, including areas of responsibility and expectations for accountability, so that they understand what they are responsible for as well as for whom and to whom they are responsible. It was also recommended that the administrator ensure that all staff members understand the role of the designated Quality Assurance staff person as a conduit to the team decision-making process. The administrator was required to provide staff training to effect this.

Evaluation of the Change Effort

The efforts of the social worker in this situation led to a major change in a large system. When change is sought in a large, complicated system, the outcome or benefit is often difficult to measure. At the same time, however, large system change offers the opportunity for long-term benefits for people served by the system.

The social worker's original concerns were satisfactorily addressed in the final report of the grievance examiner. The administrative staff and the planning task force used this report to redesign the educational program and to give more detailed attention to active treatment for program participants. One year following the conclusion of the grievance procedure, examiners from the State Department of Health evaluated the programs and services of the Education Center. Although their evaluation of the program found positive qualities, including the sincere concern of staff for program participants, the report also cited problem areas. The Education Center did not look like an adult workplace, and people's needs for relevant challenging work were mostly unmet. Their conclusions suggested that, without change, participants' work skills would remain untapped and their chances for living and working in the community would be limited.

The product of these many voices advocating for change in the system resulted in the institution changing several features of the program. The name of the educational program was changed to the Community Work Program, and more meaningful work skills were taught. In addition, the institution contracted with a number of community businesses and organizations to perform work, both on-site at the institution and in selected community businesses. Providing meaningful, realistic, paid work for program participants led to an increase in the number of institutional residents who were mainstreamed into community residences.

Ending: A Note about Large System Change

Many factors come into play when bringing about change in large systems in our society. In this case, the social worker assisted a large group of clients to exercise their legitimate rights under federal and state law. Whether working within a small group, an organization, or in change efforts in a community, social workers must be prepared to risk themselves. Although advocating on behalf of large numbers of clients is a legitimate function of social work, it is not without its dangers. Filing a grievance is confrontational and often is seen as a final step in the social worker's arsenal of social action.

Collaboration, where both client and target systems have similar interests, is preferable as a first step. When the interests and positions of client and target systems differ, as was the situation in this case (residents-institution), it is often best to attempt to mediate or negotiate agreements between these systems. When these strategies fail, confrontation or conflict is a legitimate strategy.

Although grievance procedures usually state that no one can be punished for using the procedures, both workers and clients often pay a personal price when exercising these rights. Challenges to large systems do not go unnoticed, despite measures to assure confidentiality. In large systems change, confidentiality is often difficult to preserve. The price to be paid by both clients and social workers could be anger, pressure, retribution, or personal attacks. As Saul Alinsky once suggested, when people stand up for the rights of others, they should be prepared to defend their own rights.

On the positive side, social workers engaging in large system change often find that they have made a lasting difference in the lives of others and in the institutions serving those people. Change, however, remains an evolutionary process.

Readings

Malekoff, A. (2000). Bureaucratic barriers to service delivery, administrative advocacy, and Mother Goose. *Families in Society, 81*(3), 304–315.

Mary, N. L. (2001). Political activism of social work educators. *Journal of Community-Practice, 9*(4), 1–20.

Reichert, E. (2001). Move from social justice to human rights provides new perspective. *Professional Development, 4*(1), 5–13.

Discussion Questions

1. What are some of the possible risks to social workers who try to change the system that employs them?

2. How can social workers maintain their health and integrity when dealing with this very real stress in the workplace?

3. To whom did Juan owe his greatest loyalty—the client or his employer? Why?

4. Why was it important that the clients be involved in activities similar to what they would encounter in the community?

5. What factors might contribute to an agency losing sight of its responsibilities to clients and focusing more on the needs of the organization?

6. *Juan could have decided to contact the media to focus attention on the Center's problems. Instead, he followed internal processes for handling grievances. List the possible advantages and disadvantages of each of these approaches.*

7. *Had Juan not been successful in resolving the problem, what other strategies might have been considered?*

8. *Do you consider Juan to have worked "within the system" for change? Why or why not?*

24

Self-Disclosure and Client Discrimination

Alicia R. Issac
Lettie L. Lockhart

Engagement and Presenting Problem

Alexandria Cramden was beginning to gain confidence in herself and improve her skills in her job of eight months. Alexandria was a case manager for the Step-Up program, and her job was to help mothers receiving welfare to find training and employment and become self-sufficient. Many of her clients had expressed their appreciation to her and to her supervisor, Jim Reeves. Several of her coworkers said they were learning from the innovative ideas Alexandria had been using with her clients.

On Alexandria's sixth visit to Mary Carpenter, a young mother in the Step-Up program, she was informed that Mary did not want to work with her and wanted a new case manager. This request was rather shocking to Alexandria, who felt she and Mary were making significant progress together. Alexandria wondered if she had unknowingly done something to offend Mary. She remembered that during their last meeting Mary had been somewhat apprehensive and had seemed angry when she was told she would have to attend school or a vocational training program. However, by the end of that meeting, Mary seemed more receptive. Mary had a history of not following through on the tasks she had agreed to perform in their contract together.

In their last session, Alexandria had become more insistent that Mary follow through in making contacts with local schools and work training programs. Alexandria mused to herself, "I wonder if Mary is resisting some of the changes she needs to make? I can understand that she doesn't want to send her children to a daycare center. Lord knows, there have been enough incidents of sexual and physical abuse in daycare centers reported in the national news lately. I can understand her reluctance to trust someone else with her children. Asking for a new case manager doesn't seem to be a productive strategy for overcoming her fears about daycare." Alexandria asked Mary what was bothering her about their professional relationship, but Mary seemed reluctant to discuss the matter. The following dialogue occurred.

Mary: Look, Alex, I don't need a reason to want a new worker, I just want one!
Alex: Mary, this is a very unusual request. You need to provide me with a more specific reason.
Mary: Alexandria, I know that you are gay! A friend of mine saw you and your partner in a "gay neighborhood"

a few weeks ago. I don't hate gay people, but I can't work with "someone like that."
Alex: I'm not sure how any aspect of my personal life would or should affect my working relationship with you.
Mary: Look, Alex, I'm requesting another worker, and that's that! I've got nothing against gay people, but that's my decision. If you don't get me another worker, I'll tell your supervisor, Jim, and explain why I am making the request.

Alexandria was very disturbed by this turn of events. In a small, rural, homophobic community such as this, her job might be in jeopardy. Even Jim, her supervisor, had made derogatory remarks about gays on a few occasions.

Alexandria was not sure she wanted to "come out," for news of this could reach friends, families, clients, and colleagues. Also, she had to consider the feelings of her partner, with whom she had lived for several years. How would she take this news? Would a self-disclosure about their relationship jeopardize her employment or her relationships with others in the community? More than anything else, Alexandria felt her professional values were being compromised. She felt she had a right to be treated in a professional manner, since she had acted professionally with her clients and colleagues. She somewhat resented being pressured into discussing her sexual orientation when this was not required of her peers in the organization. This did not seem fair.

Assessment: Organizing the Information

Alexandria's first impressions were that Mary was unhappy about having to pursue a job and that she was reluctant to follow through with placing her children in daycare. She felt that Mary was making this request to manipulate her and to sabotage the work they had done to resolve the issues that had kept Mary dependent on welfare. In retrospect, Alexandria was able to identify the evening that Mary's friend had seen her and her partner together. This incident had occurred several weeks ago. Mary must have known this information before now, but she had chosen not to bring up the issue until now.

Alexandria was unsure of what to do. Because of the complex and sensitive nature of the issues raised, she felt she had few choices. She could either process Mary's request, discuss the request with her supervisor, or do nothing and wait for Mary to carry out her plan. She felt pressured into making an involuntary self-disclosure.

She resented having to divulge personal information about herself that had no bearing on the quality of her work. Above all, Alexandria felt discriminated against because of her sexual orientation. This was the kind of thing that people in the real world experienced. She had been taught in her BSW education that clients who experienced discrimination need to be supported and protected; however, she never thought she would be in this position herself, especially in a social services organization. She worried about the potential for discrimination by her supervisor and peers, yet she had no way to measure the support she might or might not have in the organization without telling someone about her dilemma.

Lastly, Alexandria felt manipulated and coerced by Mary. Because of Mary's resistance to change, Alexandria would either have to continue with Mary's treatment plan and risk being "blackmailed" because of her sexual orientation or process Mary's request for a new worker and risk further attempts on Mary's part to manipulate a new worker. The situation was complicated further by trying to understand some of the ethical issues involved for her client.

Alexandria was keenly aware of the NASW Code of Ethics, which supported the client's right to self-determination. She also knew that professional social workers needed to put the interests of their clients above their own needs, but she was unsure of whether this standard applied in this situation.

Goal Planning: Considering the Options

For better or worse, Alexandria made a decision that, despite Mary's right to self-determination, she did not have the right to manipulate the situation and coerce her into compromising her professional standards. She felt strongly that Mary did not have a problem working with someone who had a differing sexual orientation; rather, this was Mary's attempt to resist the changes they had planned together. A telephone conversation revealed that Mary continued to be adamant in her request for another worker.

Alexandria decided not to process Mary's request. She did not want to establish a pattern of being threatened by clients each time her lifestyle came into question. She knew that Mary had a number of friends in the Step-Up program, and even if she did process Mary's request, she felt Mary would share this information with her friends.

After many hours of soul searching, Alexandria devised the following action plan:

- she would discuss the situation with her partner and find out what her feelings were;

- she would inform Jim, her supervisor, about Mary's request and the reasons she had given for the request;
- she would seek support from two of her best friends in the agency; and
- she and Jim would make a home visit to Mary to discuss her request in more detail.

Intervention: Confronting the Issue

Alexandria's discussion with her partner, Jean, went very well. Jean told Alexandria she felt that eventually both of them would confront this issue, and rather than run from it, they should try to resolve it within their relationship. Jean pointed out that neither of them had the ability to control the feelings others might have about their sexual orientation. Alexandria felt relieved and supported by Jean's comments. She felt lucky to have such a supportive partner.

Jim's reaction to Alexandria's presentation was not as supportive. He showed obvious discomfort, and his nonverbal communication indicated that he did not know how to respond to Alexandria. As the conversation progressed, he was able to verbally express some of his feelings. He stated that all of this was quite a shock to him and that he had no idea that she was gay. He related that he had very little experience with "these kinds of people." Jim also related that he felt a bit betrayed by her as she had been present when office personnel were engaged in discussion about gays and she hadn't acted as if she were a part of this group. He also was concerned about how other service consumers and her colleagues would relate to Alexandria if they knew she was gay. He stated that it would be very difficult to defend her and the organization if a female client lodged an allegation of sexual misconduct. Jim stated that the agency did not need that type of publicity, and he would have to think about what to do in the present situation and get back to her.

Alexandria's conversations with two of her colleagues were much more supportive. Both noted that if they were in Alexandria's position they would not let Mary manipulate them. They felt that if Mary continued to insist on having a different worker, Alexandria should let Mary process this request with Jim.

It took a week before Jim scheduled a conference with Alexandria. During the conference, he informed her that he had done some reading on the subject and felt a bit more equipped to handle the situation. He stated that he could support Alexandria in not processing Mary's request for a new worker. He warned Alexandria that she should be prepared for trouble because Mary had been in the system for a long time, was familiar with the rules and regulations, and knew whom to contact if she did not get her way. He told her he had struggled with the issue of whether or not to contact the organization's director about the situation but had decided not to. Although he felt he might eventually have to do this, to do so now might be prematurely inviting additional difficulty. He ended their conference by supporting Alexandria's position and offering to make a home visit with Alexandria to discuss the issue with Mary. Alexandria and Jim made a home visit to Mary on the following day. Although Mary had agreed to meet with Alexandria and Jim, she appeared apprehensive about inviting them into her home. The conversation proceeded as follows.

Mary: You all are welcome to come in. But I just want you to know that I am not feeling very well, and this will have to be a short meeting.

Jim: We appreciate your meeting with us, and we will try to make it as brief as possible. We think it is important to deal with this issue as soon as we can. Since we are all aware of why we are here, maybe we don't need to go over all the details. Alexandria, will you give us a brief summary of your last meeting with Mary? Mary, I'll ask you to respond when she is done, if that's OK?

Alex: It was during our last regularly scheduled meeting when this issue was raised. Mary and I were discussing the absolute last date she could begin her training program, when she informed me that she wanted a new case manager. I was quite shocked and perplexed, and I asked her why. In the beginning, Mary stated that "it was personal." Later, if you recall, Mary, you said that a friend had seen me with my partner in a "gay neighborhood." Mary, you stated that you could not work closely with "someone like me," even though I did not acknowledge to you whether or not I was gay. What I did say was that I did not think my personal life would keep me from doing my job in an effective and professional way. As I told you, Jim, Mary refused to change her mind at that point, and she said that if I did not process her request, she would call you.

Jim: Mary, is this account accurate? Is there anything you want to add or change?

Mary: Yes, this is what happened, except she did not tell how nervous and upset I was about her being here.

Alex: As a matter of fact, Mary, I noticed that you seemed to display hardly any emotion during our last meeting.

Mary: Maybe that is just what you thought.

Jim: Before we go on and talk about our options here, perhaps each of us can share what we are feeling about this situation. As for me, I'm still not sure what is the right thing to do in this situation. Mary, I understand your request, but I also know that Alexandria is the best case manager in my unit. I think you have made more progress toward reaching your goals than you have with the last two case managers you have worked with. I don't see anything about Alexandria's lifestyle that has interfered with you reaching your goals.

Alex: This incident has really upset my life and has made me wonder whether this is the right profession for me. I feel that my lifestyle is not the real issue here, but it is being used to keep me from doing my job. I am afraid, confused, and deeply concerned, because this does not only affect me but others. I somehow feel that whatever happens, I will be the loser.

Mary: All I have to say is that I'm sorry if this has caused problems for you. I have my rights and feelings too, and I shouldn't have to be around gay people if I don't want to.

Jim: This has been a learning experience for both Alexandria and me. We have made some decisions about how we would like to handle your request. Our organization has specific policies that must be followed when requesting a worker change. Because Alexandria has made the decision not to ask to be reassigned, you will have to initiate the process yourself, in writing. I have brought a list of necessary steps, which I will leave with you today. I understand that this may not be what you desired, but I agree with Alexandria that the real issue for you may be fear about the new direction your life may be taking.

Mary: I'm not sure that I agree, but I don't know what to do. I can't let you know right now what I am going to do.

Jim: I want you to know that change is frightening, but you will not have to go it alone. We will be here to support you. The other women in the program will support you. I can remember how involved you were in working with the school when you thought they were discriminating against "welfare mothers." I think this situation is very similar to what Alexandria is going through now.

Alex: Mary, I hope you will really think about what we have said. I hope you know we want to continue to work with you. You and I have our regularly scheduled visit next week. Unless we receive something from you in writing, I will be here. Jim, is that appropriate?

Jim: Yes, I think it is.

Evaluation: Ending

Mary did not respond in writing, and Alexandria made the home visit as scheduled. Although it felt like starting over with Mary, Alexandria did her best to help Mary move along in the Step-Up program.

Readings

Lewis, R. J., Derlega, V. J., Berndt, A., Morris, L. M., & Rose, S. (2001). An empirical analysis of stressors for gay men and lesbians. *Journal of Homosexuality, 42*(1), 63–88.

Newman, B. S., Dannenfelser, P. L., & Benishek, L. (2002). Assessing beginning social work and counseling students' acceptance of lesbians and gay men. *Journal of Social Work Education, 38*(2), 273–289.

Van Voorhis, R., & Wagner, M. (2001). Coverage of gay and lesbian subject matter in social work journals. *Journal of Social Work Education, 37*(1), 147–160.

Discussion Questions

1. *What is meant by client self-determination? In this case, was Mary's right to self-determination violated when she was not allowed a change in worker?*

2. *How could Alexandria have worked with Jim to help him overcome his attitude about gay men and lesbian women? What possible remedies might there be for institutionalized homophobia in the organization?*

3. *What rights do social workers have in protecting their personal lives? Do social workers need to sacrifice their personal safety or well-being to satisfy the client's right to self-determination?*

4. *Should service consumers routinely be given the right to determine who will work with them, or should organizations make assignments based on the expertise or skill of the worker?*

5. *What responsibility does a professional social worker have to help change clients who are overtly discriminatory, racist, sexist, or homophobic? What responsibility does the social worker have to change coworkers, supervisors, and organizations that are openly or institutionally discriminatory?*

6. *What federal regulations guide "welfare reform"?*

7. *What is the role of a case manager?*

8. *What did Alexandria mean when she said she did not want to "come out"?*

9. *What risks might coming out pose for Alexandria?*

25

Managing Margaret's Care
Kimberly Strom-Gottfried

Margaret Benham slumped back in her chair. Her desk was littered with piles of brochures from insurance companies, and today was the deadline for selecting one to provide her health insurance for the coming year. Each October, Margaret's employer, Ace Accounting, held "open enrollment" so workers could make new insurance choices for the year ahead. Like many other employers, Ace put together an array of plans and allowed employees to select the plan that best matched the worker's life circumstances and personal needs. Ace provided its employees with a fixed amount of money for health coverage, and employees could then "spend" the amount any way they chose. Some workers elected to buy the lowest cost insurance and use the leftover funds to purchase dental insurance or prescription coverage. Other employees were willing to pay extra, to supplement the employer's contribution, in order to get the particular services or family coverage they needed. In some ways, Margaret's choice was simple. As a single, 38-year-old without children and without a history of health problems or risks such as smoking or high blood pressure, she had no particular or special needs for her health plan.

Margaret had always had traditional insurance before, but because she used so little health care, she found herself paying "out of pocket" for routine exams and prescriptions in order to meet the $500 deductible required before her insurance would begin picking up the costs. As she skimmed through the insurance companies' slick brochures, she wondered why she should continue to pay for services that other plans were promising to provide for free. She had narrowed her choices down to three managed care plans, two of which were offered through Health Maintenance Organizations (HMOs) and another that was a "Point of Service Plan." The last was quite costly, and since she was determined to stop overspending on health care, she ruled out that option. The other choices were two plans within the same HMO, "Health-Mate." They both offered low-cost prescriptions, so that no medication would cost her more than the $5.00 copayment. They both offered a number of clinics with locations near her home and her office, and extended hours, so if she needed services, she could go before or after work. Since both plans covered mental health services, home care, and hospitalization costs, Margaret felt she would be protected in case of a catastrophe. After spending an exhausting hour scanning the materials, she could find no real distinction in the plans that would account for the difference in cost between the "Bronze Plan" and the "Platinum Plan." In fact, the price of the Bronze Plan meant that she would get money back from her employer, since the monthly rate was less than Ace had allocated for her insurance. Margaret selected the lower cost plan, completed her form, and carried it to the Human Resources Department.

December 1, 1998

Margaret received a letter welcoming her to Health-Mate, her new insurer. Along with it she received a packet of information the size of a small phone book. The book listed a lot of information about her coverage, the policies about getting care, and what to do in emergencies to make sure that HealthMate would pay for needed services. Margaret glanced at the material, but was most concerned about the information that listed all the doctors at the various clinics. She was alarmed to find that her regular physician wasn't listed, and she called the consumer help line for assistance. The woman who eventually answered confirmed that Margaret's physician was not a preferred provider. She would need to choose a new doctor from the available list. The representative offered to provide information about the credentials and availability of various doctors, but agreed with Margaret that it felt like a pretty random choice. She assured Margaret, however, that she could change physicians later, but urged her to make a decision of some type so that her enrollment in the HMO could be processed.

HealthMate was glad to have Margaret as a member. HMOs are paid though "capitation," where employers pay a certain amount of money, per employee per month, for a range of services, regardless of whether the employee ever uses them. This provides incentives to HMOs to offer preventive and other services without copayments or deductibles, so that for members who use them, illnesses and more expensive services are avoided down the line. HMOs calculate the risk of covering certain populations, and enrollees like Margaret are prized. With her good health and limited use of medical care, the funds saved on the care she doesn't use could be pooled to cover other "high-users" of care and to provide profits for the HMO.

January 1, 1999

It didn't take long for Margaret to become acquainted with HealthMate! Walking to her car one snowy evening, she slipped on the ice and fell sharply on her wrist. The next day, convinced it was not a mere sprain, she called her new doctor. The woman answering informed Margaret that urgent care calls went to the "Care Line" for triage and that only standard appointments were made directly with the physician. Margaret was transferred to the Care Line and a nurse asked her a series of questions about her injury, the level of pain, and the range of movement in her wrist. The nurse agreed that it warranted examination and arranged an appointment for Margaret within the hour.

When Margaret arrived, she learned that the appointment was with a "pool" doctor, since her physician was booked for the day. Nevertheless, she was grateful to be seeing someone, and she set about completing the forms required for a first-time visit. The doctor's demeanor was brisk but kind. She agreed that the injury needed to be X-rayed and sent Margaret to the Radiology Department upstairs where a staff person was waiting. Within an hour, Margaret's injury had been diagnosed and her wrist set in a splint. As she left the clinic with a follow-up appointment and a low-cost prescription for pain, Margaret marveled at the efficiency and economy of her HMO compared to her earlier form of insurance and her care from a private physician.

September 22, 1999

As Margaret undressed for her aerobics class, she felt a slight tugging in her chest. Her breasts had always been "lumpy," but lately she'd felt a hard lump, and this surge of pain reminded her that she should have the lump examined. During an annual checkup over the summer, she had mentioned the lumps to her doctor. He assured her that his examination had turned up nothing unusual and said that the HMO policy for scheduling mammograms was that they were to be done at age 40 and every five years after, unless family history or examination indicated otherwise.

Margaret was a little annoyed at his statement that he'd "found nothing unusual." Since this was the first time they'd ever met, how could he compare his findings to anything? She understood the policy for selectively recommending mammograms, though. For one thing, she wasn't exactly eager to have one, and she knew that by using protocols about when to do certain types of testing, the HMO could manage expenses better and avoid unnecessary costs or services. In addition, she trusted the doctor and was relieved when he gave her a clean bill of health.

Now, however, she wasn't so sure. She called the Care Line, and as she waited on hold, her apprehensions mounted. The nurse finally came on, asked about her concerns and, because the situation was urgent, referred Margaret for an appointment. Margaret tried to put her worries aside as she awaited the appointment. She reasoned that if there was any real cause for concern, they would have had her see someone immediately. As it was,

she had to see a Dr. Strunk, since her physician was booked far in advance.

Dr. Strunk shared Margaret's concern and, after a brief examination, referred her immediately for a mammogram. On this day, the HMO operated with the same calm efficiency, but Margaret felt her fear swelling up and her life spinning out of control. When she returned to Dr. Strunk's office, she knew the mammogram results were not good. The internist had consulted with a team of other physicians who specialized in cancer and described Margaret's condition to her. He believed her cancer was at an early stage and recommended a mastectomy to ensure that the tumor and any remnants were removed.

Margaret, still stunned by the news of her cancer, reacted with disbelief to this recommendation. Weren't there other, less radical options? What about a second opinion? The doctor reviewed Margaret's chart and left the room to make a phone call to the Care Review Department. He returned to tell her that her level of coverage allowed for a second opinion, but only if she bore the cost of it herself. Furthermore, he felt that a mastectomy was clinically indicated to eradicate the cancer and he stated that the HMO had determined other options to be less effective or experimental.

Secretly, Dr. Strunk was reluctant to say more. He truly believed that the mastectomy was the best alternative for Margaret, but he also knew that there were other alternatives, with different risks and success rates. Unfortunately, Margaret's coverage with HealthMate would not pay for any of those procedures, and HealthMate's policy was that physicians should *not* discuss alternatives that were not part of HealthMate's services. The organization felt that it was divisive to HealthMate and upsetting for patients if doctors were "turning patients against their HMO." Dr. Strunk had never been happy with these "gag rules," but he was certain that, if necessary, he would not let them come between him and his duty to his patients.

September 23, 1999

Margaret had decided to forego the second opinion, not wanting to waste money or precious time in dealing with this problem. She called HealthMate and scheduled the mastectomy. However, the admiration she'd once had for HealthMate's efficiency was turning to aggravation as she had to speak with several staff before getting the person who specialized in scheduling breast cancer surgery. The nurse who answered had not been involved with Margaret's previous care but she gathered information on the case by pulling up Margaret's file on the computer. As she waited, Margaret pondered the ease with which her records were available—anywhere, anytime—and wondered distractedly if every HealthMate employee could so easily learn about her situation.

As they were making the arrangements, Margaret asked how long she would be hospitalized for the procedure. The nurse replied, "six hours." She went on to explain, "We believe that there is a high risk of infection when people are in hospitals. It is much better to return home the same day, where you can rest without all the distractions and interruptions of the hospital."

Margaret's rage, fear, and incredulity merged. "Do you realize I live alone? I can get a ride there and back, and I have friends who can look in on me, but *I am alone*!! You want me to leave the house in the morning with two breasts, and come home at the end of the day with one . . . just like it's a regular work day, or a splint on my wrist? What then?" The care manager was not unaccustomed to such reactions, and in her heart she understood. She tried to soothe Margaret and assured her that the social worker assigned to her case would arrange follow-up care, counseling, and all the other services needed so she could heal at home. As Margaret hung up the phone, she snapped, "And I suppose she'll arrange a cook and housekeeper for me, while she's at it!"

September 26, 1999

It was a sunny Monday morning as Margaret joined an array of people being processed for various forms of "day surgery" at the HMO. As with her other visits, she moved seamlessly through the filling out of forms, the check of vital signs, and the meetings with various people involved with her care. Her sister-in-law Linda had flown into town to be with her during the surgery and the beginning of her recovery. Shortly, the two were visited by Karen, the social worker in charge of discharge planning.

Karen greeted the two and escorted them to her cubicle adjacent to the waiting room. "I understand this is a difficult day for you. My role is to work with the nurses and physicians in letting you know what to expect during the procedure today and when you return home. In particular, I'll be making the arrangements for your home care and follow-up services, and I'm also here to help with the emotional or psychological aspects of your condition." Karen asked what questions or concerns Margaret had and went on to outline some of the common reactions to a diagnosis of breast cancer and to the loss of a breast. Recognizing that the information was likely overwhelming, she left Margaret with a booklet of information and a list of services within HealthMate and in the community, such as support groups, educational programs, and stores for post-mastectomy products. She noted that many of the services were free or involved a nominal fee, and added, "Of course, you can see one of the therapists in HealthMate's behavioral health unit for support, but they're pretty backed up, and your plan would require you to pay half the fee. If you decide you want individual counseling, it may be best to seek that out in the community." Suddenly, the "benefits" in Margaret's health plan didn't seem as comprehensive after all.

Karen then asked Margaret about her home, her support systems, and her plans following discharge. She said, "You'll be leaving here today with enough bandages, gauze and tape to change your dressing for the next two days. You'll need to pick up more for the rest of the week. We'll give you a week's worth of pain medication and an information sheet on all the do's and don'ts for taking care of your wound. A home health nurse will be visiting every three days to check on you until your follow-up appointment next week."

"Wait," Margaret interrupted, "what about showering and meals and medications? Who is supposed to change my bandages on the days the nurse won't be visiting?"

"Well, that is why I was asking about your supports and how long Linda will be available. We urge you to use your own network for help in your recovery . . . to supplement your health plan."

Linda made a face. She did not want to upset Margaret, but she had come to offer help with meals and transportation and emotional support. The idea of changing bandages on Margaret's wounded body repulsed her. "What if I wasn't here, or if I couldn't do it?" she asked.

"Well," said Karen, "we would make arrangements for a health aide to visit Margaret, and while that would be sufficient, it wouldn't be the optimal level of care that someone in the home could provide." Margaret seemed dazed, but Linda was provoked. "Aide?! Do you mean a nurse wouldn't be taking care of Margaret at home?" The social worker nodded. "That's right. An RN's training and credentials aren't needed to do many of the patient care duties. That's why we feel family members, when they're available, can do those tasks. That way, we can conserve our nurses for the jobs where their skills are most needed."

Linda pursued, "But what if her condition got worse or if she got a fever or an infection?" Karen noted, "That's all covered on the home care instruction sheet. Our care managers will call every day to see how she is doing. If they sense something out of the ordinary, they'll ask her to come in. If at any time you or Margaret have concerns about her condition, you can call our careline and come in for follow-up."

A nurse appeared at the cubicle, holding a hospital gown and slippers. "Hi Margaret. If you'll come with me, we'll get you set up in this and the doctors will be in to go over the procedure with you." Linda gathered the resource material and instructions and followed her sister-in-law out of the cubicle, shaking her head. Karen glanced at her clipboard and went to the waiting area to greet her next patient.

October 15, 1999

Margaret returned to work and tried to restore some familiar routine to a life that was turned upside down with radiation appointments, plastic surgery evaluations, and bouts of pain and fear. On her drive to the office, she heard a report on the radio of a promising new medication, designed to reduce the risk of cancer in women with a personal or family history of breast disease. When she arrived at work, she called her doctor to ask about the drug's usefulness in her case. When Dr. Strunk called back, his tone was not promising. "Yes, I've heard of the drug, too. Actually, it has been on the market for years, but hadn't been used before for breast cancer. Unfortunately, there are two problems with my prescribing it. One, it is not carried by our pharmacy nor is it prescribed by HealthMate, as it is a very high-priced drug and we recommend lower cost alternatives. Second, its use in breast cancer prevention is, at this point, experimental, and we are very cautious about committing our resources to unproven treatments."

Margaret was indignant at the thought that a potentially life-sustaining treatment would be withheld from her to enhance her HMO's financial security. Surely there were other places to cut corners besides patient care! Dr. Strunk demurred. "If you were the only patient HealthMate had to concern itself with, the answer, of course, would be yes. But we have to balance the needs of all our patients. How do you think we can afford to provide medications and care at no or low costs? Because we cut down on other high-cost or low-impact items. Sometimes when people enroll in more generous plans, like the HealthMate Platinum instead of HealthMate Bronze, they have more options because they are paying more to begin with to buy better coverage. In your case, though, because the medication is experimental, which plan you're under wouldn't make a difference." Margaret answered "So is that the last word? Don't I have any recourse?" "Certainly," said Dr. Strunk. "The HMO has a procedure for appealing decisions. It is spelled out in your enrollment materials, but I can also have your social worker call to explain it." "Please do," Margaret replied curtly as she hung up the phone.

The call came later that afternoon. Karen explained the process for filing appeals of HealthMate decisions. "Of course, there's a form. Once you fill it out, Dr. Strunk will add his opinion. Then it goes to a panel of doctors who decide if the request is in keeping with good medical care and with the HealthMate Benefit contract you agreed to." "It sounds hopeless," Margaret replied. "Well, I've seen it go both ways. It doesn't hurt to appeal, though. I mean, they won't hold it against you or anything." Though this possibility hadn't even occurred to Margaret, the unsolicited reassurance rang hollow.

Karen continued, "So you look the form over and let me know if you need any help from me. The appeals committee meets weekly, but sometimes they're backed up, so it's best to get it in as soon as possible."

October 31, 1999

It was open enrollment time again at Ace Accounting. Margaret viewed the collection of marketing materials from the insurance companies with a critical gaze. The past 12 months had provided a powerful education on the state of health care in the United States, and she was skeptical that *any* choice she might make would really provide security in the event of another health crisis. Besides, she now had a "history" and a "preexisting condition," which would make it difficult to get new coverage without high costs, a possible lapse in service, and the need to change doctors and clinics all over again. She felt there were few choices without putting future insurance coverage at risk.

Regardless of how HealthMate responded to her appeal for better medication options, Margaret resigned herself to continuing with them for another year. She let out a cynical laugh as she checked the boxes on the form. This time, she'd see for herself if "platinum" really was better than "bronze."

Readings

Gibelman, M., & Whiting, L. Negotiating and contracting in a managed care environment: Considerations for practitioners. *Health & Social Work, 24*(3), 180–191.

Schneider, A. W., Hyer, K., & Luptak, M. (2000). Suggestions to social workers for surviving in managed care. *Health & Social Work, 25*(4), 276–280.

Sulman, J., Savage, D., & Way, S. (2001). Retooling social work practice for high volume, short stay. *Social Work in Health Care, 34*(3/4), 315–333.

Discussion Questions

1. *What pros and cons of managed care are portrayed in this case?*

2. *How can social workers help consumers like Margaret make more informed decisions when choosing a health plan? What special considerations are needed when those choosing the plans do not have the health, resources, or degree of choice that Margaret had in 1998?*

3. *How can social workers become informed about managed care? What do they need to know to help their clients?*

4. *How does the issue of informed consent apply to Margaret's decision about insurance and to her health care at various points in her journey?*

5. *What other ethical issues emerge in this case? What options are there for the professionals to avoid or resolve these dilemmas? What can social workers do when the best interests of the client conflict with agency policies?*

6. *What are the pros and cons of using natural helping networks to supplement formal health care?*

7. *How could "case advocacy" and "cause advocacy" be used effectively in this case?*

8. *What might happen to a woman like Margaret in another industrialized country (such as Canada) that provides universal health care?*

9. *If a social worker had been involved in this case, what expectations in the NASW Code of Ethics would apply?*

26

From Case to Cause: My
Name Is Jess Overton

Donna McIntosh

Jess Overton averted her eyes and said in a tired voice, "What choice do I have if that's the rule. As long as he is safe from his father, I can live with it for the time being." Valerie Gunther, the Intake and Services social worker for Safe Sanctuary Domestic Violence Services, was completing an intake interview admission into the congregate emergency shelter for Jess and her children. In the middle of explaining an admissions policy, Valerie told Jess that her eldest son Nick could not be admitted to the shelter because he was 15. "We have had to institute a no admissions policy for young adolescent males because we have found they are often aggressive and violent. This behavior makes the other residents upset and unsafe since most of our residents are trying to escape these types of behaviors. I know it's a tough call and it may feel like this policy is breaking up your family, but Nick will be housed in an emergency home host family with our youth services program. He will still be part of this agency, and the social worker for the youth services program and I will work together to ensure that you, Nick and your other children spend time together every day."

Jess thought for a minute and said to Valerie, "You have to know that I am really scared that this is going to be interpreted by David, his lawyers, and the judge, as my abandoning Nick. I am worried that David might use this to get custody of Nick." Valerie explained that the family court judges were very aware of this shelter policy and that most domestic violence shelters in the state had similar policies. Valerie handed Jess the shelter's information about the emergency home host family program for teens in crisis while she put in a call to the youth program to transport Nick to the host home. Valerie said, "I will give you a few moments to talk to Nick here in the office and then we can talk about some other services and strategies while you are here in the shelter with us."

A half hour later a youth worker came to transport Nick to the host home. The worker informed Valerie that Nick would be in a host home two towns over, near the end of the county line, so his location would not be readily known. Valerie handed the youth worker the consent for shelter care for Nick, signed by Nick and his mother. She also gave the worker at the school an enrollment form so Nick could enroll the next day at the school where the host home was located. Nick and his mother walked to the door together, and Nick looked uncomfortably aware of the workers and residents as his mom hugged him and gave him a kiss on the cheek. He said goodbye to his brother Marty and sister Shannon, and left with the youth worker.

Valerie showed Jess and the children to their bedroom, helped them get supplies, and introduced them to the rest of the residents and staff. After lunch, Valerie asked Jess to join her in the office while her children participated in afternoon play time with the other shelter children. "Marty and Shannon seem to be having fun with the other kids. I just checked on them." Jess was smiling, but Valerie could see the apprehension and worry on her face. Valerie said, "Come, sit down, Jess, and we'll talk while the children are playing." Jess sat down with Valerie and sighed, "I suppose I should tell you a little more about my background." Valerie said that eligibility for admission to the shelter really depended on what was currently going on with her family and on the presence of domestic violence which threatened members of the family. She also told Jess that residents sometimes give a history of how the problem started, so if she felt comfortable she could talk about that. Through the conversation between Jess and Valerie, the following information was developed.

Jess Overton: Her Case

Jess reported that she is the eldest of four children. She has three brothers, Peter, Stephen, and Alex. Her parents live alone on a small farm about 200 miles west. Her brother, Alex, is the closest to her age, and they remain in close contact despite the fact he lives in California. Alex is aware of the violence that has gone on in her marriage. However, she has little contact with Peter and Stephen and hasn't heard from them in years.

Jess's father ruled his family in a strict and diligent manner. Physical discipline was the rule. She was an honor student throughout school. School was important to her father. He expected all of his children to be honor students and to do their best.

When Jess was 16, she tried to kill herself by taking some of her mother's pills. She ended up in a unit of the local psychiatric hospital for six days but refused to go to a counselor. When she was discharged, she decided she wanted to get out of her house.

She was 18 and working at a hardware store when she met David. At age 19, she married David, and by age 20 she gave birth to Nick. She and David moved to another part of the state shortly after Nick was born and remained there ever since.

David was a regional marketing director for a large national firm. He did well during his early years with the company, traveled a lot, and received several promotions. He enjoyed his work. During this time, two other children were born, Marty, now age 10, and Shannon, age 6. Jess had two miscarriages between Nick and Marty, brought on from daily physical beatings from David. After Shannon was born, David stopped hitting her for a long while, and Jess was hopeful that things would improve. The physical beatings had started when she became pregnant with Nick and were the worst whenever she was pregnant. After the first miscarriage, Jess signed herself into the local psychiatric unit of the hospital because she had become obsessed with dying. She also felt like her marriage was re-creating the problems she had experienced during her childhood. She worried a great deal about leaving Nick alone with his father.

She tried to leave David once, shortly after Nick was born. Her brother, Alex, took her and the children to his house in South Carolina. Alex was a newlywed and Jess's and Nick's presence placed a stress on his relationship with his wife. She went back to David with the children after Alex learned through his job as a police officer that David had received temporary custody of the children. According to Alex, David had used Jess's past suicide attempts and hospitalizations as a means of obtaining custody.

After that, David told her she could leave anytime she wanted but "without any money, anything from the house, and certainly not with my kids." David further informed her that state law could terminate a parent's rights based solely on a parent's mental health status. Since then, Jess never tried leaving again.

But yesterday, David had gone too far when he hit Marty and left bruises all over him. Two years earlier, Marty had been diagnosed with an emotional disturbance. He was in a special educational program in his school and was receiving Supplemental Security Income (SSI) for his disability. David was always "on Marty's case," and he often told Marty that he could never do anything right. David called Marty "crazy" and "retarded," claiming that Marty couldn't possibly be his child because he would never have such a messed-up kid.

When David was hitting Marty, Jess jumped between them. David hit her several times on the head and twisted her left arm until she heard something snap. She left early the next morning and went to her physician's office. Marty's face and back were bruised and Jess's head ached. She couldn't move her arm, and it was severely swollen.

The doctor reported no broken bones and asked her how it happened. Jess told her the truth; she was finished lying for David. The doctor said that she would have to report the incident to the state's Child Abuse Hotline.

As for the abuse that Jess suffered, the doctor said that she would quietly refer her to the domestic violence shelter in the area, but officially, she was using a diagnosis under the category of Mental Health.

Jess panicked when she heard the words "mental health." Her first reaction was that she would end up being hospitalized and that David would get the children. The doctor informed her that if she reported a diagnosis of Domestic Violence to Jess's health insurance carrier, her claim would be denied. However, if she reported that Jess's injuries were the result of a home accident related to past mental illness, and if there was a follow-up recommendation for mental health services the insurance company would pay. The doctor said that managed care policies were interpreting domestic violence as a "pre-existing condition" and not a health-related illness. Consequently, they were rejecting medical claims on that basis. The doctor explained that as a physician, she was required by law to ask her about domestic violence based on the injuries she saw. However, Jess would need to go to the county mental health clinic or a private therapist if she wanted the claim for this emergency service to be paid since the insurance carrier was recognizing domestic violence under a mental illness diagnosis.

Reluctantly, Jess went to the hospital's outpatient mental health clinic. As soon as she told them she was in a violent relationship, the clinic staff told her she had no mental health problems, that it was a family violence issue and needed to be taken care of by the local shelter service. Jess wondered why it was so complicated but realized that this was the necessary route she had to take to be linked to the Safe Sanctuary Domestic Violence Services. Still, she wasn't quite sure what all of these different policies and laws meant. The bottom line for her was that David not get the children and hurt them again.

Individual and Family Needs

As Jess finished her story, Valerie quietly said, "Jess, thank you for sharing all of that with me. I am glad that despite having to go to several places, you found out about the shelter services and made it here today. The staff will be meeting tomorrow morning with you to help establish a plan, and we will be working from what you have shared with me today."

The shelter staff routinely met within 72 hours of each intake to review the information for each resident and to work with the resident to establish a prioritized service plan. Generally, a shelter stay was only 30 days, although it could be extended for up to 90 days if the local county Department of Children and Family Services approved the extension. To be eligible for services, a resident had to establish that there was some form of family violence present in the home. Together, Jess and Valerie decided that the following needs should be addressed:

1. Jess should complete an application for public assistance for supported housing.
2. Jess should enroll Marty and Shannon in the shelter's school district and see that Marty's special education plan was transferred from his previous school.
3. Valerie and Jess would need to determine the status of the child abuse report filed by the doctor.
4. Jess and the program's court advocate should file a petition with family court to advocate for custody of the children.
5. Jess should establish a plan with the shelter staff to maintain daily contact with her son Nick.
6. Jess should participate in the program's individual and group counseling services.

At the end of the process, Valerie looked at Jess in a concerned way and said, "Jess, I have to ask this question as well. You have made suicide attempts in the past and I'm concerned about that. I wonder, no I worry that you might consider that again." Jess looked directly at Valerie and said, "My children need me now more than ever. I'm scared of what David is capable of, especially when he finds out that I am filing for custody. Right now, I am fine. If that changes, I will let you know."

Staff Meeting—Day 2 in the Shelter

The staff of the shelter met early the next morning for a general staff meeting and then for Jess's case review. During the general staff meeting, Valerie reported her concerns about some disturbing policy practices brought to light by Jess's intake and history. Janet Rockwell, the Sanctuary's director and chair of the meeting, asked Valerie not to recap Jess's case, but rather to speak about the policies.

Jess Overton: Her Cause

Valerie addressed the group:

Yesterday, after I met with Jess, I learned that her physician would not properly diagnose her injuries as resulting from domestic violence. The physician noted that if she did so, Jess's insurance company would not pay for her visit because they could classify the diagnosis as a preexisting condition and not health related. Instead, she was referred to the mental health clinic for counseling, and was refused services because it is their policy that domestic violence should be handled through services such as ours. Later that night, I compiled data from our intakes for the last six months. I found that every referral from our local mental health clinic was due to a refusal on their part to provide mental health services for victims of domestic violence. My contact at the clinic informed me that it is the clinic's policy not to serve any women who disclose domestic violence as their primary problem. When I pressed him further as to why, he told me that two years ago, the State Association Against Family Violence had lobbied hard at the state level to avoid diagnosing persons experiencing domestic violence as mentally ill. The association wanted to acknowledge that persons who were violent to other family members were the ones who needed treatment, not the victims.

A different but related issue came to my attention. Over the last five years, a number of women across the state had their parental rights severed by family courts due to diagnoses of mental illness. These cases were more accurately described as domestic violence. However, in the absence of proof that domestic violence had occurred, the mothers who were victims lost custody of their children. Custody in those cases was awarded to the fathers, but many of those kids ended up in foster care when their fathers later abused them.

Valerie seemed to have gotten the attention of the group. However, the policy issues she had researched were not entirely clear to her yet. Despite spending the better part of last evening researching, she felt that she didn't know enough about the complex issues at work in Jess's case. Valerie continued,

I interviewed someone at the County Prosecutor's Office and she told me "off the record" that the County Prosecutor's Office did not acknowledge the "Battered Wife Syndrome" diagnosis used as a criterion for determining parental fitness for abused women who were seeking custody of their children. Apparently, the county prosecutor told the Mental Health Clinic director that the county legislators and many state legislators agreed that such a diagnosis would only be a sanction for women to take matters into their own hands instead of using the system that exists. However, my contact also said that if asked directly, these policymakers would "tone down the rhetoric" and cite their longstanding support of funds for domestic violence shelters and services.

I also learned that at the clinic our reputation may be in question. They feel that we have a practice of refusing readmission to former residents who were admitted to the hospital for psychiatric reasons, by claiming that we are not equipped to deal with these types of problems. My contact at the clinic expressed a desire to work on this issue, but was concerned that policies existed because of political reasons.

Janet Rockwell, the director of Safe Sanctuary Services, nodded thoughtfully and took notes. She particularly wondered about the physician's comment about domestic violence being a "preexisting condition" and wondered if this was an "official" position of the health care industry about domestic violence. She addressed the group as well as Valerie: "Valerie, I don't know. I haven't heard of such a thing, but we could call the other shelters and the State Association and find out." Janet asked if Valerie or the other staff had other concerns regarding these policies and laws.

The program's court advocate, Nancy Miller, shook her head in frustration, "I deal with these mixed messages every day in court with the women from this shelter. Valerie, if you haven't come up against this policy issue yet, you might with Jess's child, Marty. He's on SSI, and I understand that if he's not in an approved special education program, and sometimes even when children are, the federal government is disallowing them SSI. We had better work fast to ensure that Marty stays in the special individualized education plan from his previous school district."

Valerie was not sure she followed what Nancy was saying and asked for clarification. Nancy reported that in the last couple of years, the federal government had changed eligibility standards for SSI for children with emotional disturbances and was cutting off thousands of children from benefits. The premise behind this policy practice was that too many children were being labeled emotionally disturbed and receiving SSI, and that a fair number of these children weren't emotionally disturbed at all, but had been coaxed by their parents to display the behaviors that would make them eligible for SSI. In the next federal legislative session, this issue was on the agenda, and it was anticipated that the federal regulations would be modified to further tighten eligibility and eliminate several thousand more children from benefits.

Valerie had been with Safe Sanctuary Domestic Violence Services for only six months, and she never realized that she would have to know and be involved in so many state and federal policies and interpretations to do this job. She didn't want to do policy advocacy. She wanted to do her job of conducting intake and counseling services for women and children trying to escape violence in their lives. She realized that advocating for individuals and families was a complicated matter, and she felt inadequate and uninformed. She hardly understood it herself and wondered how she would ever be able to explain it all to Jess.

Sensing that the staff members were feeling overwhelmed by the complexity of the policies and laws involved in this situation, Janet suggested that the next large staff meeting, scheduled in two weeks, be dedicated to discussing what could be done about working for policy clarification and change. She also suggested that staff members who would soon be attending the next meeting of the State Association against Family Violence attempt to get their concerns on the Association's meeting agenda. Janet felt it was important for staff at all levels to understand the policies and laws affecting their work and to work toward influencing policy.

Nancy Miller sighed as she noted, "It's my job to know all of these policies as they affect our consumers of service. As I talk with other advocates in shelters across the state, I hear them saying the same thing. The policies are changing daily, and noncompliance with them is the norm. We all feel like we have to be policy advocates in addition to case advocates for our consumers. It seems like an impossible task."

Jess: Case Advocacy

Jess and the staff met to establish her service needs and plan on how to work toward her goals. Valerie began the meeting by acknowledging to Jess that her situation had brought up many larger policy issues, which could potentially affect many women in her position. Valerie did know that right now, Jess's needs had to come first. A child protective worker had called and was scheduled to come the next day in order to talk to Jess and the children. Valerie had helped Jess enroll the children in a new school district, and plans were discussed for their first day at the new school. Jess arranged for Nick to spend time with her, Marty, and Shannon at the Family Program located at the organization's main office. In addition, Jess disclosed that she would like to establish her own household and find a job or a training program to attend. The staff discussed these goals with Jess and worked on identifying a prioritized list of tasks that needed to be accomplished. Jess came out of the meeting with some optimistic feelings for a change.

Day 5 in Shelter

"Unbelievable! I didn't think this would be a problem. Since his diagnosis of a learning disability three years ago, Marty has been in the same school without any challenge to his diagnosis. Why now, when he and I need it least?" Jess's face flushed, and she paced around the office. Valerie reassured her, "We don't know yet, Jess, they might enroll him in the half-day resource room he needs or supply him with the in-class computer. If they won't, we can talk to the parent advocate at school or can request a hearing before the school board. For now, we are fortunate the school even enrolled him. The social worker from our Youth Services Department, the one who is working with Nick, told me that enrolling children in a different school district while they are in a temporary shelter didn't happen until the 1987 Federal Stewart McKinney Law mandated school enrollment, regardless of the temporary nature of residency. So Marty's in school. Next, I will accompany you, if you like, to the Individualized Educational Plan meeting for Marty next Monday."

Jess just sighed again, "I don't have the energy to fight right now. Yes, Marty is in school, and I don't want you to think I am not grateful. How well do they think he will do if he doesn't have the right educational plan. He'll fall behind quickly!" Valerie just listened as Jess yelled, "It seems like everyone knows I'm down on my luck, and they are working hard to drive me back to David!" Valerie gulped, and asked, "Is that what it feels like? Are you thinking this would all be easier if you just went back to David?" Valerie had heard this statement often in the six months she had been at the job. It was hard work and a seemingly uphill battle for women to reestablish themselves independently from their violent partners. More and more, Valerie was appreciating the impact that various policies had on people's lives and on her own abilities and skills to help women break free from violent relationships.

Day 10 in Shelter

As she returned from family court, Jess exclaimed, "I feel like it's two steps forward and one back! Today, I was granted temporary custody of the children, the child abuse report against me was unfounded, but they are still investigating David. The children's law guardians told me not to worry about losing custody because of my mental health history. They said Judge Richardson was an understanding judge who didn't stigmatize mental health problems and certainly was well aware of the effects of domestic violence on victims." Valerie questioned, "Yes, but what's bothering you?"

"This is all great," said Jess, "but then the judge granted supervised visitation with the children for David until the child protective investigation is done. I don't want him anywhere near the kids. I can't let that happen. I won't comply with that visitation order. I don't care what happens. He can't visit them if he can't find us."

"Jess, a lot of that's great and we can only take one day at a time. The person who supervises the visitation is appointed by the judge. Whatever David says or does to the children is reported to the judge. I'm sure his attorney has told David that he will have to be on his best behavior if he hopes to continue to see his children. Work with Nancy on strategy and ask her questions if you are concerned. Nancy has contacts with the Law Clinic at the local Law School. They often give free legal advice and strategy to Nancy and residents here." Jess looked a little more relieved.

Later that day Valerie received some bad news. She asked Jess to join her in the office, and she proceeded to tell her about Marty. "I had a call from Marty's school today, and I thought you should know. They decided that they do not want to have Marty evaluated by their school psychologist and that Marty will have to remain in his current classroom. They justify their position on the basis that he is technically 'homeless,' will probably be only temporarily in the school district, and they cannot justify the expenditure of time and resources for such a situation. They also reported that his school records have still not arrived from his former school. Now, I checked with Janet, our director, who tells me that this is not completely legal, but that some schools choose to interpret the federal mandates regarding the special educational rights of children in their own way. In fact, Nancy, our advocate, tells me that many school districts across the state disagree with this practice and are forming a coalition to overturn federal mandates for special education."

Valerie continued, "As for Marty, we do have a recourse. We can request a hearing with the school board and if that doesn't work, we can refer the issue to the State Education Department. Nancy will be helping you with that process." Jess fell heavily into a chair in the office and started crying. Valerie let her cry and came to sit by Jess and held her hand.

Day 21 in Shelter

The school district had rejected Marty's special educational plan after Valerie and Jess presented their case to the school board. The board noted that Marty had functioned well in a grade level below where he was placed in his other school. They felt it appeared he had no special education needs, but rather, was inappropriately advanced before he was prepared. The next step was to appeal to the State Education Department. Jess felt she wanted time to talk to Marty about the decision and to talk to a lawyer at the Law Clinic.

Day 30 in Shelter

During this past month, the job coordinator for the shelter had helped Jess enroll in a training program at the local college. Jess was going to be a lab technician. It was always something she wanted to do, but her parents had told her that they didn't have the money and that she didn't have the talent to pursue this career. She was scheduled to enter a transitional apartment on the outskirts of the city in three days. There, she would have a two-bedroom apartment and could stay for up to 18 months while she worked to get back on her feet. Valerie contacted a furniture-recycling program and helped Jess to get beds, a couch, and a small kitchen table and chairs for the apartment. Jess felt she could furnish the apartment a little at a time and was excited about her upcoming move.

David was still fighting Jess in court for custody of the children. Nick, her eldest son, had refused to visit with his father, and Jess wasn't pushing this with Nick. Marty and Shannon still went every week to the Courthouse, where in a special small room, they saw their father for an hour. Sometimes Shannon cried in her sleep for her daddy. That's when Jess found it most difficult to be on her own. For a while, Jess couldn't think about anything but the good times with David. She wouldn't tell the staff because she felt they wouldn't understand, but Jess still had feelings of love for David—even though she feared and sometimes hated him. He still wasn't paying any child support, but with the help she was getting from social services, they were petitioning the Court for back child support and future payments for the children. She still hadn't done anything about Marty's educational plan, but she intended to, after they settled in the apartment. Just yesterday, she had received a letter from the regional Social Security Office informing her that because Marty was no longer receiving special educational services for an emotional disturbance, his SSI benefits would be terminated effective the first of next month. She was sure the school had informed the Social Security Administration, though Nancy had assured her no law required the school to do so. She was still within the appeal dates for both the educational and the SSI benefits decision. She was going to appeal both. She needed Marty, Nick, and Shannon to know she wasn't a quitter, and she would fight for herself and them.

She went downstairs where the staff and other residents were throwing her and the children a goodbye/good luck party. She would miss the other women in the shelter but had already decided to keep coming to the support group. During cake and ice cream, Valerie and Janet approached Jess. Janet said, "Jess, I know Valerie has brought this up with you in the past, but I would like to extend a special invitation for you to testify at the spring forum on domestic violence. You have worked very hard in the short while you have been here and have done well, even when it all seemed uphill and people were using policy roadblocks along the way. Valerie will be staying in touch."

Janet added, "Valerie and I are attending the monthly State Association meeting soon, and we will keep you posted. It might be helpful if you come to an Association meeting; there are a number of us there who have been where you are today. The Association knows the most powerful voice sometimes comes from someone who has lived through the experience of domestic violence. Please consider joining us? Enough said, let's have more cake and ice cream!"

Jess: Cause Advocacy

Valerie, Nancy Miller, and Janet Rockwell rode in Janet's car to the State Association meeting. This was the first time in her professional career that Valerie had ever attended a statewide association meeting of any kind. She was feeling nervous but convinced that for Jess, and other women in similar situations, she had to speak up about some of the policy issues Jess's case had presented.

Janet parked in front of the building and turned to Valerie, "Valerie, it is important for you to speak up about these issues. I support you and your efforts, but I also want you to be aware that at these meetings you aren't just speaking for Jess's experience and your point of view. You are a voice for our organization, so if you are unsure about anything, I am right beside you and will help if needed." Valerie wasn't sure what Janet's real concern was, but she was starting to understand that the "politics" of her organization were also at work in this case.

Valerie's presentation included the following issues, and she requested that the Association develop positions on these issues and discuss them with legislators during the next state legislative session.

1. Managed Care, Health Care Coverage, and Domestic Violence: the status of domestic violence in the health care field. Is it considered a nonhealth-related preexisting condition and uninsured?
2. How can we ensure that victims of domestic violence are medically treated and covered by insurance? How can accurate documentation of domestic violence be established by medical practitioners?
3. How can we ensure that victims of domestic violence and their children receive necessary mental health services and domestic violence services without receiving a label that could hinder their legal rights and their well-being?
4. What are the legal rights of parents with mental illness, and how does the child protective system evaluate their abilities to care for their children?
5. How can the association help to clarify the diagnosis of "Battered Wife Syndrome," and how do the legal and mental health definitions differ?
6. What are the rights of children who are homeless and who need special education placements in schools? How can their rights be upheld, especially if they are receiving SSI benefits?
7. What are the educational barriers faced by children from families who are homeless, including issues of school enrollment, transportation, transfer of records, and safety issues?
8. Is it possible to revisit the policy of not admitting male children who are 14 and older to shelters for domestic violence?

Association representatives in attendance discussed these issues briefly, many of them noting that they had also experienced some of these policy issues. Valerie learned that some of these concerns were being addressed with the State Coalition for Mental Health. Both groups were planning to appear at a legislative hearing next spring.

The Association president, Amanda Greenfield, asked Valerie if she would be willing to supply written and oral testimony at that hearing. She also asked Valerie if she could find someone who could testify about these policies from a "service consumer" perspective. Valerie said that she had a person in mind and would get back to her about her willingness and availability to testify.

Amanda Greenfield told Valerie that many programs were being asked to look at aggregate data for the past year to see if their consumers were encountering difficulties with the policies Valerie had noted. She also noted that the Association was working with BSW students from a Social Work Research course at the local college and that they were hoping to develop a survey to be used to collect data on some of these policy issues.

Jess: From Case to Cause

Spring the Following Year

Valerie was standing in the foyer of the legislative hearing room watching hundreds of people from all walks of life streaming into the room in anticipation of the domestic violence forum. She couldn't believe how involved she had become in policy issues in just a few short months. It certainly was not where she would have envisioned herself. She derived her greatest satisfaction from working directly with the women and children. However, Jess Overton had taught her that one or two people can start a "chain reaction" of good and necessary policy changes. In the past several months, the State Association Against Family Violence had held several "talking sessions" with the State Coalition for Mental Health, with representatives from the health care industry, as well as with members of the local bar association and local law school. As a result of these meetings, representatives from these groups were here today to submit written and oral testimony. Not everyone agreed on how to address these policy issues, but all agreed it was important enough to continue dialogue and to raise public awareness. The Association, along with the Bar Association, had just submitted a legislative initiative for a Legal Advocacy Law Project for Family Violence, where social workers, lawyers, and other helping professionals would work together on individual cases and on legislative monitoring and advocacy.

Valerie turned to go into the hearing room when, from the corner of her eye, she spotted a familiar face in the crowd. She looked again. Jess Overton approached her; they hugged and walked into the hearing room together.

Valerie escorted her to the testimony table, introduced her to the Association president, Amanda Greenfield, and sat down directly behind Jess.

Valerie thought back several months to the first time she had met Jess during the intake assessment at the shelter. She had worried then that they might be overwhelming Jess with abstract policy information at a time when Jess only needed to know she and her children were safe. Valerie worried now if encouraging Jess to testify today was exploiting her for the benefit of the shelter or for some abstract cause. She realized as Jess prepared to testify that this was Jess's way of being strong for herself and for her children, a means of self-empowerment.

After the Association president spoke to the legislative committee members, she turned to Jess and introduced her as a special guest speaker. Jess looked at the group and said, "Thank you for allowing me this opportunity to speak. My name is Jess Overton, and I'd like to share with you what I've been through."

Readings

Carlson, B. E., McNutt, L., Choi, D. Y., & Rose, I. M. Intimate partner abuse and mental health: The role of social support and other protective factors. *Violence Against Women, 8*(6), 720–746.

McCaw, B., Bauer, H. M., Berman, W. H., Mooney, L., Holmberg, M., & Hunkeler, E. (2002). Women referred for on-site domestic violence services in a managed care organization. *Women & Health, 35*(2/3), 23–41.

Zweig, J. M., Schlichter, K. A., & Burt, M. R. (2002). Assisting women victims of violence who experience multiple barriers to service. *Violence Against Women, 8*(2), 162–181.

Discussion Questions

1. *What levels of generalist practice and system sizes are evident in this case?*

2. *The first policy issue that confronted Jess and Valerie was the shelter's requirement that Nick could not be admitted. Do you think that this problem should have been confronted first? Give reasons for your answer.*

3. *What were some of the issues that were responsible for Jess's considering returning to her husband, David?*

4. *Compare Jess's experiences to those of other survivors of domestic violence. What is your reaction to Valerie's statement that young adolescent males "are often aggressive and violent"? Do you agree with this assessment?*

5. *The term "interlocking systems of oppression" has been used to describe situations in which oppression in one institution is connected with and can create oppression in other institutions. Do you see any evidence of these systems in this case?*

6. *What strengths did Jess demonstrate in this case?*

7. *What do you think of the physician's decision to give Jess a mental health diagnosis in order to ensure that the health insurance carrier would pay for Jess's treatment?*

27

Community Work with Refugees

Terry L. Singer

"I have everything." That was the response to a question asked of Sabri, a Kosovar refugee, who, with his family, had just arrived in Louisville, Kentucky, for resettlement. Only a few weeks earlier, Sabri and his family had lived in Kosovo, a part of the country that had once been Yugoslavia. Now, Serbians and Albanians were in the midst of hostilities that had roots dating back centuries, and Kosovo was war-torn and dangerous. To underscore the danger, a bomb had recently claimed the lives of Sabri's father and uncle. Then, without warning, he and his family had been given five minutes to leave their home under threat of death. The family escaped Kosovo, moving to a refugee camp in nearby Macedonia where they remained for two weeks. This time, Sabri's family, including his wife and two children, sister-in-law, and her two children, was transported to a completely unfamiliar city and country. Josh, a recent social work graduate and a church volunteer, had been asked to coordinate the family's resettlement and to prepare for the influx of other Kosovo refugees.

To be honest, Josh knew little about the country other than what he had learned in the newspaper and on the evening news accounts of atrocities. As an outspoken social worker on issues of social justice, he had been his church's logical choice to lead this effort, working in conjunction with the Kentucky Refugee Ministries, one of the state's primary refugee resettlement agencies. His hometown, Louisville, was chosen as the first place to begin resettlement efforts in the United States in relation to the war on Kosovo.

As a midwestern city, Louisville was not generally perceived as a center for refugee resettlement. In reality, however, the largest national resettlement agencies had been placing refugees in the region for a number of years. This was the case because the region was welcoming and also tended to provide jobs to help those from other lands get a start. As a result, Louisville had become one of the fastest growing refugee population centers in the country. Over the years, ethnic pockets of diverse neighborhoods had quietly evolved throughout the community. Yet, this was the first family from Kosovo and would require a lot of skill to facilitate the beginning of a new community in the city.

This work would challenge all of Josh's organizational skills, sensibilities, and, in particular, his patience in collaborating with a human service and health system that did not easily respond to change. Much of that challenge would involve understanding the special needs associated with ethnic and religious diversity. Sabri's family members were Muslim Albanians, who were now forced to live in a predominantly western Judeo-Christian culture. Josh's task would require eliciting the system's sensitivity to the needs of a family being resettled as a result of war, violence, and policies of ethnic cleansing. In addition to these traumas was the personal grief arising from the loss and deaths of family members. To complicate matters, only one family member spoke even a few words of English. And finally, because Josh had been asked to head up this volunteer effort for his church, he would have to tap into all the organizational skills necessary to help this family effect a successful transition to its new life.

Engagement

One month before the family arrived, the church had asked Josh to coordinate a volunteer effort to assist Kentucky Refugee Ministries in the likelihood that some families would be relocated to Louisville. At this point, there was little certainty that any refugees would find their way to the city; nonetheless, the agency, which works with local churches, wanted to be prepared. An organizational meeting was held at Josh's home where the refugee agency briefed about 15 volunteers about what they might expect. At this meeting it was explained that the group might be called upon to find housing, provide initial transportation, and in general, begin orienting families to this new environment. They were told that a family could arrive in town without much notice, so they needed to be prepared. And the volunteers were warned that although their normal response would be to smother the family with attention and concern, they needed to respect the family's privacy and to avoid creating unnecessary dependence at all costs. The group's job was to be a transitional one.

Task Identification, Data Collection, and Assessment

Without knowing exactly what to expect, or when to expect it, the volunteer group began to identify some initial tasks. Like many other theoretical stage models, the various stages of the problem-solving method do not easily fall into discrete activities. Understanding this fact, Josh realized that some plans would need to be in place before accurate information could be had. This volunteer effort would entail fluid movement between task identification and data collection, and assessment would be ongoing.

As coordinator of the volunteer group, Josh would be the contact person, facilitating communication and ensuring that the group stayed on task. It is important to note that the coordinator's role is crucial to the success of this type of community effort. All members of this group, including Josh, were volunteers, many of whom had "day jobs." Therefore, volunteers could not always be available when needed, and a number of backup systems needed to be developed. One volunteer agreed to begin searching for a place where a family could live—this without knowing how many family members would be arriving. Another began collecting food items, and several others proceeded to search for furniture and other necessary accessories. Josh worked to keep the church informed of the group's needs and progress to ensure both the church's support and its ownership of the volunteer effort. He also maintained close contact with the refugee agency.

Within several weeks, word came that a family would be arriving shortly and that the volunteers needed to finalize arrival plans. Not all of the planning and anticipation could allay the fears about wanting to do what was right and helpful. The announcement was not precise about the family composition, but it was projected to include a father, mother, two young daughters, a sister-in-law and her young daughters. The refugee agency told Josh and the other volunteers that all of the children were under seven years of age.

Armed with this information about family composition, the volunteers were able to crystallize housing needs. It is never easy to find adequate housing for such a large extended family. Recognizing that this family had been in emergency and transitional housing since fleeing their homeland, the group wanted to plan for a settlement that would not require another immediate move. Gary, one of the volunteers, had called numerous realty agents and read every apartment and home rental listing in the weekend papers. Many requests for housing information were met with rejections, particularly once the situation of need was disclosed. Gary was sensitive to the desire of the volunteer group to avoid some of the more dangerous areas of the community. Josh went to several sites with Gary to ensure that the best possible housing arrangements could be secured.

Josh used the Internet to communicate with the volunteers. The common understanding was that others were to post activity on the distribution list to keep everyone informed of progress and identify any difficulties. For the most part, communication arrived to Josh in his coordinator role through telephone contacts. He posted the messages to others at their Internet addresses to help coordinate the

work. Although Josh was the coordinator of volunteer activity, those in designated work groups were free to initiate any activity that seemed to be needed. Given the extent of intervention required, this sharing of responsibility was the only way the work could be accomplished. Refugees, by agency policy, are to be relatively independent within a 90-day period. To even approach that goal requires a lot of work on the part of the refugees. In many ways, in the case of the Kosovar family, it was unrealistic to achieve complete independence and autonomy, but the effort did seem to produce a positive outcome. The role of the volunteers was to assist in this objective, so each volunteer had to be able to act as necessary to meet any recognized needs. For a community to be responsive in the face of little expertise and knowledge, creative and imaginative problem solving becomes essential. Josh knew that the role of communicator was one of his most important functions. Ultimately, it kept the volunteer group working off the same page, and the work did get done.

During this period of anticipation and preparation, the volunteers had tried to prepare by reading material on Kosovo as well as on the Muslim faith, just as many Americans would find themselves wanting to know more about the Muslim faith after the tragedy of September 11, 2001. Josh wanted to ensure that the group could relate to the needs of a family that would find itself in a community with a very small Muslim population.

In assessing what resources the family would need to negotiate the move, it was clear that the program's housing allowance was so marginal that it would not support this family's space needs. This problem required close coordination with the church to secure sufficient supplemental funds. With the arrival plans of the family complete, the planning started to fragment. For example, a final check of food supplies in the home indicated that the baked beans that had been donated contained pork. Do Muslims eat pork? Would they be offended to be given such food? One volunteer was therefore assigned to inventory all of the donated food to ensure no insult would be given. In cases of doubt, the uncertain foods were removed.

Another unanticipated activity involved the media. This was going to be one of the first families of the war to be resettled in the United States, and the media of course wanted a part of the action. Since Josh was the announced point person, he was soon besieged at both work and home for information. Who was the family? Where would they live? What would they do? Josh was aware that he should protect the family; at the same time, he saw this as an opportunity to promote the cause of refugee resettlement in the community. In his role as spokesperson, Josh found that he needed to keep two perspectives in balance.

First, without knowing much about the family, Josh wanted them to have the proper time to heal and adjust to the recent turmoil of their lives. This meant that he had to protect their confidence and privacy. Knowing that reporters would be relentless in "getting their story," he found himself making deals. Explaining the personal space that family members would need to adjust, Josh agreed to arrange with television, radio, and print reporters to provide information. Frankly, he was surprised at their understanding.

The second perspective had to do with the community response to the experience of refugees in their city. Citizens had been bombarded on the evening news with pictures of Kosovars, particularly children, fleeing their homes in terror and desperation. The community response and interest was overwhelmingly warm and generous. At the same time, Josh was aware that many Cubans, Haitians, and African refugees had settled in Louisville without the same fanfare. He wondered how much of this difference in response had to do with skin color, and he had even shared this observation with colleagues. Rather than confront the community with this charge through the media, Josh decided to use his media opportunity to address the overall extent and needs of refugees in the community, hoping to broaden interest. He began to appreciate how important it was for those in high-profile work to think ahead about what one might communicate. To be caught unaware or in a thoughtless mode could affect outcomes negatively.

Another aspect of fragmented plans played out in relation to the family's arrival. The last-minute announcement of travel plans at a designated time of arrival at the airport conflicted with Josh's prior scheduled activity for his agency. When efforts to find alternate volunteers to meet the family did not materialize, he was forced to choose this volunteer effort over his work responsibilities, believing that this family took precedence over a more routine agency activity. In addition, Josh knew that he had to coordinate the presence of an agency interpreter and to arrange with the airport authorities for assistance in getting the family members to a secure room and quickly away from reporters. Being on site would ensure a better chance of success at these tasks.

With a frenetic beginning, Josh and the refugee family members made their way to the new family apartment where volunteers had been waiting to greet them and orient them to their new environment. An interpreter from the Kentucky Refugee Ministries agency who spoke Bosnian helped facilitate communication. Though Bosnian was not the language of the family, Sabri and his family understood it. The church volunteers had been able to secure enough furniture for the whole apartment. Stuffed animals were presented to the children, flowers adorned the home, and friendly faces provided welcome. It was in this context that Sabri, when asked what else he needed, responded that he had everything. He had lost his home and several family members; a brother was lost and unaccounted for; and his family had only the clothes on their backs. But he had everything. It brought tears to Josh's

eyes as he thought about the things he took for granted in his own life and his own expected comforts. He was not the only one in the room feeling tearful. None of the volunteers had anticipated the power of this meeting. These are the sacred moments that reinforce the importance of civic involvement. Josh knew that he would never be the same after this moment, but he had no idea how much would change.

Sabri's sister-in-law, Fexhrije, and her two children had to be located several miles away because a large enough dwelling could not be found to house everyone. It was difficult for the family members to be separated. Fexhrije's husband, Sabri's brother, had not made the trip; in fact, he was unaccounted for. There was some question about whether he was even alive because he had been a "rebel fighter" against the Serbian army. So, this separation from family posed one of the first areas of concern for the volunteers, but at this point, there was no alternative. It was a sad separation for a family that had stayed together through a flight from their homeland, through Macedonia's refugee camps, and finally to Kentucky.

After the First Day

Josh thought that everything that would follow this beginning would be anticlimactic. In fact, the pace of work accelerated. The family had virtually no communication skills, and interpreter time was limited. Josh had to coordinate information gathering and advocacy activity to facilitate this transition. Even with agency support, new community programs that were launched to accommodate refugees had to be developed as resources. New legislation created housing and cash support, but it was not easy to find information about access. Health programs were also available but very difficult to navigate.

The volunteer group knew that it would be without an interpreter for the whole weekend that followed, so it carved out questions for consideration. These questions were based on an assumption that the family would want to engage in some activity but might well want to be alone for some quiet time after the hectic beginning. Therefore, these questions were meant as possibilities:

1. Might the family wish to be alone all weekend? Would they want to explore their neighborhoods alone?
2. Would they like visitation with other refugees? If this were so, how would we organize it?
3. They only had the clothes on their back. Should we take them to a local department store for underwear and other immediate clothing needs?
4. Should we consider driving them around the city to get a sense of the city's layout?
5. Should we coordinate visitation by members of the church? If visiting were to take place, how many

members should visit? The church members were very interested in helping in any way possible at this time.

6. Should we coordinate special activities for the four young girls?

7. Would any of the family wish to attend church to meet their sponsors?

These questions were the foundation for careful planning by the volunteer group, attempting to consider all of the possibilities. When Josh went to visit the family mid-morning the next day, they were already being visited by a Bosnian refugee family that had seen the news on television and had tracked them down through a community network. It was amazing to Josh that such a network existed, particularly since there were no other Kosovar families in the city, and Sabri and his family had no connections to anyone before arriving. Conversation with Sabri determined that the family would be able to manage through the weekend with their new friends.

Linking to Resources

The Kentucky Refugee agency asked Josh to transport Fexhrije and her children to the agency to begin the process of obtaining social security registration and other legal documents. It was an experience he had not anticipated and for which he was not prepared. He found their apartment and, after knocking on the door, realized that he had very few communication avenues. (The interpreter could not travel with him that day.) Josh was faced with convincing Fexhrije to accompany him with her children to a place unknown to her. After numerous attempts at hand signs and slowly enunciated language efforts, Josh finally recognized that she knew no English at all. When he mentioned Sabri's name, however, she instantly understood that she should accompany Josh. The trip in the car was another awkward experience. Josh had the radio playing music for the 20-minute trip, while his company sat silently without any means of language communication. That moment was another of the many powerful moments that he would experience. The power was in the recognition that this woman was willing to get into a car with a stranger thousands of miles from her home, with no knowledge of her husband's safety, no way to communicate with her driver, and wondering what would come next. Josh wondered the same thing and was overwhelmed by her seeming vulnerability. Unexpectedly, soon thereafter Fexhrije decided that she and her family would move in with Sabri and his family, even though the space would not easily accommodate them all. Sabri explained that it was better for everyone to be together. This news prompted the housing subgroup to move into action again to help the family find larger quarters. They would eventually secure larger lodgings but not until the Kosovar family lived in close conditions for another month.

In another situation, Josh was leaving his office on a call from Sabrije, Sabri's wife, to help her get to the hospital clinic for a physical. It took three hours for her to be examined because the clinic, contrary to federal law, refused to see her without an interpreter. It was the health facility's responsibility to provide interpreter services, but it was unprepared and ignorant about the law. Later Josh learned that many refugees had to rely on their children, who had greater language facility, to interpret very personal and intimate health matters for their parents. Josh therefore realized that he had to become more conversant about the rights of refugees, and so his role as advocate quickly began to take shape. During his wait in the hospital clinic with Sabrije, Josh happened to see a physician whom he knew and asked for his intervention to expedite the appointment. Without that assistance, it might have taken even longer. Since this particular experience, Josh now serves on a community committee set up to ensure interpretation services for all people. He had learned early in his social work education that workers need to maintain a broad perspective in bringing services to people in need. Political action and advocacy are both key components of responsible care.

Through spending time in the hospital with Sabrije and the interpreter Josh came to understand some of the horror the Kosovars had experienced in their flight. One very moving story told of a mother who held her child tightly to her breast, refusing to release it to the Serbian soldiers. The soldiers responded by cutting off the woman's arms below the elbow so that she would never hold a child again. When Josh heard more such stories, he wondered how this family and others like them could ever return to a normal life.

From this point on, some of the coordinating activities involved helping the adults secure employment, find clothing, identify health care providers, arrange for schooling of the children and English-as-a-second-language classes for the adults, secure bus schedules and help the family learn how to use the public transportation system, establish a budget, and introduce them to others in the community. One particularly significant resource that Josh secured for the family was passes to the public library where they would have free computer web access. Sabri soon began his routine visit to the library where he would go on the Internet and read papers from his home country. During this time, the children looked at books in the children's section of the library. This flow of information for Sabri was important for a family that had been virtually cut off from any communication from Kosovo.

The refugees quickly made natural linkages to earlier Bosnian refugees to the community, since they shared language to a large degree. These linkages provided more insider information to help the family negotiate the complexities of life in a new community. They encountered many difficulties in their new country. For one thing public transportation did not easily get the family where it needed to go. In its planning for the family, the volunteer group had considered the importance of finding an apartment on a bus line, but they had never anticipated that so many important destinations would require complex transfers. In addition, Sabri had difficulties getting a driver's license because the test was not given in his native language. When he tried to take the test in Bosnian, he failed. It took considerable time for him to master enough English to pass the test.

During this intense three-month period, the volunteer coordination was genuinely tested. After the initial planning and engagement, many of the volunteers had less time available, and so a great deal of the burden fell on Josh's shoulders. Even though he had mastered the skills of group work and had served effectively in community problem solving on many committees and boards of directors, he had not anticipated how difficult it would be to hold a group of volunteers together to follow through on the needed tasks. His various phone numbers became frequent avenues of assistance for the refugee family. He now found himself torn emotionally. On one hand, he had great empathy for what the family had to endure, and he wanted to be helpful; on the other hand, he often got little rest and was increasingly frustrated in the struggle to sustain the volunteer commitment of others. Investment and commitment to any volunteer effort has a natural life. At first, the volunteers were tripping over themselves to be helpful; after just one month, however, volunteers began to fall away. Understandably, the pressures of work and family take precedence, and volunteer work becomes secondary. With the remaining volunteers, the smaller group agreed to share continuing transportation support. Other church members were good about inviting the refugee family to their own family events; several others made sure there were seasonal changes of clothes.

Sabri, Sabrije, and their children eventually found their way and developed their own community networks. Employment was secured, and the children made good progress in school. They had another child, the symbol of the hope they harbored for their new land. A year after resettlement, Sabri's brother was able to join his wife and children in Louisville.

Evaluation

One year after the beginning of the project, Josh met with the volunteer group and members of the refugee resettlement agency to ponder the lessons learned. Even though frequent gatherings had been held during the course of the experience, the whole group had not been together since the initial planning. It was important now to assess the experience and to build a framework for understanding refugee work and the role of community coordination.

Josh realized that we seek to understand general principles about groups of people such as refugees from Kosovo, but when we are dealing with the individual, we are faced with the narrative that unfolds at the smallest level. That is, we think in concepts, but we work with individuals who are unique. He reminded himself not to lose his focus on that central fact.

Once Josh had identified the importance of the uniqueness of the individual, he considered other aspects of generalizable information. For example, refugees, who by definition come from homelands that pose a threat to their lives, are often teetering on the brink of uncertainty about what they want: comfort and solace; time alone; desire to make a new start; hope of returning to their home once the conflict ends; constant assurance and assistance; and independence.

Josh understood that a volunteer effort has its own life cycle. At the beginning, there may be much exuberance and good will, and the task may be to find enough work for everyone with interest. In the middle of the cycle, the extent of volunteerism may have peaked, leaving the task to a few dedicated souls. In the end, only the coordinator and perhaps one or two others may be all who are left to bring closure. Recognizing the volunteer life cycle, Josh was able to guard against the cynicism that sometimes finds its way into conversations and the work. Josh also learned that he must be prepared to work hard and sometimes alone.

One advantage of having a social worker in a coordination role with community volunteers is the professional value placed on connections, linkages, and advocacy. Josh learned very early in this work that his social service contacts provided a wealth of resources and community information that facilitated this work. Volunteers are often frustrated in their commitments when they sense that they do not know enough to help. Although Josh realized that he did not have to know everything necessary to successfully help a family from Kosovo resettle in Louisville, he did have to know where to get information and how to make referrals and linkages. In addition, he felt sufficiently secure of his responsibility to serve as an advocate. Individually, this meant finding ways to ensure that all refugees had rights and privileges to needed health care. From a communitywide perspective, this involved employing a tactic of calling on political community leaders to help solve newly emerging community social problems.

Josh also discovered that with a sponsoring or affiliated organization such as his, he should praise and acknowledge the work of others to that organization in order to validate the importance of the work and reaffirm the decision to take on the task. In this case, he provided frequent public reports to the sponsoring religious congregation, explaining the wonderful work of the congregational members. Although it might appear to be deceitful or a bit of an exaggeration, particularly in the middle and later phases of the volunteer project, it became a lesson on what civic and religious organizations can and should accomplish and it kept the door open for other ventures.

Josh also learned to recognize the fine line between charity and professional practice. Charity is not bad and may even be the overriding framework for volunteers. In fact, vested self-interest is one of the biggest motivators for any volunteer effort. People aligned themselves with this refugee project because they were moved by the pain and plight of the refugees from Kosovo who were appearing on nightly television. The volunteers wanted to facilitate the refugees' transition to this country; indeed, this was the dominant value that directed the work. As a professional, Josh needed to maintain a perspective that incorporated a clear understanding of what needs to be done and how to do it, respecting boundaries and gaining mastery of best practices. He also discovered the value of seeking out experts when the coordinator confronts a new and challenging problem.

Technology became a principal tool in Josh's work just as it is in everyone's work in today's world. Given the complexity of keeping others informed, Josh came to accept that any volunteer effort should organize a plan of technological use. This plan might include the use of cell phones to keep volunteers, agencies, and the media informed and connected. Computers provide a source of common connection, electronic communication, and, in the case of work with refugees, immediate access to information from the homeland. Other related uses will only grow exponentially in the next few years. Coordinating community volunteer efforts will undoubtedly find new and important uses to assist in their work.

Finally, in whatever major community project is launched, it is acceptable to make mistakes. In this particular resettlement experience, volunteers began with no idea of even where Kosovo was located, not to speak of the traditions of the cultures living there. Moreover, few had any understanding of the Muslim faith. Complicating the effort was the fact that most volunteers were not social service professionals, so there were constant challenges about setting boundaries in this work. The group agreed with Josh that they should all learn together how to do this work. Humility is a great asset in bringing new understanding and careful and continuing self-assessment to one's work.

What Followed

In time, Sabri and Sabrije both found employment and purchased a car and a house. Although the seeds for this success were planted in the first three months, the outcome was directly related to this family's ability to build a network of community contacts to assist them. Louisville has become a community where this is possible because a critical mass of refugees and immigrants have come to this part of the country. All members of the family mastered English by participating in English-as-a-second-language programs.

Sabri's children were successful in school, helped in some measure by church volunteers, who served as tutors for the children. Specifically, these volunteers helped the family learn how to engage the children in completing their homework, keeping close contact with the teachers, and participating fully in their children's school life.

Following his initial stint as a volunteer, Josh took an active role in the community regarding general issues of refugee and immigrant settlement into the community. He served on the boards of several agencies, including one that focuses on a burgeoning Hispanic/Latino population in Louisville. In addition, he was asked to serve on a Mayor's Committee to address the needs of refugees and immigrants as well as a health care task force to explore creating better access to health care. The coordination activity created in Josh a sense of how important it was for communities to embrace their new neighbors, not just because of pressing social needs, but more in the recognition that a healthy, diverse community is a strong community.

Josh's experience with the Kosovars left him with two final observations. First, solving community problems means that community resources must be mobilized to respond. Volunteers provide an available pool of labor and good will to make each venture possible, and social workers possess the skills to lead this mobilization. Second, Josh learned that, for him, being a social worker was more than a professional career path. Embodied in the values of the profession is a calling to make a difference for the marginalized and powerless, and it is not easy to turn this light off when he leaves the office. So, Josh keeps that light on, just enough to see what challenge will follow next.

Readings

Becker, D. F., Weine, S. M., & Vojvoda, D. (1999). Case series: PTSD symptoms in adolescent survivors of "ethnic cleansing." Results from a 1-year follow-up study. *Journal of the American Academy of Child & Adolescent Psychiatry, 38*(6), 775–781.

Booth, K. (Ed.). (2001). *The Kosovo tragedy: The human rights dimensions.* London: Frank Cass.

Potocky-Tripodi, M. (2002). *Best practices for social work with refugees and immigrants.* New York: Columbia University Press.

Discussion Questions

1. *What aspects of Josh's work in this case would you find most challenging?*

2. *What difficulties would you envision might accompany having to adapt to a new country and way of life?*

3. *Louisville was noted as a community with a critical mass of refugees. What is the significance of this fact for future immigrants?*

4. *What purpose was served by providing sponsoring agencies with frequent reports about the refugees' situation and progress?*

28

When Life Changes in an Instant
Carla Sofka

When the phone rang shortly after 8 A.M. Saturday morning, Paula assumed it was her friend, Linda, calling to finalize plans for their outing to the fall festival in a neighboring community. The promise of New York's fall foliage would be a nice contrast to the hectic and stressful schedule of the first month of school where Paula worked as the social worker for all 900 of the students in the local school district. She looked forward to a peaceful drive across the Adirondack Mountains as the leaves were reaching their peak. When she heard the voice of Joanne Morrison, the school principal, on the other end of the line, Paula took a deep breath. She thought to herself, "She only calls me at home when it's urgent."

Mrs. Morrison explained that two popular high school seniors, Gary Weiss, and his best friend, David Sherman, were critically injured in a car accident late last night. "We don't have all the details yet, but we're being told that Gary may not regain consciousness. I'm calling a meeting of the crisis response team to talk about how we're going to handle this when the students return to school on Monday. By the time the meeting starts, we'll have more information. Can I count on you to be at the school at 10:30 this morning?" "I'll see you then," Paula said with a sigh, anticipating that this weekend was going to be very different from what she had originally planned. She called Linda to postpone their outing until Sunday afternoon and prepared for the potentially long and emotionally draining weekend ahead.

As she was driving to the school, she imagined how much harder this might be if she hadn't spent time last fall preparing for the possibility of another crisis. After September 11, 2001, Paula expressed concern to the principal about the school's lack of preparedness to handle the aftermath of the terrorist attacks that impacted the school in so many ways. The administrators, faculty, and staff at the school all agreed that things needed to change. Mrs. Morrison had given Paula the responsibility of organizing and leading a crisis response team, working closely with appropriate community resources. After locating some reference materials in the library and on the Web to help her with the planning, she had assembled a great group of people willing to come together in times such as this. She anticipated meeting with her crisis response team today, hoping that all of the members would be available on such short notice.

Data Gathering: Sharing Information from Multiple Sources

The crisis response team gathered in the conference room at the school. In attendance were the following people: Joanne Morrison (school principal), Pamela Bertman (teacher), Barbara Fitzgerald (hospital medical social worker), Joe Maloney (teacher), Jane Norwood (PTA representative), Jerry Kirby (Police Department representative), and Beth Davies (Temple youth program director).

Paula greeted everyone and asked for an update on the situation. She hoped to begin the group meeting by having everyone share information. She knew that all the members would need some time to process their feelings about the tragedy. Many members knew the students involved in the accident, and all realized an event like this would have repercussions throughout the small close-knit community.

After a few minutes of processing their initial reactions to Mrs. Morrison's call, Paula asked members of the team to contribute the information that they had gathered. Ms. Bertman began. "We learned from David's parents that they had gotten a call from David when the dance ended around 11:00 P.M. David and Gary were heading to a party for a while, at someone's house. Then, he and Gary would drive their girlfriends home, David would drop Gary off, and call it a night by 1:00 A.M. I helped chaperone the homecoming events that evening," she said. "The committee thought the prom had been a great success. The students were really excited and upbeat at the dance. Everything went off without any problems. Word was going around about a senior party, but none of us knew where it was being held."

"Gary and David almost made it home," noted Sgt. Kirby. "Officer Redmond called me this morning after clearing it with the families that it was OK to call me. About a mile before the turnoff into the neighborhood where they had both grown up, David's car crashed into a tree on that sharp curve. We suspect that the rain may have caused David to lose control of the car, but they don't know yet if there were other factors involved. The responding officers are trying to contact other students who were at the party. Does anyone know who had the after-prom party?"

Mr. Maloney noted that the party was held at the house of Vince Williams and that his house was a frequent hangout for some of the seniors. "I hope that alcohol wasn't involved," said Mrs. Norwood. "There's been debate going on at our PTA meetings about the need to form a local SADD/MADD chapter since we know that more underage kids are deciding to drink. I don't know how parents can allow that to happen, especially when the kids are getting together for parties in their own houses."

Paula stopped the discussion here to add, "Mrs. Norwood, I share your concern about the increase in underage drinking in our community. Barbara, how is David? I've gotten to know him through his work on the school paper." Barbara reported that she had met with both families earlier at the hospital emergency department. She said that David had suffered severe injuries to his spinal cord, but following hours of surgery, his condition was guarded but stable. He would survive, but it was too early to know if he would regain the use of his legs. Gary, who was not wearing his seat belt, had suffered a severe head injury. After a series of tests to determine the extent of this and any other injuries, the doctors were in the process of discussing his condition with his parents. Mrs. Weiss had promised that someone would page Barbara once they had finished the conversation with the doctor and had time to absorb the information.

"Where is Gary's sister?" asked Ms. Davies. Through her contact with the family through the Temple, she knew that Gary had a 14-year-old sister named Julie. "She's at the hospital, spending time with Rabbi Goldman," stated Barbara. "The Rabbi was called at the family's request to be there to discuss the medical options for Gary. They want to make choices that respect the values and beliefs of their faith."

"David's brother, William, is with his grandparents," added Sgt. Kirby. "His parents asked one of the officers to call them. They are staying with him at the house. Since he's only 7, they didn't want to wake him in the middle of the night. They felt he's too young to be at the hospital right now."

The conversation halted at the first sound of Barbara's cell phone. In the moment Paula had to reflect on the process that was unfolding, she was impressed that each member of the team had honored the policies and procedures that were created last September to respect the needs and rights of the people whose lives could, unfortunately, be changed in an instant. Earlier that morning, Barbara spoke with Gary and David's parents about how to ensure their rights to privacy and confidentiality and at the same time provide needed information to the crisis response team. Although they were devastated by the previous night's events, both sets of parents had given their consents to share information with the team and each had signed a release form for information to be shared freely with the team. Both families agreed with a statement made by Gary's father, "We'd prefer that people know the facts. Rumors and misinformation won't help anyone."

Barbara's cell phone conversation began. "Hello, Mr. Weiss! The crisis response team is here with me. Everyone asked me to let you know that Gary and your family are in our thoughts and prayers. Is it alright if I put you on the speaker phone so that all members of the crisis response team can hear?" Barbara asked Mr. Weiss to pause briefly while she adjusted the settings on the phone. Mrs. Morrison hoped that the audio conference system that had been purchased specifically for use by the crisis response team would not fail them when they needed it most.

Mr. Weiss noted that the last ten hours had been very difficult. The news was not good. Gary's head injury was severe, and there was little hope that he would ever regain consciousness. If he did, his quality of life would never be the same. He was breathing with the help of life support. After talking with his rabbi and Gary's grandparents, he was in the process of making a decision about continuing Gary on life support. Gary's doctors had mentioned organ donation options. He also noted that his rabbi was helping them think about both of these decisions since views about what is permissible within the Jewish faith are mixed.

Paula spoke with Mr. Weiss, introducing herself as the school social worker and the head of the crisis response team. She asked if there was anything she and the team could do for him or his family. Mr. Weiss said that his youngest daughter, Julie, was taking this very hard, and he wondered how she would adjust to going back to school. He noted that his wife, Carol, wondered if there was a school social worker available to Julie when she returned to school. Paula said that once Julie had plans to return, she would automatically see her and assess how she could help. She noted that that was standard policy for all students when a serious medical situation or a death in a family affected attendance. As the school social worker, she would reach out to Julie and help her with supportive counseling, advocacy, and other needed services. Mr. Weiss seemed grateful that the school had such a service and suggested that he and his wife would contact Paula as soon as they could. Paula added that the entire family will be in her thoughts.

Barbara spoke to Mr. Weiss about the crisis response team's duties and asked him for advice on how to proceed. She noted that in her earlier conversations, both sets of parents wanted the team to act as a communications conduit to the school community so that information could be shared with students and faculty at the school. Barbara suggested that when the students returned to school on Monday there would be a good deal of concern on their part. She had mentioned to Mr. Weiss this morning that the crisis response team had a system designed to get information out to the school community. This morning, the parents expressed their desire that the community have access to the facts. Barbara seemed uncertain whether this was still the case. Mr. Weiss noted that he and his wife had spoken to the media already and did not want to deal with further questions from the newspapers and the TV News. He added that after he and his wife finished talking with the doctor, they spoke with David's parents. David's condition was stable now, and his father Mike would like to be involved in any public statements that were made.

Barbara told Mr. Weiss that she would do everything she could to respect the privacy of the families. Mr. Weiss observed that all of the parents were a bit overwhelmed by how quickly things were happening around them. He also expressed his thanks for the concern of the team. Barbara suggested that she stop by the hospital about 5:00 that afternoon and check in with him and his family.

Paula realized that, although they had developed some information about the accident as well as the status of the boys and their families, much information remained unknown. This was especially true for members of the school community who had learned of the accident but had little information. Although the crisis response team seemed satisfied that both families had the support they needed at this time, especially considering the fact that Barbara would be seeing them in her capacity of hospital social worker, the team tried to anticipate what needs existed at different levels. They also agreed that they needed to project a "larger system assessment" and plan to provide services that might be needed within the school community.

Data Collection Update: Saturday, 6 P.M.

Paula, Barbara, and Mrs. Morrison met the families at the hospital. During their visit they learned more information about the condition of the boys and their families. Both sets of parents wanted to release information to the press and asked for help in composing a "press release." After working together on the wording, Rabbi Goldman read the following statement to the press:

> It is with great sadness that we gather here today to inform you of a tragedy that has badly shaken our families, school and community. Our sons, Gary Weiss and David Sherman, were involved in a serious car accident following the homecoming festivities Friday night. First, on behalf of our sons and all of our family members, we would like to thank everyone for the outpouring of support that we have received in such a short period of time. Your prayers and the wonderful care that Gary and David have received at the hospital have filled us with hope. David sustained significant injuries in the car accident last night. He regained consciousness for a brief period of time following surgery to investigate the extent of the damage to his spinal cord and to repair several fractured bones. Right now, he is heavily sedated and unable to help the doctors to evaluate any sense of feeling or functioning in his legs. It is difficult for the doctors to predict whether or not he will be able to walk, but we remain optimistic for his full recovery.
>
> Unfortunately, the news about Gary is devastating. Gary suffered a severe head injury that precludes the possibility that he would regain consciousness. He has been declared brain

dead but is currently being sustained on life support. Following discussions with Gary's grandparents and representatives of the temple, the Weiss family has decided that Gary would not wish to have his life maintained without the hope for any quality of life as he knew it prior to the accident. With the blessings of the temple, Gary's life support will be removed following the removal of any organs and tissue that can be used to assist one or more individuals in need. Larry, Carol, and Julie would like to express their deepest gratitude to the doctors and staff at the hospital as well as the emergency responders who have worked tirelessly to help Gary and their family during this time of tragedy. They ask that they be given time to say their goodbyes to Gary and to grieve privately prior to the public service that will be announced when specific information is available. We are grateful to Mrs. Morrison and the school's crisis response team for taking care of so many details that have allowed us to be with our sons.

Assessment and Goal Planning

As leader of the crisis response team, Paula had helped the team establish a protocol to follow that could help them organize their work. She had arranged for the team to meet on Sunday afternoon to decide on the tasks that members of the team would carry out to deal with the crisis. After driving home from the hospital she made some preliminary notes to organize her thinking. This was a complex situation, with several levels of intervention needed with different client systems. In addition, the situation not only involved responding to the individuals and families involved, but also required responding to the broader school system and perhaps to the larger community. Her notes took the form of broad questions that would need to be considered by the community response team:

> As a survivor, how will David be able to cope with the trauma he experienced?
>
> What immediate and long-term services will he need to be able to recover and rehabilitate?
>
> What supports and services will Gary's family need to deal with the removal of his life support and with his impending death?
>
> What services will Gary's and David's siblings need when they return to school?
>
> How will the team get information about Gary and David to the student body on Monday?
>
> What information about the accident will the team share with students when they arrive for school on Monday?
>
> What roles will the team play in helping students at the school deal with this crisis?
>
> Should the team organize the students into groups to discuss their reactions and to deal with their feelings about the accident?
>
> Should she and other volunteers be available for students to drop in and individually discuss their feelings about the accident?

These and other questions would have to be worked out tomorrow with the team. Paula knew that the immediacy of the crisis would dictate that some tasks and goals would need to be prioritized as immediate and short term. However, she couldn't help but raise other important questions that seemed important but less immediate. These would need more long-term investigation:

What role might alcohol have had in the accident?

To what extent did any after-prom parties contribute to the tragedy?

What role should the crisis response team play in investigating and dealing with teen alcohol use by students?

How can the team research whether or not alcohol and substance abuse is an emerging problem at the school?

What role should parents play in helping the school investigate and respond to this larger social problem?

What larger issues exist in the community that impact on the safety of children in the school?

What would need to be done if conversations with students who attended the party and David's discussions with his parents revealed that he had been drinking prior to getting in the car to drive home?

Concluding Comments

Social workers often expect to deal with individual problems such as those encountered in this case. The fatal injury of one student and a serious injury to another is clearly a trauma for their respective parents and families. The nature of generalist social work practice, however, means that what begins as an individual problem will not necessarily end there. The case discussed above is an excellent example of this and illustrates the enormous breadth of generalist practice.

The social worker in this case, Paula, was called upon to perform several tasks related directly to the automobile accident described above. She assessed the situation by collecting data, meeting with others who could provide information, and worked with a team of colleagues to create a plan that would guide their activities over the next few days. In addition, she personally provided support for traumatized family members and assisted them in preparing a "press release" dealing with the students' situations. However, as a competent generalist practitioner, Paula accurately saw her role as much more complex, going well beyond the responsibility to work with this family.

In many ways, this case epitomizes the breadth of generalist practice. Although the accident experienced by the two boys was an individual problem for their parents, Paula quickly saw the many issues that would arise from such an event. Earlier, she had advocated for establishing a crisis response team that would be capable of managing a variety of traumas that might affect her school and community. By doing so, Paula was engaged in macro practice as she worked to develop a program that would benefit an entire group of clients, namely, members of the school and community. Her use of advocacy was an appropriate macro practice activity and would prevent the problems associated with being unprepared when a catastrophe strikes. The team would be prepared to assess, plan, and act in a timely fashion.

Paula recognized that this family tragedy would also have potential impacts on other areas. For example, it was clear that larger issues would need attention. This included such considerations as the role that alcohol played in the lives of high school students, ways to prevent similar problems in the future, and how to help students who may have participated in the events leading up to the accident.

She also used group work skills in her actions as part of the crisis response team. These included seeking information from other members and respecting the contributions each could make to the challenges facing the team. She also displayed critical thinking skills as she helped the group avoid making decisions based on conjecture. By keeping the focus on the facts of the situation, she helped ensure they would reach better decisions. She also helped them identify a variety of tasks that they would face in helping the school deal with this trauma as well as considering what assistance family members might still need.

Interacting at the micro, mezzo, and macro levels is typical of good generalist practice. Paula demonstrated how a single event can involve multiple challenges and require skills for intervening at all levels. By her efforts, she illustrated that generalist practitioners can bring about change at different levels without losing sight of the needs of individual clients.

Readings

Hillman, J. L. (2002). *Crisis intervention and trauma: New approaches to evidence-based practice*. New York: Kluwer Academic/Plenum Publishers.

Martin, L. R. (2001). Constructing a community response to violence. *Smith College Studies in Social Work, 71*(2), 347–355.

Schonfeld, D. J. (2002). Supporting adolescents in times of national crisis: Potential roles for adolescent health care providers. *Journal of Adolescent Health, 30*(5), 302–307.

Stevenson, R. G. (2002). Sudden death in schools. In N. B. Webb (Ed.), *Helping bereaved children: A handbook for practitioners* (2nd ed.). New York: Guilford Press, pp. 194–213.

Discussion Questions

1. *What immediate tasks would a social worker like Paula need to carry out to respond to the individuals and families in this crisis?*

2. *What interventions at a mezzo level (family and small group) would Paula need to consider?*

3. *Beyond the effects of this crisis on the individuals and families involved, how might this crisis affect the school and larger community?*

4. *What tasks would a social worker carry out to meet the needs of the school and the larger community?*

5. *What policy practice issues might the crisis response team become involved with to avoid this type of crisis in the future?*

6. *What factors would need to be taken into account when planning ways to commemorate Gary's life and death with members of the school community?*

TO THE OWNER OF THIS BOOK:

I hope that you have found *Case Studies in Generalist Practice*, Third Edition useful. So that this book can be improved in a future edition, would you take the time to complete this sheet and return it? Thank you.

School and address: _____

_____

Department: _____

Instructor's name: _____

1. What I like most about this book is: _____

_____

_____

2. What I like least about this book is: _____

_____

_____

3. My general reaction to this book is: _____

_____

_____

4. The name of the course in which I used this book is: _____

_____

5. Were all of the chapters of the book assigned for you to read? _____

   If not, which ones weren't? _____

6. In the space below, or on a separate sheet of paper, please write specific suggestions for improving this book and anything else you'd care to share about your experience in using this book.

_____

_____

_____

_____

_____

_____

OPTIONAL:

Your name: _____ Date: _____

May we quote you, either in promotion for *Case Studies in Generalist Practice*, Third Edition, or in future publishing ventures?

Yes: _____ No: _____

Sincerely yours,

Robert F. Rivas

Grafton H. Hull, Jr.

FOLD HERE

- -

BUSINESS REPLY MAIL
FIRST CLASS   PERMIT NO. 34   BELMONT, CA

POSTAGE WILL BE PAID BY ADDRESSEE

ATTN: Shelley Gesicki, Editor

WADSWORTH/THOMSON LEARNING
10 DAVIS DRIVE
BELMONT, CA   94002-9801

**NO POSTAGE
NECESSARY
IF MAILED
IN THE
UNITED STATES**

FOLD HERE